Conversations with Clint

ADVANCE PRAISE FOR *CONVERSATIONS WITH CLINT: PAUL NELSON'S LOST INTERVIEWS WITH CLINT EASTWOOD*

"An amazing find! Hip journalist Paul Nelson's lengthy, detailed, casual yet riveting, long-believed lost conversations with the iconic director-producer-star Clint Eastwood, who has had one of the most extraordinary careers in the history of the American screen. A must for any true film lover."

—**Peter Bogdanovich**, director, writer, actor, critic

"At a time when most critics didn't take Clint Eastwood seriously, he had no admirer more prescient or loving than the late Paul Nelson. And Nelson—still insufficiently appreciated for his stubborn indifference to fashionability, but a smoke-wreathed legend to his 1970s colleagues—will never have a posthumous rescuer more devoted and scrupulous than Kevin Avery. Unguarded, searching, and occasionally very funny, the uniquely intimate interviews collected in *Conversations With Clint* morph as we read into the ideal script for a lost Eastwood movie on the nature of friendship. I'm sure Paul would be pleased that the alternate title that kept springing to mind was that of a John Ford Western: *Two Rode Together*."

—**Tom Carson**, critic for *GQ* and author of *Daisy Buchanan's Daughter*

"This is what happens when an artist interviews an artist: Nelson's acute critical engagement with Eastwood's films yields more insight from the moviemaker than any reader could have hoped for. Can a collection of interviews be called poignantly brilliant? This one is."

—**Ken Tucker**, *Entertainment Weekly*

"Kevin Avery has performed a great service to film lovers by bringing to light Paul Nelson's remarkable interviews with Clint Eastwood. Nelson was an appreciator of Eastwood in the seventies, before he had won wide critical recognition. In these fascinating and wide-ranging conversations, the actor-director discusses with complete candor both the art of his films and the realities of filmmaking in Hollywood."

—**Andrew Sarris**, author of *The American Cinema: Directors and Directions 1929–1968*

"I found that *Conversations with Clint* is invaluable reading, not just because it's a uniquely in-depth series of interviews with someone who always had a sense of himself as an enduring figure. It also takes us inside the head of Paul Nelson—the interviewer himself—whose states of mind complete the story. The best interviews have always been two-sided—a conversation—and *Conversations* is just that: a compelling look at an extended eyeball-to-eyeball encounter, complete with blinks and flinches."

—**Elvis Mitchell**, host of KCRW's *The Treatment*

"Paul Nelson was the first serious film aficionado who, way back in the early '70s, turned me on to the importance of Clint Eastwood as an actor, filmmaker and American icon. He showed me the S&W Magnum .44 he kept under a pile of sweaters in his closet. 'Same as Dirty Harry,' he said, explaining that if he was going to write about men with guns he had to know how it felt in his hand. We were both devoted to F. Scott Fitzgerald and hoping that Clint Eastwood would play Gatsby in the upcoming film, which, of course, he didn't.

"The repartee between these two straight shooters is more revealing of the inner workings of Hollywood and the creative process of Clint Eastwood than anything I've ever read before."

—**Elliott Murphy**, singer-songwriter

Conversations with Clint

*Paul Nelson's Lost Interviews
with Clint Eastwood
1979–1983*

EDITED BY KEVIN AVERY

continuum

Continuum International Publishing Group

80 Maiden Lane	The Tower Building
Suite 704	11 York Road
New York	London
NY 10038	SE1 7NX

www.continuumbooks.com

Library of Congress Cataloging-in-Publication Data
Avery, Kevin.
  Conversations with Clint : Paul Nelson's lost interviews with Clint Eastwood, 1979–1983/edited by Kevin Avery.
     p. cm.
  Includes filmography.
  ISBN-13: 978-1-4411-6586-2 (pbk. : alk. paper)
  ISBN-10: 1-4411-6586-X (pbk. : alk. paper) 1. Eastwood, Clint, 1930–Interviews. I. Nelson, Paul, 1936-2006. II. Title.
  PN2287.E37A84 2011
  791.4302'8092–dc23
                                        2011019700

ISBN: PB: 978-1-4411-6586-2

Typeset by Fakenham Prepress Solutions, Fakenham, Norfolk NR21 8NN
Printed and bound in the United States of America

for Deb,
for making it all possible

ALSO BY KEVIN AVERY

Everything Is an Afterthought:
The Life and Writings of Paul Nelson (2011)

*Thank you to Jann Wenner and Rolling Stone
for the use of Paul Nelson's unpublished interviews in this
form, and to Mark C. Nelson for everything else.*

CONTENTS

FOREWORD

I never sat in a movie theater with Paul Nelson. We watched movies he'd taped off late-night television broadcasts, from neatly hand-lettered VHS tapes. He often had two or even three old movies on a cassette, many with sequences of static, and vintage late-night commercials, intact. Later we watched laserdiscs, but those never supplanted his tapes. For Paul, I suspect that when we met—I was nineteen—I struck him as a remedial case. I liked Godard and Truffaut and Kurosawa, directors who'd taken a lot from classical studio-era Hollywood, but I'd seen little of the real thing. My taste, shaped by my parents' viewing habits, leaned to foreign films and counterculture "classics" like *King of Hearts* and *Harold and Maude*. The only Western I'd seen was *Blazing Saddles*. Fortunately, I don't think Paul found my prodigiously confident opinions (some, in retrospect, wrong, and some right) unworkable, but he wanted to rewind my viewing habits, like one of his treasured tapes, and start me over again. I remember that we screened Hawks's *Red River* in slow motion, as Paul stopped the film at various points to describe what he found remarkable or characteristic in a given sequence, or just wanting to linger over details. We did the same thing with Welles's *Citizen Kane* and *Lady from Shanghai*. Other movies—*Ride the High Country, The Long Voyage Home*—we'd just put on and watch, and I'd feel the force of Paul's regard, the extraordinary pressure-field of his devoted gaze, guiding my own. Certain other films I never saw in Paul's company—*Heaven's Gate* comes to mind—yet no matter how long it was until I finally saw them, when I did they were enclosed in the terms with which Paul had described them to me, his projections and insights, his abiding gaze. I watched them with Paul even though Paul wasn't with me at the time.

We never discussed Clint Eastwood. I'm guessing now, having read Kevin Avery's terrific reconstruction of Paul's conversations with the actor-director, that this was more than happenstance. Given the size of Paul's engagement with Eastwood's work, and seeing the extent and intimacy of their friendship, the way it tested the bounds of journalist-and-subject, and understanding the disappointment of the encounter's failure to find a home in the "real world" of publication, I suspect it was too sensitive a matter for Paul to want to acknowledge by the time he and I were spending time together. There were zones of silence in Paul. Some covered what you'd have to guess were the most important pieces of his life. I could barely get him to mention Bob Dylan, for instance. I never knew he had a son.

This book is a miracle. It reads so naturally—a testament to Kevin Avery's editorial skill, and his own devotional attention to Paul's voice—that you might suppose it's an example of something. But it's not. There aren't books like this, because I doubt any other interviewer could ever have this sort of effect on a human being as (justifiably) well-defended as Clint Eastwood. (For comparison, see Lester Bangs, Paul's friend, jousting with Lou Reed.) Here, you feel the seduction of good conversation, of genuine friendship, overwriting the task at hand for both participants. As someone who's done an interview or two, getting too much is nearly as bad as getting too little, and getting too close is dangerous. Paul may have believed he was still heading for a *Rolling Stone* cover story, but at a certain point this encounter became something like the screenplay Paul worked on for years, after his journalistic career was through—a companion, a shelter against loneliness. I doubt it would have felt safe for him to subject this companion to the exigencies of a magazine's editorial offices, where ninety percent would have been judged slack or irrelevant, with the contemporary references, including those to Eastwood's own films, aging rapidly. If only Paul could somehow have known he was writing a book instead—a book as much about himself as about Clint Eastwood or his films (though you'll learn as much about the Hollywood film from it as any book I can think of). In fact, this book could be seen as a sort of screenplay, for a plotless movie on the subject of what it sounds like when two men discover kinship in the process of getting (or not getting) a job of work accomplished, like John Wayne and Dean Martin in *Rio Bravo*, or Walter Huston and Tim Holt in *The Treasure of Sierra Madre* (which, I suppose, puts Warren Zevon in the Humphrey Bogart role). But then if Paul had thought he was creating a book it's possible this book would never have existed.

I suppose it's safe to say I'm Paul's creature entirely, when it comes to my preferences and appetites as a film fan. Not that I've caught up to him and his bottomless collection of VHS tapes. Clint Eastwood, in particular, is one of my blindspots, but last night I discovered that Turner Classics was showing *The Outlaw Josey Wales*, and captured it with my DVR. That's a technology Paul would have delighted in, though he'd have been irritated, as I am, by his inability to put the results on any kind of shelf. Tonight I'll watch *Josey Wales* and, thanks to this book, I'll be watching it with Paul.

JONATHAN LETHEM
Claremont, California
April 19, 2011

FILMOGRAPHY

This list only includes those Clint Eastwood films discussed in Paul Nelson's conversations with the actor-director. It does not include Eastwood's half dozen or so television appearances during the Fifties, the eight seasons he spent on the TV series *Rawhide*, or, most notably, the twenty-six movies he has acted in or directed since these interviews took place.

1955

Revenge of the Creature
Directed by Jack Arnold
Screenplay by Martin Berkeley
Produced by William Alland
Universal-International
Cast: John Agar, Lori Nelson, John Bromfield, Clint Eastwood
   (uncredited, Jennings, the lab technician)

Tarantula
Directed by Jack Arnold
Screenplay by Robert M. Fresco, Martin Berkeley
Produced by William Alland
Universal-International
Cast: John Agar, Mara Corday, Leo G. Carroll, Clint Eastwood
   (first pilot)

1958

Lafayette Escadrille
Directed and produced by William A. Wellman

Screenplay by A. S. Fleischman (based on a story by William A. Wellman)
Warner Bros.
Cast: Tab Hunter, Etchika Choureau, Marcel Dalio, Clint Eastwood (George Moseley)

1964

A Fistful of Dollars[1]
Directed by Sergio Leone
Screenplay by Sergio Leone, Duccio Tessari, Victor A. Cantena, G. Schock (adapted from *Yojimbo* by Akira Kurosawa)
Produced by Harry Colombo, George Papi
Jolly Film/Constantin/Ocean/United Artists
Cast: Clint Eastwood (Joe, the Stranger), Gian Maria Volonté, Marianne Koch, Pepe Calvo

1965

For a Few Dollars More[1]
Directed by Sergio Leone
Screenplay by Luciano Vincenzoni, Sergio Leone (based on a story by Sergio Leone and Fulvio Morsella)
Produced by Alberto Grimaldi
Produzioni Europee Associates/Constantin/Arturo Gonzales/United Artists
Cast: Clint Eastwood (Monco, the Stranger), Lee Van Cleef, Gian Maria Volonté, Klaus Kinski

1966

The Good, the Bad and the Ugly[2]
Directed by Sergio Leone

---

[1] Not released in the United States until 1967.
[2] Not released in the United States until 1968.

Screenplay by Luciano Vincenzoni, Sergio Leone (based on a story
    by Age-Scarpelli, Sergio Leone, and Luciano Vincenzoni)
Produced by Alberto Grimaldi
Produzioni Europee Associates/United Artists
Cast: Clint Eastwood (Blondie, the Stranger), Eli Wallach, Lee Van
    Cleef, Aldo Giuffre

1967

The Witches[3]
Directed (Part Five: "A Night Like Any Other") by Vittorio De
    Sica
Screenplay by Cesare Zavattini, Fabio Carpi, Enzio Muzii
Produced by Dino De Laurentiis
Dino De Laurentiis Cinematografica/Les Productions Artistes
    Associés
Cast: Silvana Mangano, Clint Eastwood (Mario, the husband),
    Armando Bottin, Gianni Gori

1968

Hang 'Em High
Directed by Ted Post
Screenplay by Leonard Freeman, Mel Goldberg
Produced by Leonard Freeman
United Artists/The Malpaso Company
Cast: Clint Eastwood (Jed Cooper), Inger Stevens, Ed Begley, Pat
    Hingle

Coogan's Bluff
Directed and produced by Donald Siegel
Screenplay by Herman Miller, Dean Reisner, Howard Rodman
    (based on a story by Herman Miller)
Universal Pictures/The Malpaso Company
Cast: Clint Eastwood (Walt Coogan), Lee J. Cobb, Susan Clark,
    Tisha Sterling

---

[3]   Not released in the United States until 1969.

Where Eagles Dare
Directed by Brian G. Hutton
Story and screenplay by Alistair MacLean
Produced by Elliott Kastner
Metro-Goldwyn-Mayer
Cast: Richard Burton, Clint Eastwood (Lieutenant Morris
 Schaffer), Mary Ure, Michael Hordern

1969

Paint Your Wagon
Directed by Joshua Logan
Screenplay and lyrics by Alan Jay Lerner (based on the musical
 play by Alan Jay Lerner and Frederick Loewe)
Adaptation by Paddy Chayefsky
Produced by Alan Jay Lerner
Paramount Pictures
Cast: Lee Marvin, Clint Eastwood (Pardner), Jean Seberg, Harve
 Presnell

1970

Kelly's Heroes
Directed by Brian G. Hutton
Screenplay by Troy Kennedy Martin
Produced by Gabriel Katzka, Sidney Beckerman
Metro-Goldwyn-Mayer
Cast: Clint Eastwood (Kelly), Telly Savalas, Don Rickles, Carroll
 O'Connor

Two Mules for Sister Sara
Directed by Don Siegel
Screenplay by Albert Maltz (based on a story by Budd Boetticher)
Produced by Martin Rackin
Universal Pictures/The Malpaso Company
Cast: Clint Eastwood (Hogan), Shirley MacLaine, Manolo
 Fabregas, Alberto Morin

1971

The Beguiled
Directed and produced by Donald Siegel
Screenplay by John B. Sherry (Albert Maltz), Grimes Grice (Irene Kamp) (based on the novel by Thomas Cullinan)
Universal Pictures/The Malpaso Company
Cast: Clint Eastwood (John McBurney), Geraldine Page, Elizabeth Hartman, Jo Ann Harris

Play Misty for Me
Directed by Clint Eastwood
Screenplay by Jo Heims, Dean Reisner (based on a story by Jo Heims)
Produced by Robert Daley
Universal Pictures/The Malpaso Company
Cast: Clint Eastwood (Dave Garland), Jessica Walter, Donna Mills, John Larch

Dirty Harry
Directed and produced by Don Siegel
Screenplay by Harry Julian Fink, Rita M. Fink, Dean Reisner (based on a story by Harry Julian Fink and Rita M. Fink)
Warner Bros./Seven Arts/The Malpaso Company
Cast: Clint Eastwood (Detective Harry Callahan), Harry Guardino, Reni Santoni, Andy Robinson

1972

Joe Kidd
Directed by John Sturges
Screenplay by Elmore Leonard
Produced by Sidney Beckerman
Universal Pictures/The Malpaso Company
Cast: Clint Eastwood (Joe Kidd), Robert Duvall, John Saxon, Don Stroud

1973

High Plains Drifter
Directed by Clint Eastwood
Screenplay by Ernest Tidyman
Produced by Robert Daley
Universal Pictures/The Malpaso Company
Cast: Clint Eastwood (the Stranger), Verna Bloom, Marianna Hill,
   Mitchell Ryan

Breezy
Directed by Clint Eastwood
Screenplay by Jo Heims
Produced by Robert Daley
Universal Pictures/The Malpaso Company
Cast: William Holden, Kay Lenz, Roger C. Carmel, Marj Dusay

Magnum Force
Directed by Ted Post
Screenplay by John Milius, Michael Cimino (based on a story by
   John Milius and characters created by Harry Julian Fink and
   Rita M. Fink)
Produced by Robert Daley
Warner Bros./The Malpaso Company
Cast: Clint Eastwood (Detective Harry Callahan), Hal Holbrook,
   Mitchell Ryan, David Soul

1974

Thunderbolt and Lightfoot
Directed and written by Michael Cimino
Produced by Robert Daley
United Artists/The Malpaso Company
Cast: Clint Eastwood (John "Thunderbolt" Doherty), Jeff Bridges,
   George Kennedy, Geoffrey Lewis

1975

The Eiger Sanction
Directed by Clint Eastwood
Screenplay by Warren B. Murphy, Hal Dresner, Rod Whitaker
  (based on the novel by Trevanian)
Produced by Robert Daley
Universal Pictures/The Malpaso Company
Cast: Clint Eastwood (Jonathan Hemlock), George Kennedy,
  Vonetta McGee, Jack Cassidy

1976

The Outlaw Josey Wales
Directed by Clint Eastwood
Screenplay by Philip Kaufman, Sonia Chernus (based on the novel
  The Rebel Outlaw: Josey Wales by Forrest Carter)
Produced by Robert Daley
Warner Bros./The Malpaso Company
Cast: Clint Eastwood (Josey Wales), Chief Dan George, Sondra
  Locke, Bill McKinney

The Enforcer
Directed by James Fargo
Screenplay by Stirling Silliphant, Dean Reisner (based on a story
  by Gail Morgan Hickman and S. W. Schurr and characters
  created by Harry Julian Fink and Rita M. Fink)
Produced by Robert Daley
Warner Bros./The Malpaso Company
Cast: Clint Eastwood (Detective Harry Callahan), Tyne Daly,
  Harry Guardino, Bradford Dillman

1977

The Gauntlet
Directed by Clint Eastwood
Screenplay by Michael Butler, Dennis Shyrack

Produced by Robert Daley
Warner Bros./Malpaso Productions
Cast: Clint Eastwood (Ben Schockley), Sondra Locke, Pat Hingle,
William Prince

1978

Every Which Way but Loose
Directed by James Fargo
Screenplay by Jeremy Joe Kronsberg
Produced by Robert Daley
Warner Bros./The Malpaso Company
Cast: Clint Eastwood (Philo Beddoe), Sondra Locke, Geoffrey
Lewis, Beverly D'Angelo

1979

Escape from Alcatraz
Directed and produced by Donald Siegel
Screenplay by Richard Tuggle (based on the book by J. Campbell
Bruce)
Paramount Pictures/The Malpaso Company
Cast: Clint Eastwood (Frank Morris), Patrick McGoohan,
Roberts Blossom, Jack Thibeau

1980

Bronco Billy
Directed by Clint Eastwood
Screenplay by Dennis Hackin
Produced by Dennis Hackin, Neil Dobrofsky
Warner Bros.
Cast: Clint Eastwood (Bronco Billy McCoy), Sondra Locke,
Geoffrey Lewis, Scatman Crothers

Any Which Way You Can
Directed by Buddy Van Horn
Screenplay by Stanford Sherman
Produced by Fritz Manes
Warner Bros.
Cast: Clint Eastwood (Philo Beddoe), Sondra Locke, Geoffrey
Lewis, William Smith

1982

Firefox
Directed and produced by Clint Eastwood
Screenplay by Alex Lasker, Wendell Wellman (based on the novel
by Craig Thomas)
Warner Bros.
Cast: Clint Eastwood (Mitchell Gant), Freddie Jones, David
Huffman, Warren Clarke

Honkytonk Man
Directed and produced by Clint Eastwood
Screenplay by Clancy Carlile (based on his novel)
Warner Bros.
Cast: Clint Eastwood (Red Stovall), Kyle Eastwood, John
McIntire, Verna Bloom

1983

Sudden Impact
Directed and produced by Clint Eastwood
Screenplay by Joseph C. Stinson (based on a story by Earl Smith
and Charles B. Pierce and characters created by Harry Julian
Fink and Rita M. Fink)
Warner Bros.
Cast: Clint Eastwood (Detective Harry Callahan), Sondra Locke,
Pat Hingle, Bradford Dillman

Introduction
The Good, the Bad ...

"I'll say that you can see the man in his work just as clearly as you see Hemingway in A Farewell to Arms *or John Cheever in his short stories. Hell, yes, he's an artist. I even think he's important. Not just a fabulous success at the box office, but important."*

Literary heavyweight Norman Mailer no doubt caused some eyebrows to skeptically rise when he penned these enthusiastic words in *Parade* magazine in 1983. But more than eleven years earlier in *Rolling Stone*, critic Paul Nelson had already come to the same conclusion. Reviewing *Dirty Harry*, he wrote that Eastwood "promises to be a major force in the films of the next decade, both as an actor and a director ..." Screenwriter Jay Cocks, then a critic for *Time* magazine and a good friend of Paul's, remembers that this was in the days of "pre-Clint idolatry," when not too many people—especially critics—were prepared to come out and confess that they were Clint Eastwood fans. "There were not a lot of us," writer John Morthland says. "Not like today. Clint Eastwood had not really reached his pop critics of any kind. Paul was one of the few who really liked him."

It took until 1979, but Paul finally convinced his editors at *Rolling Stone* that a cover story was in order. Paul, who was the magazine's record-review editor, had a special arrangement with publisher Jann Wenner: in addition to his usual editorial duties, he would occasionally contribute feature stories (sprawling, sometimes award-winning pieces) about those artists whom he considered special. Even though he was legendary as a music critic—in 1960 he had cofounded *The Little Sandy Review*, a homemade journal devoted to the consideration of serious folk music; but in 1966 he alienated many of his folk brethren by championing the electrification of Bob Dylan and the arrival of adult rock & roll—movies were his first love. In the early Seventies, he'd written a string of a half dozen memorable film reviews for *Rolling Stone*.

Friends with Eastwood, Cocks and his wife Verna Bloom provided Paul with his entrée to the star. "He either asked or we volunteered," Cocks says. "Verna had been in two movies with Clint. So we called Clint." Not only did the actor-director say yes, but Paramount Pictures loved the idea and wanted to tie Paul's proposed piece to the studio's upcoming release, *Escape from Alcatraz*. Eastwood had starred in the film and was now lending a hand to the director, his old pal Don Siegel, with the editing. Paul could fly out to LA and snag some quotable Clintisms from him when he wasn't busy at the Moviola.

But such flackery wasn't the kind of piece Paul had in mind. "It's like your between-shows interview with a rock star or something. You go backstage and you might get something." After a pause—probably to take a drag on the ever-present Nat Sherman Cigarettello—he added: "You never get anything." Paul's MO when it came to interviews was to show up, hang out, and soak up the atmosphere, allowing interviewer and subject to get comfortable with one another. He wouldn't even think about pulling out his tape recorder until a day or two later. Once they began, the interview sessions themselves usually ran two or three days, minimum.

No, he would rather hold off until Eastwood was back in the saddle again as actor and director on his next film.

Which was why, in October of 1979, Paul Nelson flew from the increasingly meaner streets of Manhattan to Boise, Idaho's Wild West, where arguably the most recognizable man in the world was making a movie called *Bronco Billy*. His first time on a set, he watched with a fan's fascination as Clint worked both sides of the camera. Back at the Red Lion Inn, where Eastwood and company had set up camp, Paul conducted lengthy, in-depth interviews, not only with the lead but also two of his co-stars: Clint's leading lady (personally and professionally), Sondra Locke, and Sam Bottoms. Paul took an immediate liking to the young actor ("Billy Budd as a cowboy"), who, fresh from his experience of filming *Apocalypse Now*, had more to say about working with Eastwood than he did about working with Francis Ford Coppola: "We'll be studying Eastwood like Bogart, in the future, for sure." Paul also sat down with Fritz Manes, Clint's longtime friend and key member of his production team, and *Bronco Billy*'s co-producer, Dennis Hackin, who wrote the screenplay.

By the time he returned to New York City, Paul had plenty to write about. He and the star had hit it off. Unlike the laconic characters he was famous for portraying onscreen, Eastwood with Paul was often loquacious, patiently answering questions he'd undoubtedly been asked dozens of times before, but also confiding in him about subjects less frequently discussed. He spoke honestly about his influences and strengths, both as an actor and director. He reminisced about the early years he'd spent trying to break through as a contract player, as well as his hopes for the future as a director. When Paul traveled to Los Angeles the next month to interview singer-songwriter Warren Zevon (for another *Rolling Stone* cover story), Eastwood made time for him. And when Clint came to New York in December to shoot a few scenes for *Bronco Billy*, he invited Paul to his hotel room and, in between watching football on TV, drinking beer (Clint, not Paul, whose drink of choice was Coca-Cola), and visiting with Jay Cocks, they talked some more.

What more could a journalist ask for? On top of it all, he liked his subject and his subject, by all indications, liked him. Paul came away from the experience feeling, "Jeez, Clint Eastwood is a real best-friend type." As taken as he was with the man, though, when *Bronco Billy* opened the following June, its release was unheralded in *Rolling Stone*. Paul had failed to deliver his article.

Fast forward a few months. Cocks received a call from Eastwood, who was already wrapping up work on *Any Which Way You Can*, the sequel to the immensely popular *Every Which Way but Loose* (two movies in the same year was not unusual for Clint, who in earlier years had sometimes released three). Someone at *Rolling Stone* had contacted him about sending someone—not Paul—out to interview him about the new film. A year has passed since the original round of interviews. What's up with the piece? If Paul was going to finish it, Clint wanted to go that route rather than start anew. Cocks says, "This was the first real sign I had that Paul was having serious problems." He reached out to him to find out what was going on.

Paul assured Jay that he was indeed going to finish the article—in fact, it would be great if he could interview Eastwood some more about the new movie. The fire beneath him once again burning, in October Paul headed to Los Angeles where, in Eastwood's Malpaso Company office on the Warner Bros. lot, another series of interviews commenced. By December, however, when *Any Which Way You Can* was released—six months after *Bronco Billy*—Paul still hadn't turned in his article.

What happened after that, from the end of 1980 until early 1983, could be the subject for another book (and in fact is). Paul, falling victim to problems both personal and professional, struggled more and more with his writing. Even under the best of conditions, he was slave to his own obsessive-compulsive, perfectionist tendencies. As his old friend Kit Rachlis says, "As a writer, he was a real diamond-cutter kind of person." But this was something beyond his usual OCD-like inability to suffer a typographical error on the page, which had to be absolutely perfect before he could proceed. In the pre-PC and pre-word processing days of the Seventies and Eighties, Paul's only recourse was to rip the paper from the typewriter and start over on a clean sheet. This was writer's block in the bleakest sense, a paralysis that deadened not only his writing but his entire being. The inability to arrange words on the page in ways that pleased him often rendered him horizontal and unable to function.

By the time Paul quit his job at *Rolling Stone* in 1982, his colleagues had long stopped asking how the Eastwood piece was coming along. It was less awkward that way—for both parties.

This wasn't the first time that Paul's perfectionism had wedged itself between him and a piece of writing, nor would it be the last. A few years earlier, a similar fate had befallen an interview with Kenneth Millar, who, under the name Ross Macdonald, wrote about private eye Lew Archer. He also never satisfied a book deal to write a biography of Neil Young, and a book about Rod Stewart only came to pass when Paul's friend and fellow critic Lester Bangs came on board and filled most of the blank pages. Marathon interviews with Leonard Cohen and Lucinda Williams would yield nothing. And, at the same time Paul was wrestling with the Eastwood piece, he was experiencing similar difficulties with the Zevon article (more than a year passed until he finally finished it).

As different as all these projects were, they were also similar in that they all dealt with artists whom Paul admired as much personally as he did aesthetically. Their opinions undoubtedly meant as much to him as did their work and, fearing that he might fall short in his understanding of them and what they did (for Paul, writing was discovery in the truest sense), the argument could be made that perhaps he was afraid to disappoint them (to say nothing of himself). In terms of the sheer volume of material he gathered on them, just where to begin was daunting. He admitted that sometimes he just had "*too much* to say." If this were the case and it was beyond him to find the right words to describe these artists and their work, well, then he'd rather just say nothing at all.

As much a fan as he was an objective journalist, the frissons that came from spending so much time hanging out with his heroes, talking with them, *trying* to understand them, must have been considerable. (After all, this was a man who, as a result of seeing *Dirty Harry* in 1971, purchased—by way of not entirely legal means—a .44 Magnum.) Maybe, to put it bluntly, writing-wise he'd come too soon. Perhaps his reasons were the same as why, when he worked at Mercury Records in the early Seventies, scouting and developing talent, he'd laid his job on the line with the company brass until they finally relented and allowed him to sign the unruly New York Dolls to the label: "I just wanted to be around the damn band—it was as simple as that."

But the story didn't end in LA in 1980. Over two years later, in January of 1983, galvanized by the need for cash, or the need to complete a piece he desperately wanted to write, or the desire to apologize for what he'd failed to do—maybe, probably, all three—Paul Nelson reached out once again to Clint Eastwood. For whatever reason—perhaps his relationship with Cocks and Bloom, who were good friends with Paul, or maybe because he just flat-out liked Paul and wanted to believe he could come through—Clint said yes once more. In October, shortly before Norman Mailer's article appeared in *Parade*, Paul was back in LA with Eastwood, who was putting the finishing touches on his fourth Dirty Harry film, *Sudden Impact*.

Of course, as the subtitle of this book suggests, Paul never turned in his cover story. Despite running over seventeen and a half hours of tape with Clint (not including all the time, on the set or over lunch and dinner, they hung out together when the recorder was turned off) and almost another ten with his associates, he was never able to get past page four of his manuscript. When Eastwood once again called Jay Cocks and suggested that perhaps Paul could relinquish his tapes to another *Rolling Stone* writer so that he could do the cover story on whatever Eastwood flick was coming up, Cocks understood, "but Paul's not going to want to do that." Eventually another writer was assigned to the cover story, which finally ran in 1985.

In the four years that passed since they first sat down across from each other, when Eastwood was forty-nine and Paul was forty-three, Clint completed five films. The Seventies, that most directorial of decades, had been winding down when the interviews began, but for Eastwood that's where he saw his future. Using a series of small, often rough-around-the-edges but energetic films to better learn his craft, still aggressively making the transition from actor to director, he was laying the groundwork for what has become one of the most iconic careers in the history of cinema.

As for Paul Nelson, he died in 2006. Six months later, while researching my book *Everything Is an Afterthought: The Life and Writings of Paul Nelson*, his son Mark Nelson and I spent three days exploring Paul's apartment. Paul had spent the last fifteen or so years of his life here and, from the looks of it, whatever he'd brought into the dwelling pretty much remained there. The sixth-story walk-up was dominated by videotapes and CDs and books. There was barely room to navigate. It had not been so much a place for living as it had been for enjoying those things that mattered to him most: movies, music, and literature.

Our first night there, sorting through all of Paul's mementos, papers, and photographs—some hidden away, some in clear view—doing our best to divine all that was personal from all that was not, Mark undid the flaps on a cardboard box, peered inside, and found four years of his father's life. He said, "I found the Eastwood tapes."

KEVIN AVERY
Brooklyn, New York
February 28, 2011

Editor's Note

Because Paul Nelson's interview technique tended to be less guided than it was roundabout—more conversational, if you will (he knew that to get to the heart of A, sometimes it required jumping ahead to K or S, or even Z, and coming back again)—the material has been reorganized to follow Clint Eastwood's career, and the events of his life, as chronologically as possible.

Most importantly, even if their reason for getting together in the first place was never until now realized, I wanted to preserve the tone of the talks between two men who, for a period of time, enjoyed what was basically an ongoing, four-year conversation between friends.

The Telephone Call

PAUL NELSON'S APARTMENT
NEW YORK, NY
JANUARY 1983

FADE IN:

Paul Nelson was always difficult to reach by phone. A devout screener, he almost always let his prehistoric answering machine, which many a friend grew to despise, pick up his calls. This one, though, he answered himself.

PAUL NELSON: *Hello?*

SECRETARY: Hi, Paul. Here's Clint Eastwood.

CLINT EASTWOOD: How you doing?

PAUL: *Hi, how are you?*

CLINT: Good, Paul. What's up with you?

PAUL: *Oh, a lot of dramatic things. I thought I should call, first of all, to fill you in and apologize for the holy mess at* Rolling Stone.

CLINT: I heard it was a little bit of a problem. Jay [Cocks] brought me up to date.

PAUL: *And to tell you that I thought* Honkytonk Man *was just great. It's one of your best pictures ever. I saw it again last night actually for the third time, and it just gets better and better.*

CLINT: Ah, I'm glad you liked it. It's not going to be a big hit movie, but I didn't make it expecting it to be a big hit movie. I just made it because I wanted to make it. Sometimes you've got to make a few things like that. I can always pick up a gun and go racing through the streets.

PAUL: *The* Rolling Stone *thing, the last two years I was there was just a running battle with the publisher. Basically the trouble was with the music section where my main job was editing record reviews. So I just figured, To hell with this. This is silly, you know? [sighs] I sort of took a line from you. I remember you saying there's a time when you have to make your move—and my move was just to get out of there.*

CLINT: Cut and run on it, yeah.

PAUL: *So I sold a lot of my first-edition Hammetts and Chandlers and sold some records to get some kind of stake to stay alive, and just quit. But since I left, they have sort of come around and want me to write freelance for them. Anyway, I'm awfully sorry it didn't appear yet, but they do want it again now—*

CLINT: [chuckles] Oh, really?

PAUL: *—and I'm certainly willing to do it.*

CLINT: I thought it was good material. We were getting along. In fact, I was kidding Jay: "Boy, if I ever decide to sit down and write a biography, I'll just call Paul up and say, 'Paul, would you mind printing that stuff up?' We've got it." [laughs]

PAUL: *That was another thing that I wanted to talk to you about, because I'm going to try to write books from now on basically. What I was thinking—and you maybe don't want to do this— writing not a biography but something called* Conversations with Clint Eastwood. *It wouldn't be a biography per se, it would be the stuff we talked about. Uh, what's your feeling on that?*

CLINT: Well, someday. I'm not ready for one yet, but someday when I am I'll call on you because you've got half the material all there.

PAUL: *I felt you probably wouldn't want to do a full-scale biography at the moment.*

CLINT: Seems maybe a little early. I think I've got one or two more projects left in me.

PAUL: *That's what I figured. This book, more or less, would all be in your own words. But I wouldn't want to do it unless you wanted to do it.*

CLINT: [hesitates] I'd rather wait a little bit. Maybe coordinate with you on one that is a definite thing. But everything else is cool, though, huh?

PAUL: *Yeah, except for money. You don't get a regular check this way. It was good to get out. In the long run it'll be the best thing I ever did, if I can get through the next year.*

CLINT: Oh yeah, you will.

PAUL: *I've got a deal for a Neil Young book, which will probably keep me going for six months' worth of paying the rent and everything, and then I hope to get another one on Ross Macdonald. You have to do a lot of them to really make it. You don't get royalties until after the book is published, and my rent's almost a thousand dollars a month here. So it's a bit sticky. It's exciting, I must say.*

CLINT: They [*Rolling Stone*] just gave up on the story, huh?

PAUL: *They didn't want to do it for Firefox, and at that point I was in such a bad mood I didn't want to cooperate with them at all for a while. Now we've sort of made peace on a freelance basis and Jann [Wenner] really wants the story again. So I'd like to do it.*

CLINT: But what do you want to tie it in with? Would you want a cover story on nothing?

PAUL: *No, I think it would be a cover story. I just think he wants it. Oddly enough—or maybe it isn't odd if you're as crazy as Jann is—he seemed to goad me into quitting for two years and the minute I did quit he went completely nuts and wanted me to come back. I know he likes my writing a lot, and it's I guess some sort of crazy love/hate respect/non-respect thing. I know once you're out of the magazine you get a lot more respect than when you're working directly for it. As long as you're working there you're dirt under their feet.*

CLINT: I remember the same thing years ago being a contract player with a studio. Boy, as soon as you left they seemed more interested than when you were there.

PAUL: *I just think they're interested—period. The whole premise anyway was going to be what a good director and actor you are. It wasn't going to specifically focus on one picture.*
Is there any time we could talk more about Honkytonk Man?

CLINT: Sure. See if those guys want to do it and then give me a holler.

PAUL: *Okay. And if you do decide you'd like to do this* Conversations *book, boy, I would love to do it. Or if you want to wait, or whatever you want to do.*

CLINT: I'm not certain about it at the moment. Let me think about it a little bit.

PAUL: *So are you going to be in LA this week? I could ring you back in a couple days or I'll just leave a message.*

CLINT: Ring me back. I'll be here.

PAUL: *Say hello to Sondra [Locke] and everybody.*

CLINT: I will, Paul.

PAUL: *I'll talk to you soon.*

CLINT: Talk to you later.

FLASHBACK TO:

The Conversations

CLINT EASTWOOD'S AND PAUL NELSON'S ROOMS
RED LION INN, BOISE, ID
OCTOBER 1979

CLINT EASTWOOD'S HOTEL ROOM
NEW YORK, NY
DECEMBER 1979

CLINT EASTWOOD'S OFFICE
THE MALPASO COMPANY, BURBANK, CA
NOVEMBER 1979, OCTOBER 1980,
AND OCTOBER 1983

1

PAUL: *I'm sorry, I've forgotten your father's name.*

CLINT: His name was Clint Eastwood, too. I'm junior, actually. Clinton Eastwood Jr. I don't have a middle name. My dad didn't have a middle name either.

PAUL: *Fritz [Manes] told me that your father was a real athlete who went to the U of Cal for about a year and then got tired of it.*

CLINT: I think he went a year or two. He was a big-time high school football player. His mother had died of cancer and then, living alone with his father, I guess he just decided to move out and get a job and get married. There were no scholarships.

PAUL: *He died quite some time ago? In the Sixties, was it?*

CLINT: Early Seventies, I think. Sixties. Hard to keep track of time now.[1]

PAUL: *I don't know if you've seen your entry in this book by Ephraim Katz, The Film Encyclopedia. But it sounds to me, from what you've told me, that he rather romanticized and exaggerated this. It says: "A child of the Depression, he spent his early boyhood trailing a father who pumped gas along dusty roads all over the West Coast." From what you told me, I hadn't gathered it was quite that bad.*

CLINT: It wasn't quite *The Grapes of Wrath*, but it had enough of the struggling to do well that probably influenced me to do *Honkytonk Man*. In the early days, in the Thirties, it was definitely job-to-job in some cases. We moved over to Sacramento from Redding and then we packed up all our gear and came all the way down here from Sacramento to Pacific Palisades just to have a gas pump job. That's how tough the times were. The guy had a year or two of college and that was the best job he could get. I remember those times, I remember the houses that we lived in. And I remember chicken houses. People would take chicken houses and convert them into houses and live in them.

PAUL: *Your father, he was a stevedore and a dockworker.*

CLINT: We moved around a lot until we got to Oakland. We stayed in the Bay Area, where they were from, where they had started out. During the war years, in Oakland, he worked for Bethlehem Steel as a pipe-fitter and a lot of jobs like that. But in between that he was also a jewelry salesman. He tried a lot of things. For a few years it was kind of so-so and then he finally started doing pretty good.

My parents both worked for a while, so I went and lived

---

[1] Clinton Sr. died in 1970 at the age of sixty-four.

with my grandmother for a while. That was out in Hayward, a suburb of Oakland. Sunol, I lived out there for a while. My mother worked as an operator for IBM when IBM was really small. She should've bought the stock then, except nobody had the money to buy it with. When I was in high school, my dad went into the container business, selling. Container Corporation of America, it was called. During the late Forties, after I got out of high school, he went to Seattle and he took over a plant. He was very good at taking plants in trouble and bringing them back. He became a success doing that. Later on, the company never really came through with a lot of their promises to him, so he moved on to Georgia-Pacific, which he liked very much. Finally he retired. But he had about ten years, maybe more, of doing well in the final result.

PAUL: *My father started with a gas station and apparently was smart enough to make a fair amount of money in the stock market, then he lost the whole works in the crash. He then built it up again from a gas station to an auto dealership and owned some farms. I really wish I could remember that period because after that it seemed to take something out of him, the crash.*

CLINT: A lot of guys it did. It busted them down.

PAUL: *He became quieter. My mother probably influenced him. My mother was quite religious. I was brought up to consider movies a sin, which probably explains why I like movies.*

CLINT: For resisting your parents, huh? But that was your escape, too. That was probably your way to take a trip somewhere.

PAUL: *Oh, it was.*

CLINT: Unfortunately that's one of the problems with religion: the fear aspect. My parents would send me to various churches as we'd go. They were all different, whatever was convenient, because they wanted me to get a religious education. But I had a hard time picturing God as being quite as sadistic as being made out by some of these groups, as somebody who couldn't wait to punish you and couldn't wait to make you grovel for some indiscretion you made. I just never saw him that way. I wanted my vision of him, so I just asked my parents if I could *not* attend. That was the day when I guess they realized I'd made up my mind that I had a philosophy about it. Anyway, it's all in what the mind makes it.

PAUL: *I'm not sorry that I grew up that way. I learned a lot probably by having to think for myself from a very young age.*

CLINT: No, it was good because it made you make decisions about things or gave you thoughts about things at a stage in life where you started saying, "Wait a second, I'm not sure I agree with that. It may be written in some scripture that's very, very old, but I'm not sure that I want to look at things with that outlook. I may want to later on, but I'd like to know a little bit more about it before I go putting myself on the line." I felt pretty much the same way.

PAUL: *And your mother is Ruth?*

CLINT: She's alive and doing well.[2]

PAUL: *You have a sister also. A younger sister or older sister?*

CLINT: Younger. Jeanne.

PAUL: *I talked to Fritz a little bit and he was very impressed by your parents and that your home was a home in which you and your sister were talked to as adults at all times. What do you think your parents gave you?*

CLINT: You're lucky if they draw you from a lot, and they're lucky if they've drawn you from a lot. I guess I was lucky. They were just good people. My parents dealt straight across to me, they didn't condescend in any particular way. Their parents were nice, fairly well-adjusted people, not too many problems.

PAUL: *It was quite a happy and comfortable home?*

---

[2] Margaret Ruth Runner Eastwood passed away in 2006 at the age of ninety-six.

CLINT: I think it was, yeah.

PAUL: The Film Encyclopedia *goes on to say: "Young Clint rarely spent more than a semester in one school, and after graduating from high school, he worked as a logger, steel furnace-stoker, and gas pumper."*

CLINT: I've done all those jobs plus a hundred others.

PAUL: *You got into acting at the Army camp in Fort Ord with Marty Milner and David Janssen.*

CLINT: Yeah, all those guys were up there, though I had a friend who had been into it before and I had another friend who was an assistant film editor. He was like an apprentice. These guys were all drafted during the Korean campaign. We had all kinds of good talent up there. André Previn was at the same base, and all these great musicians and a lot of actors. I forget who all was up there. I think Richard Long was there.

PAUL: *You were really seriously thinking about it as a craft at that time?*

CLINT: I was getting interested, but I wasn't aggressive about it. I was thinking that it would be a satisfying way to have a career, but it wasn't something that had been a lifelong burning since I was a child.

PAUL: *Had the years before* Rawhide *been pretty tough in the anonymous world of smaller pictures?*

CLINT: They were very tough because you'd do a few bits and then you wouldn't get any parts for months. A lot of times guys'll do either theater or television. In the old days they'd bounce around live television shows and then finally somebody'd give them a break. From that they'd springboard into something.

I can remember when I first got in. Hell, the movie business is so strange anyway. You first go on interviews, and a lot of the people who are making the decision on whether you are going to work or not are people who really have no knowledge of the business anyway. Ninety percent of them, I'd say, whom I've met along the way aren't even in the business. They've gotten in through real estate or are salesmen or they've gotten in because of some deal they've been in. You'd go on interviews where they'd have ten guys your size and age bracket in the office. You'd feel like an asshole sitting there. "Cattle calls" they used to call them for the theater. What are the odds? Now there's ten: that's a one-out-of-ten shot. Maybe they ran two sets of ten before that: that's a one-out-of-thirty shot. Then you'd go meet whomever was casting, and they'd all sit around you and go, "Humph."

You'd get pretty depressed. I was working, and running down to the gas station to call my agent. "Anything for me?" "No, no." "Okay." Boy, I used to call and bug those guys. They were always out of the office, but you knew he was sitting right there.

Sometimes they'd send you on a snore interview. It would be one where you knew damn well you weren't right for the part. When you got there, you found out that they'd sent you just to keep you in action. Sometimes you'd go on an interview where you knew the agent had called on a promise and sent you.

I had an agent do that to me recently. He called and said, "Would you see so-and-so?" I said, "I don't have a part for the gal." "That's all right, I promised her an interview. You'd be doing me a great favor." I said, "I can't do that. I'm not going to mislead this person into thinking there's something there and get her all excited about the possibility when there's absolutely nothing there. It's just a fake. All fakery. You made the promise, you get out of it." I'm sure he probably told her that I was a bum or something. Those guys are scummy sometimes.

PAUL: *The money wasn't so good, I guess, if you were a contract player for the studio back then.*

CLINT: When I was a contract player at Universal, I made seventy-five dollars a week. I was there a year and a half. When I left there I was maybe making a hundred or something like that, but even then that wasn't a hundred because you got forty weeks a year, then you were on layoff for the rest of the time.

PAUL: *I imagine it was also very hard to make an impression in a small role where your only line was "Here's the test tube, doc" or something like that.*

CLINT: Exactly. You'd come in to play a pilot and they'd throw the mask on you, a helmet, the goggles, and so-and-so and such-and-such, and you're a body wig. There's no impression—and you don't fool yourself by thinking there's an impression. You do the job, you're glad to have the credit, and you're glad to be just working, even for the fun of being in on the action. You know you're not going to set the world on fire.[3]

PAUL: *I gather this is the period that made a considerable mark on you. In other interviews I've seen, the cattle calls and the crushing of the ego seem to come up a lot. This was a period where some hurt was done and hasn't been forgotten.*

CLINT: Oh, I guess it's forgotten, but I don't know. It's sad, too. I find people come up to me now and they say, "How do I break into the acting business?" I say, "What have you been doing up to this point with it?" Sometimes they've been in schools or they've been in little theater, and other times it's nothing, no experience, and they want to start from scratch. Boy, you hate to really burst the bubble. You hate to say, "Don't do it," because somewhere you might be talking to a really great potential talent. At the same time, you think, Boy, you'd better be ambitious and be able to hang in there, because if you think you're going to try it for six months and you're going to be an overnight hit, you've got a lot of fun coming. We all know the old joke about being a ten-year overnight success. Once in a while some guy comes along and makes it when he's a teenager or something like that, but even then who knows how long that lasts? You go along and then you get a lull.

PAUL: *Did you ever consider giving it up at that point?*

CLINT: Oh, sure. After about the first five years or so, four years, I started really getting to the point where I started wondering.

---

[3] Eastwood played such a part in 1955's *Tarantula*, leading the jet squadron that successfully exterminates that giant arachnid.

You go through periods of really liking it and wanting to be involved—but struggling. It's one of the few professions where you struggle to work. Most of the time, you just go out and hire on the job and you learn something about it, and you stay with it or you transfer to another company. But in the acting profession you've got thousands of people all wanting to do the same job, so there's a tremendous amount of competition involved. And I wasn't a very good competitor on the outside. I mean, I was a good competitor—I'd make all the interviews—but I wasn't a terribly extrovertish guy. Some of these guys would come in and they'd have all the latest jokes and they really could get in and sell and do a nice job putting themselves over. But if I went into somebody's office, it was just "How do you do, so-and-so?" and that's about the best I could come up with. I wasn't going to sit there and bullshit the guy. I always felt a complex about taking up the guy's time. I always felt I was a lousy handshake, you know?

PAUL: *I know that feeling exactly. It's the same with writing. If the work is good, you should get the damn job.*

CLINT: If you can get it on film, that's more like your correlation with writing, because you can lay the writing right in front of them and say, "Now read that and see how you like it. If you like it, you like it. Don't expect me to give you all the patter." If I ever had a chance to test for roles where I made film tests, I usually got the parts. But if it meant coming in and giving some jive to a couple ad men, I was a washout. Before *Rawhide* came along, I struck out on a lot of series just at the door—and I was sure that I would have been good for them if I'd had a chance to be on film or even if I sat around a bit. But naturally you can't expect the people who are putting on the shows to sit around and wait till you loosen up, till you all become buddies, so you can go out and have a few beers. They have to look at hundreds of people every day, so it just doesn't work like that.

PAUL: *It's still a horrifying feeling to know that, if you even get on that stage, you have one minute to knock this guy cold, and there are 300 guys behind you.*

CLINT: And out of the 300, what are the odds that somebody else isn't going to knock him cold?

PAUL: *When did it hit you that "I'm pretty good at this. I feel good doing this"?*

CLINT: I guess after. I was a contract player at Universal and I didn't know whether I was good at it or not. I probably wasn't [laughs], but I just thought that I had something to bring. I didn't know what it was, I didn't know on what level or what magnitude along the way, I just thought I had something that I could develop.

The more you go to acting classes, the more you study, you realize the less you know. It's like laying bricks: it looks pretty easy to see a guy slapping the mortar down and dropping them in, but you don't realize until you start doing it yourself that there are some techniques and knacks to it. Acting's a very strange thing to learn because it's not an analytical or intellectual art. It's a very instinctive and animalistic art, and you have to just do it, to *feel* yourself and then catalogue those feelings away. After a few years of it, once in a while you'd do a scene and you felt like you were cooking. You started thinking, Well, now that's not too bad.

Then you just bash your head on doors because half the time, when you go on casting calls, nobody knows what they want anyway—unless you happen to be a specific type or have a specific reputation as an actor; then they just hire you. There are an awful lot of people whose doors you have to knock on who don't really know what they want or what they're doing there. So it's a very frustrating thing.

PAUL: *I taped* Revenge of the Creature *the other night, but I think you were cut out. Is that the one where you have the mouse in your pocket?*

CLINT: Yeah.

PAUL: *I stayed up until 5:22 in the morning to tape it. That scene was gone from the version I taped.*

CLINT: Ah, well. Nothing's sacred anymore. They take that fabulous scene out of the picture. That was my very first part. A four-liner or something like that.[4] I remember it was Jack Arnold directing and William Alland was the producer. Alland called me into his office and read me the scene and gave me the part. And that was it. He said, "I'll take you down and we'll meet the director." I walked on the set and the director said, "What the hell is this? I told you I don't want to do that goddamn scene! Who's this guy?" [laughs] I thought, I'm going to get punched—he was screaming and yelling—or else I was just going to wilt to the floor. Probably the latter. Alland made me realize that it wasn't anything against me—the director just didn't want the scene in the movie, so he didn't see any reason for shooting it and thought they should cut it out.

PAUL: *Well, they did in the version I saw [chuckles].*

CLINT: The producer won the argument. He just said, "That's in. Shoot it first thing in the morning." That was the final word, so I said, "I'll see you in the morning." But it was a hell of a way to start your acting career: walk on a set and you *know* that the director hates the scene. Therefore you know he hates *you*.[5]

2

> The television series *Rawhide* debuted in 1959 and ran until 1966. Eastwood starred as ramrod Rowdy Yates, charged with driving 3,000 head of cattle from Texas to Missouri.

CLINT: *Rawhide* was the first series I got, the first decent break.

PAUL: *That was when you were about twenty-eight, I guess.*

CLINT: Yeah.

---

[4] Eastwood was being modest. He actually had seven lines in the 1955 film, the first of two sequels to *Creature from the Black Lagoon*. Eastwood, uncredited, played a lab technician.
[5] Eastwood and Arnold, who also made *Tarantula* together with Alland the same year, would reunite a few years later when Arnold directed four episodes of *Rawhide*.

PAUL: *You directed some second unit stuff on* Rawhide *every once in a while, right? Like a cattle stampede once and things like that?*

CLINT: Yeah, some trailers and stuff like that.

PAUL: *Even then you pretty well knew that you wanted to be a director.*

CLINT: Oh yeah, I had been involved with a lot of things on the set.

PAUL: *It's been described as a* Red River/Montgomery Clift *type of role.*

CLINT: He was much more naïve. He was like the sidekick guy, a little hotheaded. It was a great experience to play that. I got to work. There's something you can do in a series if you're really selfish that you can't do in theater or anything else: you can every week play the same character, then look at it and pick and choose. You see things that you do and you think, Yeah, that worked. You see things that you do that don't work. And after you do that for seven or eight years you build up a file in your brain as to what works and what doesn't work for you.

Paul was good friends with singer-songwriter Warren Zevon, whom Clint had met two years earlier. In addition to comparing the musician to the actor in print ("seeing the man onstage was like experiencing—what?—[Jackson] Browne's 'For Everyman,' the works of F. Scott Fitzgerald, Sam Peckinpah's *The Wild Bunch*, the New York Dolls, Norman Mailer, Clint Eastwood in *Dirty Harry*, and Ross Macdonald/Ken Millar's Lew Archer novels at a very impressionable age. Rightly or wrongly, your life got changed"), Paul was responsible for taking Warren to see his very first Clint Eastwood movie, *The Outlaw Josey Wales*. Zevon left the theater a fan for life. "After that I was determined to see all the Eastwood pictures, and I thought they all were great."

PAUL: *Warren Zevon tried acting actually. His girlfriend is in* Knots Landing. *There was a small part on that and he said he'd like* *to read for it. His manager is Irving Azoff, who's a powerhouse rock & roll manager. He said, "I don't want a call from my rock manager to get me an audition. If I am any good, I'd like to think people think so because I have some talent, not because I was a spinoff of something else." It was sort of a* Psycho/Tony *Perkins-type part where he had to be soft-spoken but menacing at the same time. He didn't get it. I don't know whether he's got any talent along those lines in acting.*

CLINT: He probably does. Anybody can develop it or work with it. You just have to spend some time.

PAUL: *Warren's girlfriend, Kim Lankford, the stories she tells about how they shoot are just horrific. The director turns up Monday with a hangover, he's got five days to shoot an hour, and he says to the cast, "I'm sorry, I haven't read the script yet." Was it that bad?*

CLINT: If a guy showed up drunk and hadn't read the script, I think we would've kicked his ass out of there. If a guy showed up and he wasn't prepared and he started fumbling around, he quickly lost the enthusiasm of the cast because the cast was there week in, week out, all year long, year after year. Especially in the later years, we wanted guys who were very, very efficient.

I don't know why a lot of people are hired. It seems like the movie and television business is almost masochistic at times. What I resent is the general disrespect for the profession of acting. I guess it delves [*sic*] down from the top, from the producers or whatever, but they'll hire directors who don't know much. Maybe that's because the producer doesn't know *anything*. He'll have to have somebody who at least razzle-dazzles him. They'll get bluffed into thinking this guy knows something, then they find out he doesn't. They'll allow him to hire actresses or actors sometimes who really haven't had any experience at all.

Not that everybody should be experienced. You have to get experience somewhere, but so many pictures get scuttled because they're not properly cast. It's not a question of the actors being bad, it's just a question of—instead of being cast in a role that really suits them, they're cast in something that's a stretch. They don't have the talent *yet* to develop to stretch that distance.

But who knows for what reason half that stuff is done.

PAUL: *That's what you meant by disrespect for the actors?*

CLINT: Yeah. Every once in a while somebody will say, "We're going to use so-and-so, who's a good photographic model" or something, instead of some good actress who's been doing it for ten years and has a pretty good background and has pretty good capabilities. By and large, most of it's a fad. There are so many good actors and actresses around, but everybody's faddist around town here. It's who's the TV-Q of the moment? If there is such a thing as TV-Q. I guess there is.[6]

PAUL: *Did you know Steve McQueen in the television days?*

CLINT: He was doing a series before I was, before *Rawhide—Wanted Dead or Alive*—but I didn't know him.

PAUL: *Did you know Jim Garner back in those days?*

CLINT: He and I lived across the street from each other out here in Sherman Oaks. I knew him before he became an actor—I used to see him around town now and then—but not well. One of those guys who pops up now and then and you feel a camaraderie because you're both struggling in the same direction.[7]

3

In 1964, Eastwood made the first of his legendary trio of "Spaghetti Westerns" with director Sergio Leone, *A Fistful of Dollars*. A cowboy re-imagining of Akira Kurosawa's *Yojimbo*, because Leone had failed to secure the rights necessary to remake the film, a lawsuit ensued that prevented *A Fistful of Dollars* from being shown in the US until 1967. *For a Few Dollars More* (1965) and *The Good, the Bad and the Ugly* (1966) followed, though in both instances there was a two-year lag before their US release.

---

[6] The TV-Q measures the appeal and familiarity of a celebrity or television program.
[7] In 1959, Eastwood appeared in an episode of Garner's TV series *Maverick*. In 2000, Garner would co-star with Eastwood in the director's *Space Cowboys*.

CLINT: After I did the series about six and a half years, I had the chance to do *A Fistful of Dollars*. When they sent me that script to do it, I wasn't interested at all. But when I read it, I was interested because, as a Western, I saw the possibilities in it, provided the director was as good as people said. [Sergio] Leone only directed one film before, a thing called *Il Colosso di Rodi—The Colossus of Rhodes*—and that wasn't my favorite picture. It was a Rory Calhoun tits-and-sandals thing. He was considered by people I knew in Rome to be a man with a great sense of humor and a very imaginative guy, so I just took a chance and it turned out that he was great. I had a chance to build a character who was really fun to play. Because the *Rawhide* episodes were all very open and forward kind of things, this character, you could hold all his background in abeyance, let the audience figure out who he is.

In fact, his whole background *was* drawn out. There were reams and reams of dialogue talking about where he came from, why he was there, what he was going for, et cetera, et cetera. But that was boring and it would've just bored the audience no end. What he *didn't* say was much more interesting than what he *does* say, creating the whole mystique thing. That was more important to me. It was hard to convince Leone of this because Italians are used to explaining things with great detail. It's just more of their natural makeup. We finally compromised by doing it that way, though it wasn't too much of a compromise [laughs].

I went to Europe and did *A Fistful of Dollars*. Boy, I came back to big headlines in *Variety*: "Westerns Are Out" and "Westerns Are Finished," they said. Some so-called expert was pronouncing them dead and gone for the next ten years or so. I picked that up—I was back here doing *Rawhides*—and I thought, Gee, how about that: Westerns are finished and I've just come back from making one?

PAUL: *You made three before they even showed the first one in America.*

CLINT: Finally it came out in Europe and it just went smash. I didn't even know it was that film. They changed the title, they didn't even tell me. It was called *The Magnificent Stranger* when they released it over there. It was a little tiny production company that had made it. They were forced into releasing it because they'd snuck the film in Milan or Naples or somewhere and sneak-previewed it. It became just a *huge* sensation all over the country. Then they sold it to Spain—Spain was a co-producer on it—and Germany. It was doing real well in all those places, but they couldn't release it over here due to all the litigation on *Yojimbo*.

I remember seeing that picture long before I ever did *A Fistful of Dollars*. I saw it with a friend of mine, a kid named Bill Tompkins, who was nuts over Japanese film.[8] I thought, God, what a great, exciting film. Of course, I love Kurosawa. In his prime he was one of the better directors in the world. In *Yojimbo* he captured a great excitement. I thought, God, this is just like a Western, but, jeez, they'd never have the nerve to make that here. In a Western they couldn't have that kind of punch and that kind of violence and that kind of antiheroics with the hero, who was totally out for his own gain. But Leone was smart enough to put it all together in his mind.

When I read the script, I recognized it right away as *Yojimbo*. He'd made a very good conversion of it. After I read it, I thought, What the hell, maybe a European director's the ticket on this thing. He didn't know you weren't supposed to tie up the shots of the guy shooting a gun and then somebody else getting hit by a bullet. It was just an old unsung rule: you didn't do it on television. We didn't do it on *Rawhide*.

PAUL: *You weren't legally allowed or you just didn't do it because you might get into trouble?*

CLINT: It became a thing you just didn't do because of the old Hays Office rules. It was a silly rule, an archaic one, much like a husband and wife in the movies couldn't sleep in the same bed.

PAUL: *So this was like a breath of fresh air.*

CLINT: Oh, it was great, yeah. All the pent-up frustrations of years of doing television, years of watching American Westerns decline

---

[8] An old Army buddy, Eastwood got Tompkins a job as stunt coordinator on *A Fistful of Dollars*.

because they were repeating themselves—and he's doing every crazy thing you'd want to do. I got a chance to just get right in and be with that style. I enjoyed it. Sergio knew how to build things up, too. He has a childlike imagination sometimes. That's what you need to express yourself in the movie business. After that he became the great expert supposedly on Westerns and the West, but he was no expert on the West. Leone's study of the West was looking at old tintypes. As he grew up, he'd seen all the same films we'd seen, in Italian. John Ford pictures would run in Europe and I guess he became influenced by some of these movies, but he didn't know about the Hays Office and the taboos that had been put on Westerns in America. He didn't know any more about the West than anybody else. He just happened to be very, very clever with his visual eye.

PAUL: *Had you ever read any of the Dashiell Hammett books at the time?* Yojimbo *seemed to be almost based on Hammett's* Red Harvest, *in a way.*

CLINT: I don't think I was influenced by Hammett, though he's done some marvelous things. Not consciously, but I think you're subconsciously influenced by a tremendous amount of things over your lifetime and they could be anything from who knows what.

PAUL: *You never felt consciously influenced by either Don Siegel or Sergio Leone in your own directing?*

CLINT: I'd say Leone because working with the European scene and the European style, and the difference in approach to pictures was great. Then coming back and working with Siegel, who was maybe not as much a composition kind of guy, more a hard-hitting, efficiency type guy. Both of them are good at editing in their own ways, their own styles, and both of them are totally different. But you have to go off and embellish on your own.[9]

I've learned from every director I've ever worked with, even the directors I worked with on *Rawhide* on television over the years. You can be influenced by what you've seen a director do and you *don't* like, that you vow you'll never do yourself.

---

[9] In 1992 Eastwood dedicated his film *Unforgiven* "to Sergio and Don."

It's an important lesson, as well as when you see somebody do something you *do* like and say, "When I get my chance I'm going to try to use my head like that guy does" or whatever. But it all comes out in your own.

It's the same way with acting. I've never been a big aficionado of any particular actor and so I don't *think* I come off looking like I'm influenced by it. I came into acting in the period where everybody was imitating Marlon Brando. Everybody. Nineteen-fifties. There wasn't an actor on the screen who wasn't sitting around going [imitates Brando] "I'm a contender." Even when they were playing brain surgeons they'd still be acting like Brando was when he was playing a fighter.

It was a wild period, but I don't think I was ever influenced by that. To me, one performance doesn't deserve imitating like that. It's degrading to imitate somebody. Do your own thing. I don't think that Montgomery Clift when he did *The Search* imitated anybody else. I don't think that Oskar Werner when he did *The Last Ten Days* was imitative of anybody else, or Albert Finney when he did *Saturday Night and Sunday Morning* was imitative. The great performances you can think of—at least that I think are great over the last two or three decades—were all people who had a certain individuality and that was it.

PAUL: *Were you going to acting class during the time when Jimmy Dean was making his films?*

CLINT: Yeah, sure. He managed to pull it off because he had a certain magnetism that worked well. But most of them just became imitative and nobody had a soul of their own. They were soulless performances. I guess there were four or five years there in the mid-Fifties or early Fifties that took on that complexion.

PAUL: *As a kid, when you were growing up, were you obsessed by movies, a real movie nut at that time?*

CLINT: I liked movies a lot, but I wasn't a real movie buff. I had some friends—this was before television—who would go four or five times a week. I'd maybe go to a movie once or twice a week. Once in a while you'd see one you really liked, go back a few times.

PAUL: *You weren't thinking, This is a Howard Hawks, this is a John Ford, and things like that.*

CLINT: No, no. I was very much the average moviegoer. I didn't know Hawks from Ford from [Alfred] Hitchcock. To me, it was who's in it. Am I going to see a Jimmy Stewart movie or am I going to see Randolph Scott or Humphrey Bogart or James Cagney or whoever? In later years, I became more interested in films and more interested in who did them and how. As you do it yourself, you really become interested because you like to try to understand what went through the person's mind who was instrumental in bringing it to the screen.

PAUL: *Would you like to have made films with Hawks and Ford?*

CLINT: Yeah, sure. I never had the great fortune of working with any of the biggies, with any of the so-called big names of those eras. I never was in a [William] Wyler or a [George] Stevens or a [Cecil B.] DeMille or any of those things. I never even got bit parts in those. I *did* do a picture with Bill Wellman one time [*Lafayette Escadrille* in 1958], but Wellman was kind of in a cold spell at that point in his life and it wasn't one of his major efforts. The time to have been with Wellman was *The Ox-Bow Incident* and some of the great films he did. But I was never of any value to those guys at that time. Most of those guys were coming to the end of their careers as I was coming on.

Funny thing, I met Hawks one time. I was seventeen years old. I came down on the weekend with a bunch of guys from Oakland, a bunch of crazy characters, and we stopped off in San Luis Obispo and partied with some gals who went to Cal Poly there. We were just punk kids. We ran into this guy who invited us to a party at his house in Westwood. The guy's family had a few bucks. We went down to this party and we were all drinking a lot of beer and stuff, and we saw some horses running down the street. We said, "God, we've got to catch these horses." They're just running down the boulevard—Sepulveda. This was before freeways and all that. We ran out and we stopped these horses and we herded them all back up the street. We saw this man come running down the street and he said, "Oh God, you got the horses. Thanks, you guys." The guy who lived down there said, "That's Howard Hawks, that guy we were just talking to. A big movie guy." I was really impressed.

PAUL: *Where did the horses come from?*

CLINT: They were his and they got out of the corral at night somehow. But that's the closest I ever came to anybody in the movie business at that time of life. I had no ideas about anything. Later on, I ran into Howard Hawks one time at a party and I reminded him, but he didn't remember it. It wasn't much of an incident to him, but to us it was an event.

4

In 1968's *Hang 'Em High*, directed by Ted Post, Eastwood is lynched for a crime he didn't commit. Surviving the noose, he sets out to find the nine men who placed it around his neck. The year before, Clint established his own production outfit, the Malpaso Company (later changed to Malpaso Productions).[10] Named after the creek that runs south of Carmel-by-the-Sea, California, *Malpaso* in English means *bad pass* or *bad step*, which is what Eastwood's agent had told him he'd be making if he traveled to Europe to shoot the Spaghetti Westerns.

CLINT: *Hang 'Em High* was actually the first film I worked on as a protagonist in America, and that was after the *Dollar* films. There was something great about going over and doing those little pictures with those characters. Each one of them was a tremendous hit. I just decided, Maybe it's time to move on to a few other things. Even after they came to America and did well, still I wasn't getting a tremendous amount of action. I wasn't getting the action that the trade magazine stars were getting, the kind of people you read about a lot—whomever Joyce Haber

---

[10] Although none of the films that Eastwood made during the course of these conversations—*Bronco Billy*, *Any Which Way You Can*, *Firefox*, *Honkytonk Man*, and *Sudden Impact*—bore the Malpaso brand, they were all made with the usual Malpaso personnel.

liked, just to name an example, not a specific. But I just kept whittling away at it and finally I did *Hang 'Em High*, which was low-budget.

PAUL: *Did Leone ask you to be in* Once Upon a Time in the West?

CLINT: He asked me to be in *Duck, You Sucker!* and *Once Upon a Time in the West.*

PAUL: *I assume it was the Charles Bronson part for* Once Upon a Time, *right? And the James Coburn part for* Duck, You Sucker!?

CLINT: Uh-huh. But I felt at the time, after *The Good, the Bad and the Ugly*, that he was going in a different direction than I wanted. He wanted to go more into a kind of spectacle thing. I think Leone more envisioned himself as a David Lean *à la Italiano*, and that's understandable. He just wanted to make bigger, more elaborate projects.

PAUL: *They kept getting bigger and more elaborate and longer and longer and longer.*

CLINT: There was no challenge for me anymore. In *The Good, the Bad and the Ugly* there certainly wasn't as much of a challenge as a performer as there was in *A Fistful of Dollars* or *For a Few Dollars More*. In each one progressively the impetus became on the production values rather than the story.

PAUL: *You had two movies in '68 after the Italian trio, and that's when you formed Malpaso, if I remember right. Was* Hang 'Em High *a Malpaso?*

CLINT: Yeah, though it wasn't in the same style as those. I liked the story because it wasn't quite so satirical, and I liked the way the script had been laid out: the analyzing of capital punishment without making a statement for or against. I liked the way the hero started out *against*, became *for*, then became *against* again, and went around in circles due to various things that happened to him in his life. Just like, I suppose, if every judge sitting on the bench had been a victim of a violent crime—or every juror, for that matter—capital punishment would be handed down quite often. This was the case of a guy who becomes a victim of violent crime and then all of a sudden he finally becomes the devil's advocate, arguing for letting one of the guys off who strung him up unjustly. It had some nice stuff in it, but it was a very inexpensive film. When I did *Hang 'Em High*, it was funny because the agency wanted me to do a film called *Mackenna's Gold*.

PAUL: *Oh, that turkey. That was one of the worst.*

CLINT: I talked to Carl Foreman [*Mackenna's Gold's* producer and screenwriter] on several occasions, but I didn't care for the script. They kept saying, "Wow, but you get to work with a lot of well-known actors"—Omar Sharif, who was real hot stuff then—"and it will be a big showcase." I said, "Yeah, but I just don't like the script." I think the agency had a little apoplexy when I turned that down to do a one-and-a-half-million-dollar film, and this picture was a big six-, seven-million-dollar extravaganza. It was just my feeling that it was better to do a smaller script that had at least some merit.

PAUL: *I'm sure it made more money by far than* Mackenna's Gold.

CLINT: Oh yeah, it was in the black. It made a lot of money, it didn't cost very much, and it was a very good bargain for the studio. They tacked it onto the Leone trilogy, running foursomes of the picture all over the country.

Then from that, all of a sudden everybody started saying, "We ought to use this guy. Maybe he isn't just a European deal." They looked down on it like it was a European deal. First, they look down on you because you're from television—television was the real black sheep of the family as far as movie people were concerned at that time.

PAUL: *You and McQueen both managed to get out of it.*

CLINT: Television actors were so eager about doing a theatrical film, they would grab the first thing that would come along. A lot of them flopped, so it was the saying in Los Angeles at the time that people on television didn't go on movies. Well, people on movies don't go on movies either if the movie isn't working. And people on movies don't go on television if the series doesn't work or the format isn't right. So there's no real rule on it. People just drag that cliché out of the woodwork.

PAUL: *You're not actually listed as being the president of Malpaso. You're not an employee, so you can hire out, too.*

CLINT: I'm not in a contract in any way with any studios. It's a good position to be in when you consider that actors of another era were all under contract and fighting the studios for not wanting to do some property they didn't think was particularly exciting. Actors and actresses of the Thirties generation and Forties generation all were contract players in a well-paid profession, but they did what the company store wanted to do or else they were suspended.

PAUL: *Bogart had to do a lot of junk pictures.*

CLINT: Oh sure. Usually a person is either remembered for a great body of work that they've done in their lifetime or else they're remembered for one or two really great things. When you think of Bogart, you think of *Sierra Madre* and *The African Queen* and *The Maltese Falcon*, and then there's a lot of in-between stuff that you can't even remember the name of because you purposely put them out of your mind. *The Left Hand of God* and many, many others.

PAUL: The Enforcer *wasn't very good. Bogart's* Enforcer.

CLINT: The only thing that we ever used of Bogart's *Enforcer* was the title. The story wasn't very much. But he had to do a lot of that stuff. And Cagney and Errol Flynn and all those guys had to do a lot.

PAUL: *I had heard—and apparently this is another misconception— that Post was the first director to give you a job in an American picture, but apparently it's the other way around: you hired Post for* Hang 'Em High.

CLINT: He was a friend of mine and I hired him. He did a good job. On *Rawhide* he was hired by CBS to do a few episodes. He seemed to do a little better than the average guy who came on there in some cases, for certain types of stories.

PAUL: *That seems to be one of the myths: that you let him direct* Magnum Force *because he was the first director in America to give you a job in an American film. I've heard that and read that several times.*

CLINT: No, he didn't give me a job. It just goes to show what you can believe in what you read. Believe the old none of what you hear and half of what you see.

5

PAUL: *Can you tell the story of how you first met Don Siegel on* Coogan's Bluff *[1968]? I guess it wasn't all smooth to begin with.*

CLINT: It was set to do at Universal. It was my first picture over there and they had a guy named Alex Segal who was going to do it. The story was only about eighty-seven pages; it had no ending on it. Universal had three or four scripts on it, so I read all the scripts on it and I liked the original one—or at least the one written by Roland Kibbee. His version seemed to be going in the most interesting way.[11]

Don had been brought in. He jokes about it now because I had never seen any of his work. I *had* seen his work, but I hadn't remembered. He heard that I was looking at film on him, so he went and looked at film on me [laughs]. He hadn't seen any of them. He went and looked at the Leone films and he told me about it afterwards. He said, "You know, they're goddamn good films." We were both impressed with each other's work, so we started in.

He went to New York to write. Don likes to write on the exact location; he feels it helps him. I feel that if the story's there, it can be written here and placed in India—and it can be written

---

[11] Kibbee was not credited in the final film, nor was original director Alex Segal, who dropped out of the project early on.

in India, placed here. If the story's there, it's there. But that's just one area where we differ a little bit. He went back there and he wrote a story, and I didn't care for the story too much. We got in an argument in Jennings Lang's office.[12] I said, "I don't like the story," and he said, "Well, screw you. If you don't like it, too bad." It was one of those kind of things. It wasn't a violent argument. To Lang's credit, he said, "Why don't you guys just sit down and work it out together?" So instead of going to New York to write, we sat down and worked it out. We went through all these scripts and took the best things that we liked out of all of them. We had Dean [Reisner] working with us. When we got it all, we laid it all out in a screenplay. We'd barely just finished it when we boarded the plane and headed to New York and started shooting.

But it was great fun because of the fact that everything wasn't *too* planned and *too* set up. It was more improvisational. We were both sailing. Every night we were making up stuff and adding things and subtracting things, and we were both having a great time. He felt that I had a great eye for movies and I felt he had a great one. We just seemed to cook right along. I admired his economy and efficiency. Don liked my suggestions. We worked in a collaborative way. It was a pretty good little film.

PAUL: *You did a documentary on Siegel* [The Beguiled: The Storyteller *in 1971]. What was that?*

CLINT: It was done during *The Beguiled*. It was shown on TV as a short nine- or ten-minute deal talking about Don and how he works and following him a little bit. Jeez, I haven't seen it in so many years. That might be fun to run sometime.

PAUL: *What was the reason for doing it?*

CLINT: It was more or less tied in with an idea to promote that particular film, channeling it into another avenue instead of doing just a typical large trailer.

PAUL: *Does Siegel tend to shoot a lot on location and very fast?*

---

[12] Before Jennings Lang became a vice president at Universal, he was an agent whose clientele included Don Siegel.

CLINT: Siegel is a fairly fast director, yeah. He likes sets a little more than I do, I think. He was been brought up in that era and he understands them a little better than I do maybe. Maybe he feels more of a camaraderie with that way of shooting. I don't. I'd feel great shooting in this room if this is what the scene was about. We'd move all of the stuff and zap around. Sure it's easier to knock out a wall if there's a set, but we could make this work.

PAUL: *Do you think you picked up the economy and the speed of the way you shoot from Siegel or from working on TV? Or was it always there?*

CLINT: It's just an accumulation of everything I've done. The fact that I have worked in TV and done so many hours of television series, I've seen economy with production and I've seen economy without it. I've seen waste. I've seen every aspect. Working with European directors, there was no more economical a director than Vittorio De Sica. He only shot what he was going to use. Not a frame more. He was directing the segment of a film I was in, *The Witches* [1967]. I was really surprised, I'd get halfway through a speech and he'd say, "Cut." I'd say, "Why don't I carry on and finish this momentum we've got here?" He said, "I don't want to use it over there," so I just said to him, "Would you mind, when we do it next time, let me go clean through and then you just chop it off wherever you want it?" He understood that and said, "Fine," but his way of directing was to get to a certain point, cut, move the thing around to this point, then move around to this point, and do it all in sections. It was really lean. In fact, the day after the last day we did the segment, when he got the dailies back—he had a lady who was editing along with him—he had a total rough assembly. He went in and looked at the whole damn thing the day after he finished. It was the leanest, most economical shooting I've ever seen. It was *too* lean and too economical for me. I wouldn't cover quite that lean. I'd give myself a few other outs so I could have a little bit of play room. Though there's a happy medium.

I don't want to go into the editing room and play all day. I feel that, to call yourself a director, you've got to direct on the set. If I shoot a hundred shots, or twenty or thirty or forty shots, of a scene and I haven't seen what I like yet, then I'm just guessing. I'm just going to guess along, and then I'll go in the editing room and hope that I can take a million feet of film and make it 50,000 or whatever it's going to boil down to. I don't like that theory. That's really indulgent. You have to commit yourself beforehand—commit your mind to the script, commit your soul to it, and then do it. Then when it unfolds in front of you live, you trust your eyes. If you don't trust your eyes, then hire somebody else to trust. Let somebody else direct the film, whose eyes you do trust.

PAUL: *You said on the telephone once that you visualize the whole film almost. You don't work off storyboards or off drawings?*

CLINT: No, I'm not that academic-oriented. That's how I judge the picture to begin with: I read the script. You read it and you picture it out loud in the front of your mind somewhere. Then you look at locations and see if it comes to life in your mind. If I don't see it, I just don't make it. It might be a fine story and somebody else may be able to see it and make it perfectly well, but if I don't visualize it right away, then I just feel that that's fine, I'll let somebody else do that one.

PAUL: *How much does it change when you get to the set?*

CLINT: Everything has to change by what's *there*. Sometimes you'll see a set and you say, "That'll be fine," then you get there and maybe something's a little different. You have to be able to *move*. In the old days, some guys would move things. I've heard of guys actually saying, "Move that telephone pole over ten feet" or something like that. A lot of times people will do that just to vamp and give themselves a chance to think. To me, with the flexibility of the camera, you can move and adjust anything.

PAUL: *I guess what I was trying to get at was that Hitchcock used to say that shooting the film was the anticlimax because he'd worked it all out in his head. You don't feel that way, do you?*

CLINT: No, no, no. I think he felt that he'd worked it out in his head. He also was a sketch artist. He'd sketch the film out and then lay it out for his technical people, and the AD [assistant director] could conceivably go ahead and shoot the film. [Hitchcock] would control the editing. Well, I like dealing with the actors more and watching them breathe life into it. Because I'm an actor myself, I like actors more than he did. But he's done some marvelous films over the years. His technique worked for him and somebody else's works for them, and so on down the line.

PAUL: *Sondra said that she'd never had a director before who could help a performance by the placement of the camera.*

CLINT: You have to dramatize the scene with the camera, punctuate it, get people moving towards the camera at a certain time, or get the camera into a scene or among the group at a certain time. There's a real fine line one has to weave.

The other day my cameraman wanted to circle a table with a 360 as I was doing a scene. I've seen that done a lot. Certain people like to use 360s a lot of time to give a lot of show and a lot of pizzazz. Right away it's calling consciousness to the direction and right away the audience, subconsciously or consciously, realizes that there's a camera crew as the camera's floating by there. You can see that on any commercial. You don't see one commercial on TV where the camera isn't lateral sliding. [Bernardo] Bertolucci uses a lateral slide all the time. He's always sliding, everything's sliding. Even when nothing's happening, he's sliding around. I see a lot of the directors doing that. I move without the actors sliding around. Now, there's nothing wrong with lateral sliding, but I prefer to do that sort of thing as an exception to the rule. I prefer to do that type of thing with the movement of the scene. Let something motivate you, and then you can move to the moon. But just to keep slip-sliding away, it's the director's ego saying, "Don't think because Robert Redford or Burt Reynolds is the star of the film that I'm not there, too."

They go through fads in the business. There was a fad a few years ago and it was also used on every frigging commercial you saw, too: it was using the rack focus thing.[13] I've used it occasionally, but I don't use it anymore. You get so tired of looking at it. Yet it was an effective item at times. But people

---

[13] Racking the focus involves changing focus from one object to another within the same shot.

so overused it, it almost became a thing where every picture had that. It popped up on every commercial on TV, on every documentary and everything else. The people were racking all over the place. One of the earlier pictures that influenced that was *The Ipcress File*, I think. It was a very successful film, it was well-photographed, but you were very conscious of the photography and the direction because of that. I think a lot of directors thought, Oh, this is great. It's a chance to give a little pizzazz to a film, take weak stories and jazz them up.

Not that there isn't room to do anything. There are really no rules. You can do anything you want that works for you, and if it affects the audience and makes your film work, then that's fine. If you look at people who have been terribly successful, like Hitchcock or John Ford, they kept economy. John Ford could be really still. He'd hinge on shots, he set a lot of very fixed portraits. You look at some of those Ford movies and some are just very simple.

PAUL: *Oh, they are.*

CLINT: You see a picture like *Cousin Cousine*, and it's fixed portraits with people coming in this side, coming in that side, playing a scene, exiting this side, exiting that side—and that camera never moves at all. It was conspicuous by its lack of moving. The whole picture, I don't think they ran a dolly more than two times. That's another way of doing it. It seemed to work for that picture, which is a marvelous picture and has a great charm. One of the reasons is the director had great confidence in what he was trying to tell and so he starred the people. When you think back on that film, you think of all the people and their relationships. But in a lot of movies you don't, in a lot of movies you just remember the colors or the camerawork or a scene here and there—but you don't remember the people much.

6

PAUL: *A couple of books that I've got have two birthdates for you: one is May 30, 1930, and the other is May 31, 1931. Are either of them right?*

CLINT: May 31 is correct and '30 is correct. So part of each was correct. When you get to that age I guess most people start knocking off a few years here and there or start going back to thirty-nine like Jack Benny, but I've been enjoying every one of them. I never celebrated birthdays when I was in my twenties, so why should I bother celebrating them now? As long as I feel fit and think fit.

PAUL: *I do know that every once in a while you get the scary feeling that you've passed the halfway mark—*

CLINT: [bursts out laughing] Yeah.

PAUL: *—and that, God, I better do something pretty quick. Does that happen to you?*

CLINT: I've never even thought about it. You think about it, all you can do is laugh about it. Who knows, the halfway mark could've been when you were twenty-nine years old, or it could've been when you were ten if you get hit by a bus when you're twenty. You have to be a little fatalistic about it.

I keep myself fit for my general feeling of well-being and my general lifestyle. It isn't for any longevity craving. My grandfather lived to be ninety-seven and my father passed away in his sixties, so I don't know. Everything is relative to how things work out for you. Some of these guys who live down in the Andes live to be a hundred and ten or something, but, Jesus, their life may be so boring it may seem like two hundred years. Errol Flynn only lived to be fifty, but he was actually a hundred and fifty by anybody else's standards. Not that that's the ultimate way of living—that was the way *he* chose.

PAUL: *I read someplace—I don't know exactly where it was—but you connected acting with being physically fit; that at the end of a long day, if you're not physically fit you don't have enough to give the scene. Do you think it actually does make a difference in your work?*

CLINT: I train up for a picture whenever I'm on it. Like, *Bronco Billy*, I went off and I was running every day and working out every day and getting a lot of rest. I get my mind and my body in shape to attack it because I know I'm going to be preoccupied with every scene, every sequence, and I'm not going to have a chance to really maintain like I usually do. So I try to get tuned up as fine as possible before every show.

If I'm feeling good, I don't get tired easy and I enjoy the whole project. Your mind is sharper, your memory is sharper, you function sharper, your concentration is sharper, and those are all things that are very important to acting. The basis of good acting is being able to receive well, being able to listen well, to respond well. People who can't listen as actors are usually poor at it. Oh, they may be able to be showy and pound their head against the wall and transmit a great scene, but they can't work on the audience's inner feeling about them because the audience is listening *with* them, absorbing with them. So all those things boil down to just general mental and physical health.

PAUL: *Running has a real calming effect. It's like an American version of meditation—sweating on the road, the movement.*

CLINT: Sometimes, just jogging, you can get mesmerized. You can start daydreaming and you get away from the exertion of training. Both of them are good. I think meditation's terrific.

PAUL: *Is it something you try to do every day also?*

CLINT: Yeah. It's just a very relaxing thing. There *are* forms of it, I guess, where you can do it in groups, but I'm not much for anything that's encounter or group. I like private things. Running or meditation or any of those things you discussed, you can do them with a partner or a friend, if you want to, but you can do them also by yourself and just hear nothing but the breeze.

PAUL: *I noticed you had a Jack LaLanne exerciser.*

CLINT: Oh yeah. It's a handy little thing in the daytime if I'm in between appointments. I usually eat lunch in there or else I make my own lunches. I don't go out except on rare occasions. When everybody takes off, I have them lock it up and I'll do a few exercises just to get the circulation going.

PAUL: *When you're running, what do you do a day?*

CLINT: Three or four miles. I have a three-mile layout that I cover and sometimes when I'm really getting feeling good I'll come off of it and do a series of sprints: sprint/jog, sprint/jog, sprint/jog. That's when I really start feeling good again. Really get opened up. I'll run even when I don't feel like it, but to me it's strictly exercise, not *that* much of a sport. Then I'll come back and I'll usually do some gut work and maybe some miscellaneous things like that. Maybe in the evening I'll go in and do some chins and dips and stuff like that and maybe some presses.

PAUL: *I guess you've had this sense of order and common sense from the beginning, right?*

CLINT: I don't think so. I've been through some strange periods in my life. My parents were people of militant common sense and maybe I just inherited a little bit. My father liked things kind of orderly, I guess. I can be undisciplined about things I don't like. There are a million ways to circumvent self-discipline, it seems to me.

PAUL: *To me, you gain as much mentally from running as you do physically. Or more, I would say. To me, it's a substitute psychologist or psychiatrist.*

CLINT: I agree with you. It wipes a lot of things out of your brain, leaves it fresh for new things to come into it, it seems. It's like, you look at a horse that sits around the track, grazing the field, and does nothing. It's fat. The one that is out there running is sleek and it feels good. Obviously, that horse is alive and full of zip and everything. You know right there that the difference between being in and being out of shape is day and night.

7

CLINT: The agency thought that I ought to do a picture with Richard Burton because I'd never done one with another internationally known figure. So I did that. *Where Eagles Dare* [1968] was not a

Western and they felt, because Burton was well-known, it would be a project to do. Brian Hutton, who was directing it, wanted me in the thing and I felt, okay, I'll give it a try.

PAUL: *It's wonderfully stylized. It's a lot of fun.*

CLINT: To Brian's credit. He felt the script was a pile of crap. Burton felt the script was a pile of crap. We got over there and Burton said he was doing the picture because I was in it; and I was doing the picture because he was in it. It turned out to be one of those things.

"Brian," I said, "there's so much exposition in this thing." He had a couple of scenes with Richard shooting that he didn't think looked too good. I was in really good shape then. "Burton talks good and I'm good with the action stuff," I said, "let him handle the talk and I'll handle the killing and we'll just do a wild film." So we did it and everybody had fun doing it, and it did real well.

PAUL: *I haven't the vaguest memory of what it's about. I just remember in the last hour that you must have shot about 500 Germans.*

CLINT: I was in it and I can hardly tell you what it was about.

PAUL: *Was Taylor around at that time?*

CLINT: Yeah, she was around. They came to Salzburg and I met them both. She stayed there the whole time. She was great fun.[14]

PAUL: *I gathered you must've gotten along because* Two Mules for Sister Sara *[1970] was supposed to be a project for her.*

CLINT: Universal had told me about it. She ironically asked me about it as they were telling me about it. She asked me if I'd look at it, so I read it and I told her I liked it. We shook hands and said, "Great, okay, we'll do it." She felt she could play a Latin.

---

[14] Elizabeth Taylor was married to Burton from 1964 to 1974, then again from 1975 to 1976. For her fortieth birthday in 1972, he gave her a 69.42-carat, pear-shaped diamond.

I promptly struck up a deal with the studio and I understood she was striking up a deal with the studio. Then all of a sudden, pow, it all fell apart.

What happened is I guess their salary got big. They'd been doing a lot of pictures together that hadn't been clicking, like *Boom!*, that Joe Losey film based on *The Milk Train Doesn't Stop Here Anymore*, Tennessee Williams's thing. That came out to be a real turkey.

It was really funny, we were shooting some interiors in London and we were invited to this little tiny private screening [of *Boom!*]. So they ran it. I didn't know what to say. You're sitting right next to the leading lady and Richard's sitting two rows down with a cousin or somebody. You start to think of the usual things you'd say—"The cinematography in there was just ...," "The sound effects were interesting ..."—and she turns around and says in this loud voice, "This is the worst piece of shit I've ever seen!" [laughs] Everybody went [heavy sigh of relief], "Okay, now let's go have a drink!" and then went out and had a cocktail on the show.

But anyway, getting on to the other stories, *Boom!* didn't do well and the price was high and they always had to work *together* and near each other. It just became complicated, and Universal finally said, "We don't want any part of it."

We went over all the Mexican possibilities, you name it. Don and I liked the idea of Sophia Loren, too, because she *is* Latin, Even though she's Italian, we thought she could play Mexican. Then the studio kept saying, "What about making her an Irish nun who's working in Mexico or something like that?"

PAUL: *I thought MacLaine was really good in it.*

CLINT: Yeah, MacLaine was good. I like Shirley. She's a terrific gal. But it was a quite a bit of a change in casting idea. Now we're making her an Irish nun instead of a Mexican nun as written by Budd Boetticher, who wrote the original story. It was originally a pistolero and a Mexican who was posing as a nun but was a hooker. So a lot of revamping had to be done to make that show work. The film's made some good dough.

PAUL: *You and she strike off more sparks than I think you and Taylor would have. It's hard to remember because Taylor was* *really quite, quite good at one time and could've played that part—*

CLINT: Oh, she could've played it.

PAUL: *—and then later she couldn't play anything, it seemed like, and she got into a lot of bad movies.*

CLINT: It's hard to tell. I guess there's a certain time for everybody to do a certain role, but Taylor could certainly have done it at that time. She would've played it real earthy, but there were just complications in their life and so it wasn't the time to do it.

PAUL: *That must've been somewhat disappointing to you. Did you like Burton?*

CLINT: We got along great. He was great fun, a very amusing guy. They lived a totally different lifestyle than me. I couldn't stand that lack of privacy. I showed up in Austria in a pair of Levi's with a B-4 bag and went to the hotel, and they showed up in a private jet with six people and—

PAUL: *A million-dollar diamond.*

CLINT: —a big rock and a lot of furs and a lot of clothes and a wardrobe man for him and a wardrobe man for her and whatever. It was fun for me to watch them from afar.

8

CLINT: *Paint Your Wagon* [1969] was tough. It was a nice location— it was beautiful country up in Eagle Creek there, out of Baker [Oregon]—but to be on a picture that long [five months], every day going out there and waiting hours for setups to happen, it was a very uncoordinated film. Invariably on those things the scenes that are shot the fastest and move along turn out to be the best scenes in the movie.

PAUL: *I never saw it. I don't have much respect for Josh Logan as a movie director at all.*

CLINT: It wasn't that it was a bad movie. A lot of people just thought it was the greatest. All around it did well, but it did well if it had been done at a certain price. It did, say, twenty-five million dollars domestic in 1970. That would be respectable except that it cost twenty-two million dollars. At that price, you can't say it did well.

PAUL: *There was lots of producer trouble in that picture, I guess.*

CLINT: It was strange because they prepared that picture for a year, Logan and [producer and co-writer Alan Jay] Lerner. I remember they flew to England to see me—I was working over there on *Where Eagles Dare*—and I said I'd do it. The first script was really interesting, a Paddy Chayefsky script, and it had a certain mood about it that was tremendous. They decided they'd dump that and were going for a more fluffy kind of a musical. The Chayefsky thing was a little too serious for them, I guess. But I had said I'd have done the Chayefsky one. I liked that script. It was long, but it could have been trimmed down and been something. So they came over and they brought the new one. The new one, it was a kind of different bag, but I supposed it would work.

After a year's preparation with Logan—he was on the picture about four days—all of a sudden the rumor comes down they're going to replace him. They're sending scripts behind his back to Richard Brooks after the first few days. I called my agent, Lenny Hirshan, and I said, "Something strange is going on here. The guy's been preparing for a year and now all of a sudden they're finding out that he's not the right guy for the picture after four days of shooting? We ought to support him at least for a week or two and find out if the guy is on the beam or not." So I insisted with the producing element that they give him a try. Everybody get behind him instead of undercutting him.

PAUL: *How was Seberg? I was always sort of half in love with Jean Seberg when I was younger.*

CLINT: Ah, she was a lovely gal. I liked her very much and so did Lee [Marvin]. She was a gal from Marshalltown, Iowa. Small-town daughter of a druggist in town, and evidently she'd rebelled and gone off and gotten involved with all kinds of political causes or whatever. In Baker, Oregon, she felt like she was back in that Marshalltown kind of feeling and she was very happy there, I thought. As wild as Lee was—and Lee was having a few drinks occasionally during that show—she loved it, she thought he was great. I think she liked us all. She was a gal with a great heart who was I think used by people a lot.

PAUL: *She was in a bad situation. The way she started was unfortunate. Having no experience at all, being tossed into* Saint Joan, *which was a* very *bad film. Otto Preminger didn't do a good job with that film at all.*[15]

CLINT: Taking an inexperienced person and putting her in that kind of bad project, under that kind of pressure, it's terrible. No matter how much a person looks like she's right for the part, there's just so much a person can do. Being the protagonist of a film is a great responsibility. Everything revolves around that one character. If you're not any good, then how can anything else be any good? There's no way it can. You've got to have a certain presence and carry a certain weight, and there's no way an inexperienced young gal like that would be able to do that. It was just a Preminger fantasy going on.

PAUL: *It must be a crusher to the ego when this happens—for everybody really.*

CLINT: You get a reputation as being bad. It's not that you're really bad, you just have never had a chance to be good in the normal stepping of things. It was too bad she hadn't gotten some smaller roles. It's like going out and trying to build this building before you build a few small warehouses somewhere. There's *no* job you can jump in at the top of.

---

[15] Preminger selected the seventeen-year-old Seberg, from 18,000 contestants in a nationwide talent search, to star in his film. Four months before this conversation with Eastwood took place in 1979, Seberg, forty, commited suicide in Paris, France.

9

PAUL: *When you were shooting* Kelly's Heroes *[1970] you had a real fondness for it, but you seem to think it came out rather badly. Is that correct?*

CLINT: I loved the script on the film. Everybody I knew liked the script. Don Siegel loved it. We were doing *Sister Sara* together. I let him read it and he said, "Boy, that's the best war story I've read." I said, "Jesus, the perfect guy to prepare this is Brian Hutton." Brian had done *Where Eagles Dare*, which was a *terrible* script. It was over-explanatory, with reams of exposition, but he did a great job of glossing it over and we approached it with a tongue in cheek.

There were two sequences that told the whole story [in *Kelly's Heroes*]. I mean, they just wrapped the story up. Little poignant moments that kind of pull a picture together, take it out of just a wild shoot 'em up and humanize it. And they were cut out. We had a scene with [Telly] Savalas and myself and some of the guys: it's the whole deal about *why* and the philosophies of war. It wasn't an explanatory thing that stopped and explained what was happening; it just gave you a feeling of the guys in a different mood other than running around shooting and telling a lot of jokes. This thing had been completely dehumanized. It'd just become a massive action thing in which the special effects were great and there was a lot of action. But there was *too much* action. There needed to be some reason for this whole caper being there.

I saw the film and I said, "Brian, they cut out the most important scene in the film. Can't we put it back?" He said, "No, Jim Aubrey [head of MGM] wants to run the picture for the critics. They have a critics showing in New York." I said, "Forget the critics. They're going to hate this goddamn movie anyway. Let's put the film back in its proper order so at least it has a fair chance, so that the critics might see something—or anybody might see something. The audiences, mainly. I'll work with you on it. Just a day. A couple hours." He said, "If you can get Aubrey to do it, I'll do it." So I called Aubrey and I said, "Would you delay the New York screening and let me just work a day or so on it?" He said, "No, I can't do that." I told him the same story. I said, "The critics are going to hate the film. It's nothing but a shoot 'em up right now. Let's try to put back the values that were in that script." "No, we've got to get it out." What in essence it boiled down to is that MGM was tapioca'd and they needed the dough real fast. They wanted to get it out real quick.

We started the picture under this Bob O'Brien [MGM president] regime. The studio was taken over by the Seagram's people while [Louis F.] Polk was the president, and then it was taken over again by James Aubrey, who was releasing the picture. So it started under one regime and was released two regimes later. For that reason, it was just sloughed out. The regime that takes over the studio, they've got this product in the can and they go, "Let's get it out, let's get some revenue coming in," so they can make stuff that they want to make under their banner.

Another thing, they went out and they butted head-on with *Sister Sara*, which was out. They opened in one theater in Hollywood. *Sister Sara* happened to be out in multiple, massive release and it was just raking in dough like crazy. Why should people drive from Sherman Oaks into Hollywood—I'm just using this area as an example because I'm sure that there was a similar situation elsewhere—to see a show with Clint Eastwood as the protagonist when you've got the latest one playing right across the street?

PAUL: *I didn't realize it came out at exactly the same time.*

CLINT: Exact same time. We had the same thing with Universal with *Coogan's Bluff*. It did well, but they released it in New York on the week of the World Series, a Jewish holiday, and with *Hang 'Em High* in multiple right across the street—right *dead* across the street. *Hang 'Em High* had been doing rather good business around the country and already had a steam built up, and *Coogan's Bluff* had to start out from scratch.

PAUL: Kelly's Heroes *seemed to be marketed as the umpteenth* Dirty Dozen *rip off.*

CLINT: The script was called *The Warriors* originally and they changed it to *Kelly's Heroes*. That was another thing I fought: the title. They had a thing called *Hogan's Heroes*, very popular on television, and so they come out with *Kelly's Heroes*, which is a dumb title. For some reason *The Warriors* couldn't clear or somebody else had the rights to it. I had no control over that thing—not that I have any better taste than anybody else—but I would've liked to have done that movie with a little more control.

PAUL: *It seemed to me that the advertising and the presentation were practically* insisting *that this was absolute television series nonsense of the worst sort and that this was just a comic movie picture that had nothing to it at all. I don't think they could have turned you off more effectively if they tried, basically.*

CLINT: They were leading you to believe that this was the exact same thing you could see on *Hogan's Heroes* every week, only on a big screen. There's no reason in the world why people should go out and pay for things that they can see at home on the tube.

PAUL: *I've seen* Kelly's Heroes *and it's got some real likable things. There's something going on on the screen that's real nice.*

CLINT: It had some nice things in it. It's an all right picture. I'm not putting it down, I just think it could have been a very, very good movie with a little something added special. It was one of the best antiwar stories I've ever seen, but it was subtle, it was never preachy. But all that was taken out.

PAUL: *My reaction when I saw it was a very pleasant surprise. I went, This isn't bad, this is something else.*

CLINT: It should have been even much more so, because it had really nice things in the script. Otherwise, I would've never gone to Yugoslavia for six months. That's another thing that got me incensed: after spending six months on the road and living out of a suitcase in Yugoslavia, which isn't bad—it's a pretty country and everything—then you come back and some jerk sells the picture because he's taken over a studio that's broke and he wants to make a lot of low-budget films.

Aubrey's theory was, when he came to take over MGM, that he was going to make a lot of *Easy Riders*. He was going to make a lot of pictures with unknowns and he was going to do them all for under a million dollars. They made about five or six of them—just went in the toilet. We were just at the wrong place at the wrong time.

PAUL: *That seems to always happen in music, too: one guy hits, and then come the copies. And the reason the guy hit—his vision—isn't something that you can imitate. He is the original and audiences like* him; *and just by duplicating it again, they're not going to buy it. It just doesn't work that way.*

CLINT: Oh yeah. After *A Fistful of Dollars*, how many guys put on ponchos? There were dozens of them, smoking little cigars and hats down low. But they were doing somebody else's thing. If they had been doing their own thing they'd have had a much better break with it, a much better chance of it coming on.

10

PAUL: *You take a hand in a lot of the scripts, right? Writing scenes and dialogue in most of the films? But I guess a lot of directors do.*

CLINT: I think everybody does that. I'm a good second-guesser, like everybody in the world. I write in scenes now and then. I usually give the writer, though, the respect of telling him what I'm doing. I don't write the whole script because obviously I'm somewhat enamored with the script that I've got, otherwise I wouldn't be at that stage. But sometimes there are a few missing elements or something that doesn't quite work for me and I'll redo it. Or the writer may try to redo it and just never understand what you're trying to say, so then you've got to take it from there. A lot of them dry up. Sometimes after two, three drafts a person can just dry out on a subject and doesn't want to be bothered with it anymore. Maybe you need to bring in a new writer and do major surgery, or maybe it's just something you do yourself.

PAUL: *In the silent comedy days they always used to keep this guy around they called "the crazy" because he could pull an idea out* *of anywhere that no one could think of because it was crazy. But a lot of times it worked.*

CLINT: Yeah.

PAUL: *All the stories you hear about writers being mistreated in Hollywood, from what I know from being around you, you seem to be the complete opposite. You give the writer so much respect.*

CLINT: I try to. I don't know if anybody's mistreated. You've got to figure that if he or she is smart enough to write the concept that you want, then there's no reason why not to go with them. I can second-guess what's wrong with something and what's right with something, but I'm not smart enough to be able to sit down and write a whole script from beginning, draw the story out of midair and assemble it like that. That's a different knack, a different art, or whatever you want to call it. I'm the first guy in the world to come in and say, "This doesn't work, it needs an added sequence here," and "That scene's no good, let's take that out." I'm a great dissector. I guess a lot of people who take credit for writing on the screen are good at that, but I don't take credit for it because I respect the writer.

PAUL: *I don't mean that kind of cruelty. I mean using sixteen writers and just treating them all basically like dirt. I just don't get that feeling in general. Where they're more or less just shuttled in and out, four or five more writers, and then four or five more, and pretty soon nobody knows who's written anything. I've seen you enough to know that you almost go the opposite way. Sometimes I almost wish that you did take something out of some of the scripts.*

CLINT: Oh, I take it out if I don't want it in, if I truly believe it's not a necessary item or not an entertaining item or somehow out of character.

PAUL: *I've talked to other people who worked on your pictures and I haven't heard anybody ever say that they weren't treated terrifically or that the whole atmosphere wasn't fine on the picture.*

CLINT: I try to get the best out of people that way. You can get the best from people if they feel that they're contributing. If they feel that they're just along for the ride, then it's not productive.

PAUL: *Do you use the same crew pretty much on each film?*

CLINT: Sometimes. It varies depending on who's available and who isn't.

PAUL: *You have a different cameraman on* Bronco Billy.

CLINT: This guy's a new guy, but he's not new to cinematography. He just got in the union. That union's really hard to bust. For years, the cameraman's union has been a real hotbed of nepotism and a closed shop, so to speak. Finally, the civil rights thing helped break it open and make it a little more flexible. It's tough for me to understand a union where your peers stand in judgment on you. See, the Screen Actors Guild or the Screen Directors Guild [the Directors Guild of America], they don't have that. Anybody who is given a job is eligible to get into the union. But the camera union and some of these others are kind of a closed shop, and people who you're competing with for jobs stand in judgment of you. It's actually a moral thing really. It's a rouster system, is what it is. You have to get in and you have to sit in groups. For an employer not to be able to hire the employee of his choice just seems to me against everything that was originally founded in this country—of freedom of opportunity.

PAUL: *You do a lot of location shooting, for various reasons, I guess.*

CLINT: The biggest reason I do it is just because you're *there* on the spot. When you're on an actual location, you feel like the picture is actually happening there. It's like a piece of life rather than some cardboard sets. If you're in a studio and you can take out this wall here and take out that wall there and drop back, you think lethargic: What the hell, we'll wait and take out that. I've done it. I've used sets in pictures where there was nothing else available. I suppose I could do it in this one. I could do the New York sequences on a set and have somebody put a painting outside the window, but it doesn't seem like you're capturing much of the flavor. Maybe I'm just playing with myself, but I like to open a picture up and make it feel part of the land, or the area, where we are.

On a location it seems like everybody just pitches in because nobody lives there permanently. Everybody knows they're there to do the job—and if they have a good time on their own time, that's great, too. There seems to be more energy, more electricity in a crew. Crews work better—everybody works better—if they're all pitching in. I guess when I say "a crew," I'm including myself.

11

In this Confederate gothic, Eastwood plays a seriously wounded Yankee soldier who is rescued into an all-girl Southern boarding school headed by Geraldine Page. As he recovers, he misrepresents himself with one young woman after another—until his deceits are discovered and he's held accountable for his actions.

CLINT: I remember Albert Maltz on *The Beguiled* [1971] was really pissed at Don and me because we went back to the book ending. He had written an ending that was a very happy ending, me with my crutches and both the little girl and the girl who was my romance just happy as a lark going off all glorious and into the sunset. Because *The Beguiled* was our version of an antiwar movie, and how people's lives are affected being even on the periphery of a war and how adversely it affects the civilian population, we felt that it should have continued to be a tragedy and not had a happy ending. The book ended up just like the picture did. Maltz felt that his ending was better, and so he was a little bugged with Don and me for going to that ending.[16]

---

[16] Albert Maltz, who also wrote the screenplay for *Two Mules for Sister Sara*, was one of the Hollywood Ten. As one of the ten directors, screenwriters, and producers blacklisted in Hollywood for their refusal to answer questions before the House Un-American Activities Committee in 1947, he spent almost a year in prison for contempt of Congress.

PAUL: *That's a reversal of the usual story.*

CLINT: The ending wasn't anything related to what happened and what the statement of the film was all about. Don and I both felt it was an ultimate antiwar picture because it wasn't preachment against the horrors of war. It just unfolds in front of you. Here are these people who are trapped on the very edge of it and a stranger from the opposition side becomes part of their life. He's trying to protect himself and they start vying in between. All these things that would've never happened before.

PAUL: *Was* The Beguiled *a difficult performance as an actor?*

CLINT: I don't think so. He was a very easy guy to understand, as a performer. I just took to him. When I read the book, I liked it. A wounded soldier, he's a guy who is fortunate enough to be rescued into a somewhat comfortable situation and he manipulates it to try to stay protected. He finds himself in the difficult thing of being attracted to one party and not wanting to alienate the Geraldine Page character.

PAUL: *I would think that for that reason it* would *be a difficult part. You sort of have to be operating on two levels. I talked to Verna Bloom about that and she thinks that's an* amazing *performance, a terrifically difficult one for an actor.*

CLINT: I just projected to the actress, and the audience comes or goes.

PAUL: *Maybe I'm not putting that right. The impression you want to make on the actors is a different one from the way that the audience sees it. He's trying to fool the various women with various guises, but he's got to let the audience know that he's trying to fool them as he's trying to fool them.*

CLINT: The tricky part of the performance, of course, was to leave the audience with: did he really love that gal or was he just faking all the way? I believe he had feelings towards her, but he'd already pulled so many scams, it was too late. There was no way he was ever going to make a comeback from his mistake.

He'd blackmailed them, and then the sex scandal. And the Page character, who had been involved with incest—the decadence that had reached her from the war, her losses, and her life—it wouldn't let him up.

PAUL: *Did the critics support you on that film?*

CLINT: It was received fairly well by the critics, I think. There were a few that were dyed-in-the-wool against anything that I did, but by and large a lot of them who hadn't cared about any of my work before kind of took on a new attitude.

PAUL: *It's such a beautiful film. It's just completely different from almost any other film.*

CLINT: It was my agent's idea to drag *The Beguiled* out. That was also on Universal's hit list. It was one that was destined to become a shelved thing, so we brought it out and we worked on it. I took it and let Don read it. Don liked it, so we decided to do it.

I've been accused of falling back to action-oriented films because of the failure commercially of that picture, but that isn't the truth at all. That just happened to be a unique story. It touched me at the time, and it was a time in life to try that. I'd do it again. Maybe if we did that story today the audience might go for it, I think if presented well.

Don feels that the studio deserted us on it. We had offers to take it to the Cannes Film Festival, for instance. I think it would've won it. The studio wouldn't do that. Lew Wasserman [head of MCA, which owned Universal] said, "Absolutely not." He wouldn't spend any money on the Cannes Film Festival or get involved in that. Then we tried promotion ideas that were different than the ones for the films that I had been in before, the action and the Western films and so forth, and they didn't like that. *Clint Eastwood with a gun in his hand* wasn't the way to advertise the picture. He does hold a gun in his hand in a couple of quick shots in the film. But what it did was it alienated the people who might have been attracted to that film. It also alienated the people who wanted the other kind. The people who wanted· *A Fistful of Dollars, The Good, the Bad and the Ugly* went thinking it was maybe another film like that, and they saw it and they said,

"Oh no, we don't like this. He gets his leg cut off and he's killed and we don't want that." And the people who might've gone to it were turned off because it was Clint Eastwood: "Oh, there he is again doing that. That's not my kind of flick."

PAUL: *Sending it to Cannes would have been a great idea.*

CLINT: When we were approached about taking it to Cannes, we'd already shown it to film critics in France who were ecstatic about the film. A lot of people felt that we'd have a really good chance to do something there. It would show me in a different way; it would show Don, who was hot with French film critics anyway. We felt it was a perfect time in our lives to have this film go there. I should have stood firm on it and said, "That's the way we're going to do it."

See, I didn't have as much power at that point as far as making a play with a studio. I didn't have that much knowledge then, I didn't know much about festivals and all that. I'd agree very much with the studio heads that maybe other films aren't meant to go that way, but that particular picture at that particular time in history, it would've been very good.

I think Don's held a resentment towards the studio bureaucracy because of that. I don't hold that much resentment. They made a decision based on what they felt they knew, and we just feel that they were wrong, that's all. Today I don't think I'd allow myself to be bulldozed off of that one. I feel that if we were doing it today that we would muscle that one through because, at least where I'm situated right now with studios like Warners and Paramount, they've been much more respectful at the moment of how we follow through on the advertising and everything else. We've had some good luck.

PAUL: *Since that was a personal project for you, I would imagine that the commercial failure of that film must have hurt.*

CLINT: It hurts when you spend that much time and effort on a film. We knew it was iffy to begin with, and I told Jennings Lang before we started it—they were trying to change things in the story to make it more commercial—I said, "Look, if you have any doubts about this film, let's call it off right now.

No hard feelings. We'll do another type of film." "No, no, no," they wanted to go ahead with it. "Okay," I said, but it was very spelled out with the studio—*very* spelled out—that if we went ahead with this, it had to be approached in a totally different way. It couldn't be approached like *Coogan's Bluff* or any other film that they'd worked on. That was all fine and good, it was all understood by them and agreed by them. But then it wasn't.

The picture was going to be out at Christmas and then it was delayed till spring because they were going to present this really special advertising campaign for the film. So we said okay. They came out at Easter with a very special advertising campaign that consisted of a couple ads in the paper two or three days before the film came out, and that was the end of it. And it wasn't special at all.

Unfortunately, one of their weaknesses at that particular studio [Universal] was their advertising and promotion was terrible. That was one of the reasons I strayed away from them. Don strayed away for other reasons, I suppose. As you get a little older you realize that, to spend a year developing a film and making a film, maybe even more—some of them take more than a year, two years—and then to have just one department fail on you, it's just too frustrating, too nerve-racking, to put up with.

Even Warner Bros., whom we have a very good relationship with and whom we went with to begin with because they're a very good advertising outfit—our track record with them had been good—on *Every Which Way but Loose* they were sloughing that picture. It was one of those deals where the squeaky wheel was getting the grease. Warners had so much money invested in *Superman*, they were going to promote the hell out of that film. We kept saying, "But what about promoting this film?" Frank Wells [vice chairman of Warner Bros.] felt that *Loose* was a good commercial little vehicle that might get hot and do twenty million dollars. They were thinking maybe if they got lucky they were going to have a nice Christmas with it. Believe me, regardless of what all these guys BS you in the business, twenty million is a *lot* of money for a movie. You'd be surprised how many people who are thought of as a successful filmmaker never had a film do that much.

I made Bob Daley stay in Los Angeles and stay right on top of the advertising while we were shooting *Alcatraz* in San

Francisco.[17] I said, "Look, we're going to have to grind the studio to let them know that we've got something we think is in topflight league." Consequently we did have a good campaign on *Loose* and we got every bit of mileage out of it that was put in. *Loose* has done two and a half times what they figured they were going to do with it. It's going to be one of their highest grossing pictures in history—the third or so at the present time—based on Bob staying there and all of us staying on top of them and not letting them off for a minute. If we'd let them off for a minute, we'd have had a nice gross—maybe the movie would've done it on its own—but we weren't going to leave that to chance. And Warners is even glad of it. They've even said in hindsight, "We're glad you stayed on top of it because we got a lot more miles out of it than we expected." But all of that is just accumulation of *The Beguiled* experience and experiences we've had down the way where you just can't let up.

PAUL: *I imagine they figure, Ah, Eastwood, he's automatic. He'll get his audience. We don't have to fork out the money.*

CLINT: That can work against you sometimes. It worked against me in *The Beguiled*, even back in those days, and it worked against me in *Misty* and a lot of films. Sometimes being considered a box-office draw can be a great disadvantage because releasing organizations—*any* releasing organization, whether it's Paramount, Universal, Warners, Fox, or whatever— will say, "What the hell, so-and-so's in it and he's a big deal." There's maybe some validity in that, but not a lot. They'll get a little complacent, figuring there's a built-in audience.

PAUL: *And that you're an automatic.*

CLINT: Nobody's automatic. A box-office per se quote/unquote personality can maybe start them in for the first week or so, but then after that the picture's got to be there. You see it all the time, they desert them fast. That's why any so-called box-office big name you can mention can do ten million dollars on one picture and thirty on another. It's because the picture's

---

[17] Robert Daley produced or executive-produced all of Eastwood's films from *Play Misty for Me* in 1971 to 1980's *Any Which Way You Can*.

there—the person hasn't changed. People don't just line up just to say hello to an old friend.

If a film isn't there, you've got to market it well. Obviously, good advertising a lousy movie isn't going to do anything. It may help it for a day or two, but after that it's up to the movie itself. There's no use *really* spending *any* amount of money, whether it's a million dollars or ten million, whatever a picture costs, to make a film and then go ahead and just market it like it's a five-and-dime-store item. The process has to be creative from the writer's first concept right through to the last advertising dollar.

12

As a late-night jazz DJ in *Play Misty for Me* (1971), Eastwood finds himself the unwanted recipient of the affections of an obsessive, unbalanced listener (played by Jessica Walter), who calls him up and requests that he play Erroll Garner's "Misty" for her.

PAUL: *When I think of your own directing career, your first film was one that you wouldn't necessarily have been expected to make.* Play Misty for Me *was a twist. How do you think you've grown or gotten different from* Play Misty *to recently? What have you learned in the process?*

CLINT: I don't know. I was mentioning the other day, I'd sure love to have a story like that because I like that story. It was one of the few psychotic thrill-type pictures that I felt was actually plausible. Even Alfred Hitchcock's *Psycho*, you can't remember the story. You remember a few very important scenes that were exquisitely done, but you don't remember the plot lines. You don't really care about the plot line.

But to me that whole misinterpretation of commitment between people is something that goes on all the time. It does get sick both for male and female. I've known friends who have tried to dominate or tried to monopolize a woman's time after one date with them. They think there's an ownership stamp. I've seen women do the same thing to men. For that reason, it was fun to touch on that story. It had all the entertainment aspects and yet had a nice character relationship thing—a love story. It was a good script. It was written by a friend of mine. She's now dead.

PAUL: *Jo Heims.*

CLINT: She was a secretary back when I was trying to be an actor. We used to drink beer together. She'd say, "I'm going to be a writer someday," and I'd say, "I'm going to be an actor someday." It was one of those kind of things. She was a great girl.[18]

PAUL: *It was very good, I thought.*

CLINT: I made that picture in four and a half weeks and it was made all on location. I had optioned the property and owned it for a while, and then she had a chance to sell it. I was overseas working on *Where Eagles Dare* in Austria, and she called and asked if I'd mind if she'd sell it. I said, "Hell, no. You've got to take it. It's a shot." Universal had bought it. Then they put it on the shelf, they couldn't do anything with it. But I think that the powers that be there felt that, for the price of me making the film, they couldn't lose. I think the direct costs on it were seven hundred and some thousand dollars.

PAUL: *You didn't take your actor's fee on it, though, right?*

CLINT: No, I had a deal with them for three pictures at the time and they asked me to waive that. When they insured the picture, they said, "Because this isn't a Western or a cop drama or some action-oriented film, would you waive that and just take a straight percentage?" and I said, "Sure, I just want to make the picture." I had faith in it. And the picture did well, even though it was never sold as one of their upper echelon items. It did well despite that and surprised them all. That was fun in itself.

PAUL: *It was odd because I know I saw that picture at a screening, and it didn't come out for five, six months later. I was telling*

---

[18] Dean Reisner rewrote Heims's script, which was based on her original sixty-page treatment. A few months older than Eastwood, Heims died of cancer in 1978. She also wrote the screenplay for *Breezy*.

everybody, "You've got to see Play Misty for Me. *It's the best film of this genre since* Psycho."

CLINT: It just wasn't backed particularly well. I remember I showed it to John Cassavetes and he said, "God, if they put Hitchcock's name on this, everybody'd rave. You really ought to put your name on it"—you know, *presented by*—and I said, "No, I just want it to get out. I think the people will like it once they see it." The previews were marvelous. People were screaming and jumping out of their seats. People seemed to like the story and the characters. I knew it would work. And at the price, of course, it had to work.

PAUL: *I don't see why they saw it as uncommercial.* Psycho *was marvelously commercial.*

CLINT: You know how faddist everything is in the movie industry, and the executives throughout that movie industry are terribly fad-conscious. This was way beyond the *Psycho* period—that was done quite a few years earlier—and there was nothing like it on the market at the time. One executive I was dealing with over there, he said, "Who wants to see Clint Eastwood play a disc jockey?" I said, "Who wants to see him play anything? I dunno. It's only as good as the picture's going to be, and I think it's an exciting premise." He said, "Well, why would you want to be in a picture where the woman has the best part?" I said, "Why not? Though she has the most dramatic part, being the recipient of her obsession makes mine a dramatic role, too." Besides, I don't care about that. The main thing is the whole picture works. If the pictures work, then I work; then the bit player works and everybody down the line works. If I have a part where I'm saying every line in the movie and it's a bore, then nothing works, and people are going to hear about it and stay away from it by the droves.

Anyway, those are just some of the conversations that went on about getting to make it. Though I have to give the studio, Universal, credit. In the making of the film, they never bothered me, they never came on the set, I don't think they looked at the dailies much. They gave me complete, total control and freedom. I could never turn around and do the trick that you see a lot of times when the directors build up a jack story against the studio so they can say, "They edited out a scene, so they wrecked my movie." They build in some self-protection that way so hopefully they can get a sympathetic reviewer to turn around and say that the big-money people crushed the talent again. It's kind of the hate-with-the-front-office thing. Don does it, too. I mean Siegel. He always has an antagonism with the front office. It gives him energy to go on, and if it works for him, that's fine. I'm not saying anything out of school because I tell Don this to his face. I mean, I love the guy. He was instrumental in encouraging me into going into directing in the first place.

PAUL: *How did you envision the disc jockey character?*

CLINT: I knew a guy in Monterey who *was* like that and so I took it from there. It was written to take place in LA originally, but I felt it needed to be a smaller town. Disc jockeys many times are big fish in a small pond in a town, they're like celebrities in that particular area, so you make the guy a popular figure in a small community. He's in Monterey, which is a very nice, visual place, and he's a guy who just hasn't found himself. He's in-between somehow. He hasn't been able to get it together with a gal he likes. It's a very easy thing to visualize because almost everybody's gone through that at some point in their life—

PAUL: *Oh yeah.*

CLINT: —or is going through it or will go through it.

PAUL: *You have sympathy for [Jessica] Walter because, although she's got a crazed sense of commitment that hasn't got any reality, the DJ character hasn't got* enough *commitment it seems. It's like this perfect balance between the two of them.*

CLINT: The DJ is just afraid to make a commitment.

PAUL: *You're torn, hoping Walter won't go all the way. The way she just explodes off the screen is intense.*

CLINT: She's good. It was one of those things—she stamped the role so solid that people always thought of her as that character. I looked at a lot of film of people to use in that role. I didn't know her, I had never met her. I looked at *The Group*. Remember *The Group*? It was made some years ago. She played the gal who was always talking about sex but who was really frigid, afraid of it, and she had a deal with some ski instructor or something. I've forgotten what it was, but he made a pass at her and she froze up and he slapped her. Boy, when he slapped her there was just something in her eyes for a second there, and I thought, God, that gal has it. If I can get her to throw that switch for me, she'll be great. Another thing is, she's a fairly tall, fairly good-sized gal, so, with insanity going for her, she'd be formidable.

PAUL: *Those scenes go off like a gun at that point. All of a sudden you're just jolted out of your little world into something else. They're even more scary than the scenes with the knife. Somehow the psychological explosion is just shocking.*

CLINT: Yeah, to see a person's mind bending right before your eyes.

PAUL: *She's attractive and she's classy-looking. You don't expect this person to detonate.*

CLINT: She had to be attractive enough that the guy who meets her in a saloon wanted to take her home, and she was that. Casting is a very important thing in any film. If the people are anything but the top for their part, if they're just not right on, you can weaken yourself, you can give yourself a tremendous disadvantage.

13

In 1971, Eastwood starred as Detective "Dirty Harry" Callahan, the ultimate iconoclastic cop who, with the help of a .44 Magnum revolver, brings to justice Scorpio (Andy Robinson), a serial killer terrorizing San Francisco. Their classic showdown is arguably Eastwood's most famous scene on film: "I know what you're thinking, punk. You're thinking, Did he fire six shots or only five? Well, to tell you the truth, I forgot myself in all this excitement. But being this is a .44 Magnum, the most

> powerful handgun in the world, and will blow your head clean
> off, you've got to ask yourself a question: Do I feel lucky? Well,
> do ya, punk?"

PAUL: *Siegel likes* The Beguiled *almost better than anything he's done, I think.*

CLINT: I don't agree with him. I think that *Dirty Harry* for him will go down as one of the classic films. I think he likes to say *The Beguiled* is his best—and I think *Beguiled* is one of his best—but it's probably easier for him to overlook *Harry* because *Beguiled* was more unusual for him to do. He hadn't done a film like *Beguiled* in his career, but he'd done a lot of cop dramas. In fact, he and I had done one [*Coogan's Bluff*]. Once you've done a few, you probably feel something like *Beguiled*, then, is a far more unusual film. It may be a toss-up. It just depends on the eyes of the viewer.

PAUL: *It would seem that, if there were any justice, that film and* Dirty Harry *ought to have been mentioned in the awards—and the performances also.*

CLINT: *The French Connection,* which was also a successful film and won the Academy Award I believe, had come out prior to *Dirty Harry* that year and had a run at it. *Dirty Harry* came out at Christmas, *French Connection* came out in October or September. New York has a strong bloc about awards, too. There's a strong group there.

PAUL: *It's only a matter of time before it does happen.*

CLINT: Ah, I don't worry about it. I don't worry about that sort of thing because I don't quest it. It's not been one of my dying ambitions. I just make the product and, as Bogart said, owe the audience a good performance, to make the best films that I know how. Anybody who has, or has had periodically, the avenue to the public on a commercial level has much less chance of becoming embraced by awards and that sort of thing. It's not to put down the people who are embraced. A lot of people campaign for it and go for it and that's part of their life. They even get bigger salaries and bigger everything because of it, but it's never affected me one way or the other anyway.[19]

Don't forget that I carried a lot of prejudice over the years, but mine was based on coming up way too soon for everybody's good. It's like being in a nonpolitical party—you're not a Democrat and you're not a Republican. A slow independent comes up and does well. I came out of European-produced films and some people didn't accept it. The Hollywood community didn't accept it, the press didn't accept it—with very few exceptions anyway. Finally I started doing a few American films, and even then they got used to not accepting it, because I wasn't the prediction. They're supposed to be able to predict those things ahead of time, they're supposed to be able to bestow knighthood on whomever they want, and the public is supposed to accept it. If the public accepts you and they [the Hollywood community and the press] don't, it's a little reverse prejudice thing there. It's all right, I never minded it.

PAUL: Dirty Harry *was one of those lifetime classics that doesn't come around much. I fear no matter what you do in the next twenty years, if you make ten masterpieces, that* Dirty Harry *will still be the high point in your career. Deservedly so.*

CLINT: I think if I hadn't been in it and [Siegel] hadn't done it, it might've had even more recognition. The fact that everybody was labelizing [*sic*] there in the late Sixties and Seventies—all liberals were calling conservatives *fascists*, and all conservatives were calling liberals *Communists*—a lot of people tried to label *Dirty Harry* as a politically-oriented film. It wasn't at all. They were just showing their ignorance.

PAUL: *You mean if you hadn't been in* Dirty Harry *it would've been credited as being a better film?*

---

[19] Eastwood has gone on to be nominated for dozens of awards, both for his acting and directing, and has won several, including four Oscars: twice each for Best Director and Best Picture, for *Unforgiven* in 1993 and *Million Dollar Baby* in 2005. In recognition of his work as a producer, in 1994 the Academy of Motion Picture Arts and Sciences also presented him with the Irving J. Thalberg Award.

CLINT: I don't know if my credibility with various reviewers was as strong, though I don't think I could perform it any better today than I did then. I think I did a good job in it and Don did an excellent job in it. It was a classic cop drama. Because I came in from Westerns, playing the very quiet and mystical kind of thing, it wasn't a showy, show-and-tell performance that people liked to credit.

PAUL: *I thought it was one of the subtlest performances. I thought it was very sad. You weren't just this obsessive cop, you were this sad, likable guy whose wife had died and you were doing the job because you didn't have anything else to do. That was very moving stuff.*

CLINT: It was meant to be. That element was overlooked in a lot of the first runaround because the other, his dogmatic pursuit, was so strong. Not much ever happens good to him in the film except his relationship with his partner and his partner's wife, agreeing with them that they should get out of police work. But most of it is frustration, and right to the very end. Even when he has the satisfaction of blowing the guy away, it's a sad satisfaction.

PAUL: *He figures it's going to cost him the job, I guess.*

CLINT: He pitches the badge and figures, Screw it. They're going to ask for the badge anyway—let 'em dive for it. Though he's going back into his ritual about five bullets as opposed to six and "Do you feel lucky?" and all that, there's a sadness about it. Having to be driven to that point when he would rather have not been there at all, rather not disobeyed the orders to go after the killer. Not have the guy kidnap the children in the first place because the guy should have been put away the first time he had him. In his eyes anyway—his unsophisticated eyes as far as the legal maneuverings of this country.

PAUL: *I heard that John Wayne had once been offered the* Dirty Harry *role.*

CLINT: I don't think so. You never really know when somebody pops names like that around. I suppose they'd have gone for anybody at one time, but the first guy who had ever given it to me was at Universal. This was before it was bought by ABC, then Warner Bros. turned it around. Jennings Lang called me and said, "Would you like to do this?" Paul Newman had told them that he thought it was a great story, but he couldn't do it because he was politically opposed to it. That was the word that came to me. Now, how much truth is in that, I don't know.

PAUL: *I'd heard that one and I heard Frank Sinatra.*

CLINT: I told Jennings, who was at Universal at that time, "Buy this and I'll do this film. I don't see anything political at all about it. I see it as just one situation in a man's life. Later on he may turn around and feel the opposite about another situation in life. It has no bearing on politics." But some people line up more readily. I've never been aligned politically, I've been very much apolitical like yourself. I like certain characters who come along and I've supported a few people in my life, but only because I was against the opposition, not because I knew that much about the people I supported. All you know about anybody is the rhetoric they expel and you're kind of at the mercy of that. If you knew them all personally, you probably wouldn't vote for any of them [laughs].

PAUL: *I haven't voted for a considerable time actually.*[20]

CLINT: But Universal fumbled the ball on buying it. Somehow the deal was inadequate. So the property was bought by ABC. ABC hung onto it a while and didn't know what to do with it, and they turned it over to Warner Bros. Frank Wells was the man at Warners at the time who called me and asked me if I'd do it. This was when Warners had just turned over a new administration and they needed product badly. I was just preparing *Play Misty for Me.* I said, "I'm directing my first film and I'm determined to do it, but I'll tell you what you do: if you just hold off and let me

---

[20] Paul often boasted that the only time he'd voted for president was in 1964 when he cast a write-in ballot for his good friend Jac Holzman, founder of Elektra Records, and, "to write the story," Norman Mailer as vice president.

finish this film, I'll do it right afterwards." So finally, to make a long story short, he said no, they're going to go elsewhere. I said, "Fine. Good luck with it." So what happened is Frank Sinatra signed to do it.

PAUL: *That would've been a disaster.*

CLINT: Ashley [Ted Ashley, chairman of Warner Bros.] is a friend of his and, for whatever reasons or whatever casting ideas, they decided to go that route. So I just forgot about it. Meanwhile, I did *Play Misty*. One day Frank calls again and says, "What's your schedule?" I said, "I thought you had Frank Sinatra doing that thing?" "Looks like that's up in the air now. He has to have a hand operation or something, and he's going to retire." I said, "I might consider doing it. Give me the script again so I can reread it." They had another director on it and he was changing the script into a *completely* different direction than it was written. So I read all the scripts they had on it, which was about four or five, and I said, "There's only one that I like, it's the first one. The original one."

PAUL: *The one written by Harry Julian Fink and Rita M. Fink.*

CLINT: The Finks', yeah. So I went to Warner Bros. and sat down with them over there and I said, "I didn't like any of the rewrites, but I would like to go back to the original script and work on it with Dean Reisner. And I'd like to hire Don as the director. I haven't talked to him about it, but I know he wants to work with me and I'm sure he'd be great for it." They said fine, so I met with Don and gave him all the scripts, but I said, "Read this original one first." He was in exact concert with me. He felt that the other scripts had gone off in another direction that wasn't at all *Dirty Harry*.

The only thing that I found in the Finks' script that I wanted to change was the ending. The ending got real elaborate and went off into a production number with all kinds of explosions and Marine snipers shooting people and helicopters crashing and stuff. We felt it should be kept one-on-one with the villain.

PAUL: *The whole thing is a duel picture between those two characters.*

CLINT: We went back and rewrote it with Dean Reisner, whom Don and I had both used before, who wrote on *Coogan's Bluff* and then I used on *Misty*. He helped me rewrite *High Plains Drifter*. We whipped it into what we thought was a good script and made it.

PAUL: *How closely was John Milius involved in the screenplay of* Harry?

CLINT: Not very close.

PAUL: *I've read several Milius interviews where he takes credit for Harry and Andy Robinson being mirror images of the same character: Harry being the good side and Robinson being the bad side. But I never got the idea from you that Milius had much to do at all with the first* Dirty Harry *in any sense.*

CLINT: He maybe wrote on it when they had another director on it, Irvin Kershner or somebody like that. I guess the studio had been talking to McQueen or a few other actors about possibly playing it. I read the material and it wasn't anywhere related to the original. It was all about caliber of guns and all kinds of nomenclature.

PAUL: *I'd heard that Milius had written the .44 Magnum speech about "This is the most powerful handgun—"*

CLINT: He didn't. That scene was in Finks' script. It was basically the story that we did. All of the beginning of that script, the first two-thirds of it, play out much like they do in the original. After that it changes slightly. But Milius didn't write that part of it, no. He got off on another script with all kinds of .50 caliber guns and rifles and things. In the Finks' script, the original one, the .44 Magnum Model 29 Smith & Wesson was the sidearm that he used.

In the script, the speech where he does the "six shots or only five" wasn't written at the end. At the end he just shoots the guy.

It was only written once at the beginning. I felt it laid out the guy's character and his MO. It was my feeling that we should reprise it. Don liked it, he went for it.

At the beginning, Harry is more amused as he's got this guy down. He's had a lot of guys who have attempted armed robbery, and he says, "Well, do ya, punk?" But at the end he's a much different character. He says it because he absolutely hates this guy and wants him off the street. This guy has not only killed a victim, the girl, but has gotten out and committed more crimes after Harry has apprehended him once. His whole feeling about the criminal, and his feeling about the bureaucracy and everything he's fighting against, is all summed up in that speech using the same comedic dialogue, but with a little different attitude—less humor, of course—in the ending one. At least it was intended to be that way.

The guy did hijack a busload of adults in the original. We changed it to children. Let's face it, that's the most vulnerable thing in the world. Because we had mixed racial kids on the bus, a left-wing newspaper in Los Angeles accused us of making an anti-busing statement. Siegel and I didn't know what the hell that was all about. Siegel is not a right-wing fanatic and neither am I. That just shows you that everything is in the eyes of the beholder. We had it mixed racially because we thought it was the nice thing to do. We set it up that way because it showed that all children would be vulnerable to a maniacal soul like that—allowed out on the street by society and its bureaucracy and mishandling—and it has nothing to do with race one way or the other. They could have been all Oriental or all black or all Caucasian—who cares?

The woman who was writing the article for that newspaper was saying, "I'll never go see a Clint Eastwood movie again." Who gives a shit? I don't give a shit if she goes and sees any movie again. If somebody is that stupid and doesn't take the picture for the incident it is, well, that's the way it is. Tough shit. I doubt that person feels the same way today. I'm sure she's eight or ten years older and I'm sure she's changed. Maybe her philosophies have changed a little bit. But it doesn't make any difference anyway. You do the best you can, shoot your best shot, and walk away from it.

PAUL: *Siegel kept saying that all the authority is against Harry's methods, so how can it be such a right-wing picture when most of the police are shown to be against what he's doing? It just seemed like the criticism got totally out of hand and no one actually saw the movie.*

CLINT: Policemen liked the picture because it showed the frustration of being a police officer, which I'm sure they go through. There must be cases all over the country where people get out on a technicality after a law enforcement officer has gone to a great deal of trouble; or a judge is going to agree to it so people spend endless hours and endless reams of taxpayers' money to prosecute somebody, and a technicality gets them out. And who pays for it but Mr. and Mrs. Middle America?

PAUL: Dirty Harry *seemed to come along at a time when it was just right for centering in on something and just twisting the film's meaning.*

CLINT: That was all due to that early Seventies syndrome where everybody was finding something political about everything. That was an era of real name-calling, a kind of chickenshit era on our planet.

PAUL: *If you said you maybe weren't a liberal, you were in bad trouble.*

CLINT: If you were liberal-thinking but you had certain doubts about maybe one aspect of liberalism—maybe you *did* have doubts about overtaxing of money or the property taxes or something—it was interpreted as conservative. So those people were branded as some sort of crazy fucking right-winger or something like that.

PAUL: Dirty Harry *came out right at the peak of that.*

CLINT: It came out right at the peak of that, so everybody was going, "*Goddamn*, this is a right-wing tribute!" and all that bullshit. Of course, it wasn't that at all. You try to tell new and different stories and you try to take new and different attacks on them.

The other cop film of that year, *The French Connection*, for some reason it didn't stir people on that level. It seemed to be more straight ahead—the guy solving the case. Though Gene [Hackman] was terrific in it, he was a different kind of cop. People didn't seem to associate him with any kind of cause or any kind of crusade, whereas Dirty Harry was misinterpreted as being a right-wing crusader or a minuteman or something like that, when he wasn't that at all. He was a man with mixed feelings about law and order and the job he was doing.

PAUL: *I guess it was a case of timing. It seemed to me that had it come out later ...*

CLINT: Oh yeah, it was way ahead of its time.

PAUL: *The whole Vietnam question, like the Calley thing, about not obeying orders. The Daniel Ellsberg case, where one was moral not to do what they tell you, you know.*[21]

CLINT: Exactly. Those guys were embraced by a lot of the Left because they didn't follow orders. Here's a guy who's doing the exact same thing.

In the late Sixties and Seventies, everything was the rights of the accused, nobody cared much about the rights of the victim. Then, in England *and* here, everybody started thinking maybe there is something to the rights of the victim, too. It doesn't take much imagination to see yourself or a relative as a victim of a violent crime. How would you feel about it? If every person on a jury across the country or every judge had been somehow touched by a violent crime, I'm sure the verdicts would be radically changed. But it's easy for people to sit in a Madison Avenue apartment or a Sutton Place apartment and not really

---

[21] A US Army officer, William Calley, was found guilty for his role in the My Lai Massacre during the Vietnam War in 1968. Several hundred unarmed South Vietnamese citizens were tortured, raped, and murdered. Calley's defense was that he was just following orders.

In 1971, Daniel Ellsberg leaked the *Pentagon Papers*, a 7,000-page top secret study of the US's involvement in Vietnam, to nineteen newspapers. The study showed that the government had repeatedly lied to Congress and the public.

know what it's like down there in the less expensive areas where people are more touched by that thing.

It was the era when you had to have a lot of significance. The significance [of *Dirty Harry*] was it was an unusual case of an unusually frustrated person trying to get to the bottom of it quick. It becomes more timely now when you see people complaining of the opposite—a man gets seven years for killing the mayor of San Francisco.[22] All Dirty Harry was was a guy who said, "My God, I can't stand that shit."

PAUL: *Now it would be completely the other way around. Now it's a system of—at least in New York—plea bargaining. The guy's out on the street that night on a plea bargain. Turn 'Em Loose Bruce is a judge in New York who turns murderers loose every day.[23] The sympathy has gone completely the other way: now the sympathy would* be *for what Harry stands for.*

CLINT: The public is becoming either very callous or tolerant of this, or else they'd do more about it. Maybe they'll buy it in a movie, and then they'll go walk away and say, "Screw it, I don't want to be involved." There's that old saying: people get the politics they deserve, they get the leadership they deserve. Well, maybe we get the judicial system we deserve, too. If you get seven years for robbery and five years for murder, then that's the way our society balances out. That's not a conservative view or any other view really, it's just a view of liking living things, including human beings. It's like Albert Schweitzer's respect for humanity or for all living things. Maybe we haven't become irate enough and become up in arms enough to say we'll get these people, or whatever political regime supports them, out.

But like you say, at later dates it was brought up that Lieutenant Calley should have obeyed a higher order, he should have obeyed God and not followed the orders. We did the same

---

[22] Dan White received a seven-year sentence for assassinating, in 1978, George Moscone, the mayor of San Francisco, and city supervisor Harvey Milk.

[23] Bruce McMarion Wright was an African-American judge famous for letting poor, black defendants out on little or no bail, even though their crimes were often of a violent nature and sometimes directed toward the police.

thing in the Nuremberg Trials after World War II. We asked
these Nazi war criminals, every one of them, "How could you
have followed the thing?" "I was following orders." "But you
should have adhered to a higher order." We advocated that as
a country and we put down anybody who didn't do that. We
advocated that by jailing Lieutenant Calley.

But at the same time a guy like Dirty Harry *was* adhering to
another morality—he was adhering to his own morality. He says
to the district attorney, who says, "It's the law," "Well, then, the
law is crazy." That's a very basic feeling and there are a lot of
people who feel that way today about a lot of laws. Maybe it's not
God's law or maybe it's not Fate's law or mankind's or whatever
your beliefs are in life, yet we tried people and convicted people
on the basis of not adhering to a higher morality.

PAUL: *In* Dirty Harry *every action was for a specific reason: find the
girl before she suffocates, do this, do that.*[24] *It's just not blindly
disobeying a law. He's got a time limit to get information. It was
not a political philosophy that was determining his actions.*

CLINT: If the case wasn't solved in six hours, he had to assume,
knowing the criminal and knowing his MO and having arrested
him, that the guy would go through with his threat.

Dean Reisner, he used to get incensed at that time, in the
Seventies, when people like [Pauline] Kael would say it was
a fascist movie. He would always say that they were fascists
themselves for approaching it that way. I guess it's easy to sit in
judgment when you haven't been there yourself. It's the easiest
thing in the world. When you've been there yourself, maybe that
makes it easier but in a different direction. Who knows.

14

PAUL: *I've always thought you got along really well with black
actors.*

---

[24] Scorpio kidnaps a fourteen-year-old girl and buries her alive. Callahan chases him
down in Kezar Stadium, shoots him in the leg, and tortures him until he reveals the
girl's whereabouts.

CLINT: I don't really know that I get along with black actors any more than with any other group of actors. I was raised in Oakland, where there's a high population of black people, so I have known a lot of them. I was interested in jazz since I was a very young kid, so I've known a lot of them through the world of jazz. I don't think there's any talent in getting along with anybody other than people either instinctively take to you or they don't depending on the vibes you've got. I hate to use that expression because it's overworked.

PAUL: *I didn't mean "getting along" so much as your treatment of blacks on the screen is never Stanley Kramer-heavy.*

CLINT: Condescending.

PAUL: *You do it almost better than anyone, with less self-consciousness, and you do things other actors would be afraid to do or not be able to pull off.*

CLINT: If you're having a scene like in *Alcatraz* where you're calling each other *boy* or *nigger* or *ofay* or *paddy* or whatever, it's part of the scene, it's part of the drama. It's just two people acting out a drama is all. I don't feel self-conscious about it and none of the black actors I've ever worked with feel self-conscious about it either. There are people in life who talk this way, and I might be playing a character that talks this way. I have never played it, but conceivably if an actor was playing an out-and-out bigot, he'd have to act like an out-and-out bigot. It doesn't mean that's where his soul is, but you'd have to do it without being self-conscious about it. You'd have to think of some reason why he might have deep prejudices.[25]

Hell, I could play a Communist and, if the part was good and the story was good, I could play a dictator. Let's face it, some actor has to act out Adolf Hitler somewhere. That doesn't mean he approves of Adolf Hitler. He does the best job he can, but from an acting point of view, he tries to approach it like, Now, how does this guy think? This guy, Adolf Hitler, thought he was right and thought he was a swell guy and he thought he was

---

[25] Eastwood would play such a character in 2008's *Gran Torino*.

terrific, so how do I make myself believe that I'm terrific doing these outrageous things, these crimes against humanity? That's the thing all actors have to ask themselves on any kind of role. I ask it whether I'm playing a hero or a bum.

PAUL: *The point I guess I'm trying to make is that it really works with black audiences. They really love that stuff because I guess they're probably not used to that naturalness.*

CLINT: In *Dirty Harry*, the bank robbery sequence at the beginning, which sets up Callahan's character, was originally written just for five white guys. Stunt men. I was sitting there with Don and I was saying, "Can't we find some new faces maybe?" He started thinking maybe we could find some black actors who'd like to do it. We had some people at the studio say, "Aren't you opening up a can of beans with civil rights?" We asked, "Why? There are black renegades that run together same as there are white renegades that run together. This way it'll be a chance to use some new faces, it'll give an opportunity to new black actors and stunt men to enact the scene. Why not do it?" It worked out terrific, and blacks took no exception to the fact that it was a black guy to whom I do my speech about "Did he fire six shots or only five?" They enjoy it just as much because they enjoy the principle of the scene. It's not condescending at all. Harry's not being any nicer to him or any less nice to him because of his race. He's just a guy who was caught with his hand in the cookie jar on an armed robbery.

PAUL: *Most of the blacks I know seem to be so greatly relieved that he doesn't take that attitude. He doesn't clothe it in either a condescending or a moralistic thing.*

CLINT: That's true, I think a lot of blacks are relieved with that. Let's just talk natural and not hide anything under pseudo-liberal feelings or "the mink-coat liberal set wouldn't approve." I mean, screw it, we all come from the same place anyway.

PAUL: *That's why it's so annoying that* Dirty Harry *got bum-rapped for that.*

CLINT: Ah, well. A little bit of knowledge is a dangerous thing. Beware of the guy who gets his first feelings of guilt about racial or other things that have happened in his life. He's going to carry things to a great extreme. Beware of people who get terribly idealistic protesting too much or professing too much. People who talk too much about one thing, you've got to beware of what are the real motivations in it.

It's like religion. I was accosted the other day in a store by a guy who was religious. I was there shopping and the guy was yelling so loud finally I said, "Hey, buddy, just leave me alone." He said, "You've got to play by the rules," and went on with philosophical feelings of his. I said, "Hey, one of the rules is just leave everybody else alone." Then he started really getting incensed. I started thinking afterwards, people like that are the kind who were stringing people up during the Crusades and hacking people's heads off. When you think of the millions of people who have been killed over the years by causes—not just necessarily religious but by any causes, by people who became enraptured—and anybody who didn't believe in what they were stating was crazy. We're seeing that in Iran now with Khomeini. A person who comes in under the guise of being a savior to a country turns out to be as animalistic as the person he's accusing.[26] It goes back to those basics: sometimes your biggest faults are the ones you're accusing everyone else of having.

15

PAUL: *When you worked with John Sturges on* Joe Kidd *[1972] was that a disappointment to you? Sturges seemed to have somehow gone flat in that period.*

CLINT: I like John personally very much. He's a very affable guy. I liked some of the films he'd done.

PAUL: *I did, too. A lot. Sturges used to be a real early favorite of mine. Outdoors he was great; if you put him indoors he was*

---

[26] Ayatollah Khomeini led the 1979 Iranian Revolution, overthrowing the Shah of Iran and taking over as the country's Supreme Leader.

terrible. He couldn't do domestic drama or any of that stuff. Then he just seemed to all of a sudden get real flat and disinterested. He lost his sting somewhere in there.

CLINT: He'd done some really good things. I was looking forward to it. He's a talented guy, an imaginative guy, and he's had a lot of experience. He was an editor—and an assistant editor on *Gunga Din*—and goes way back. It's always fun to work with a guy who's got that kind of background. There's a great history there. But when John gets going on a thing, he'll keep thinking. He's an intellectualizer and he likes to think out things. Pretty soon he was changing the story every day. He never could come to a conclusion about the ending. We just kind of fought it all the time, and finally I just said, "Hey, there comes a time we've got to just settle down and make up our mind on something."

I was shooting second unit for him at one point. I was the only actor in the scene. I went off and shot it while he was doing some other stuff with some larger groups. We figured we could save some time that way, which we did. I remember I changed my direction: I took myself into the building this way—I went in right-to-left—and took myself out left-to-right because the background was so much more interesting. But you saw me enter the building and you know I'm coming out the back, so what's the difference?

He objected terribly. He asked me if I'd shoot it over again because he wanted to go right-to-left, right-to-left. I said, "Come on, John. They're going where we're taking them." "They won't understand. It'll look weird." I said, "Hey, you're the director and I want you to be happy. I'll reshoot it," so I went and reshot and took myself out right-to-left. He was much more programmed into another way of doing things than I was. I like going a lot of directions. It excites the movie rather than have everything in the A-B-C-D-E-F-G straight old fundamental routine.

PAUL: *I don't think you've ever confused anybody by flopping it around like that.*

CLINT: You're going where you're going. We used to do it in *Rawhide*. Boy, everything was right-to-left, right-to-left. "That's the way we're going because we're going south-to-north: right-to-left."

Well, you can be going south-to-north, looking into the sunset, and you're going left-to-right. When you look into the sunrise, you're going right-to-left. It's the time of day, it's a lot of things. So you just take a big, long trip. Nobody looks out one window of a car all day long—they look out both windows and round.

John, he's a different type of guy than I am. Once he edits around a little, fiddles with it, he turns over the postproduction, the music. In fact, he has a good editor, Ferris [Webster], whom I've since hired a lot of times. But he would kind of just fiddle a little bit and then walk away. He just approaches it a little differently than I do. I don't begrudge him for it. He's a guy with great talent, but he gets interested in a lot of different things. All the time we were doing the picture, he had a tuna boat he was working on.

PAUL: *Was Elmore Leonard on the set? I talked to him on the telephone a few times about his books. I think he wrote the script on that.*

CLINT: He wrote the first draft, then he was on something else. He did the script, and then John wanted to change things a lot, so Leonard was at the mercy of what was going down there. He's written some good stuff. I liked him. We've had submissions from him since then, but we've never found anything that quite clicked. We had the potential of something there, but it didn't come out as my favorite.

16

Harking back to his Spaghetti Western days, in 1973 Eastwood directed and starred in *High Plains Drifter*, once again playing a nameless, mysterious stranger. The townspeople of Lago, a small mining town, hire him to protect them from a trio of outlaws who whipped the town's last marshal to death. By the time he's finished, the stranger turns Lago into a living hell.

PAUL: High Plains Drifter *was not your average Western at all.*

CLINT: I read it as a nine-page treatment, but I was just turned on by it.

PAUL: *Verna saw your character as a ghost.*

CLINT: It was written as the brother in the original treatment and in the script, but I took out references to the brother because I felt that I wanted to present it as an apparition or a ghost. Maybe it's a ghost—I let the audience decide. The ending was left for the audience to write in with you, to imagine with you, not just give them a "This is the way it was, folks. Here's the wrap-up," and cut it off. I feel audiences are intelligent and they want to be stimulated and think about things.

PAUL: *It does seem to me to be an almost Ingmar Bergman Western. Did his films have any influence on it?*

CLINT: No. I liked some of the earlier films; I haven't been nuts about some of the recent ones. *The Virgin Spring* and *The Seventh Seal,* I used to really enjoy those. I think in later years they were mostly being held together by critics writing in what wasn't there. It was kind of like Kurosawa's films. I loved Kurosawa's work. I didn't like *Dersu Uzala*—I thought that was terrible, except it had a nice wind sequence in it. But I thought the early stuff—*Red Beard,* which wasn't too early, going back through the years to *Seven Samurai* and *Yojimbo,* which we remade as *A Fistful of Dollars,* or made a version of—were really great visual things. He had the great combination of being able to do a visual picture and have his characters come to life. You wanted to know them. Where a lot of times you get one or the other: you get somebody who's very good with the character thing and *not* with the visual, or very good with the visual and spectacle part, but you can't ever get into the people.

But it's everybody for a particular film or whatever group of films. The mark of a good director, of course, is what the body of his work is worth overall. Not just a flick—how it turns out over the years. Naturally some of them are going to stand heads above others just by the nature of spirit and all the components coming together. It's half talent/half luck or fate or whatever you want to call it.

PAUL: *Did you see* Kagemusha?

CLINT: I didn't like that. But some of his earlier things were just really fabulous. *Rashomon* was really good. I haven't liked any of his last works. But I loved his period Samurai. I'm the same way about Bergman: I'm not nuts about the later stuff. Some of the early ones were imaginative. *Wild Strawberries* I liked.

PAUL: Sawdust and Tinsel *I always liked a lot.* The Naked Night, *I guess it's also called that.*

CLINT: *The Virgin Spring,* that was the last good one I saw. Then *Through a Glass Darkly* and some of those other ones he kind of lost me a little bit.

PAUL: *I liked* Persona, *that's the only later one I like a lot. But when he suddenly started announcing trilogies and that* Through a Glass Darkly *was film number one, that's when he lost me.*

CLINT: The guy's done some marvelous things, but never advanced for the day. Overindulgence isn't limited to anybody, no matter how bright they are.

PAUL: *We probably went through the same periods in the Fifties and Sixties. You could see a lot of Kurosawa and Bergman and Godard and Truffaut.*

CLINT: And Fellini's films. He was more prolific then. The one that sticks in my mind is one of the earliest ones, the traveling circus one.

PAUL: La Strada. *I like* La Strada *a lot, too.*

CLINT: *Bronco Billy* was like an American version of *La Strada.*

PAUL: *Bill McKinney used to say* Bronco Billy *was "Walt Disney meets* La Strada.*" That was his alternate title for it.*

CLINT: Yeah, *La Strada* I liked a lot.

PAUL: *I guess it's from a Marilyn Beck column, but are you going to work with Blake Edwards on a couple films?*

CLINT: Not a couple, but we talked about one. Edwards was talking to Burt Reynolds and me about doing this one.[27]

PAUL: *I like Edwards. His work's pretty good.*

CLINT: You look back on some of the things he's done, *Experiment in Terror* and *Days of Wine and Roses*, which he got more recognition for.

PAUL: *I liked* Experiment in Terror *better myself.*

CLINT: I liked *Experiment in Terror*, too. That's one of those ones that nobody really gave credit to because it was a small little film and nobody thought much about it.

PAUL: *It's very terrifying, that nasal voice of Ross Martin.*

CLINT: Doing the asthmatic thing [breathes heavily]. And I loved those Inspector Clouseau movies. All of them. Those were always great fun.

PAUL: *Especially the first two, which were just astonishingly good.*

CLINT: *A Shot in the Dark* and *The Pink Panther.* There was always something in them that gave you great laughs. I enjoy them, too, because my kid enjoys them so much.

PAUL: *What do you watch now? Do you watch a lot of cassettes?*

CLINT: I don't get a chance to watch a lot. I'm usually just researching stuff. Sometimes I'll be watching with the kids.

PAUL: *Let me just put the old corny hypothetical question out to you: If somebody sent you off to an island, said you have to stay there*

---

[27] The film, 1984's *City Heat*, came to pass, but Edwards was fired as director and replaced with Richard Benjamin.

for the rest of your life and you could take, oh, ten or twelve films
to watch, do you have any idea what some of them would be?[28]

CLINT: That would be a tough one to answer. I don't know, I suppose
if I was going to be that isolated I would like films of expanse and
size. I'd be hard-pressed to come up with anything on that one. I
don't think if I was that isolated I'd probably look at anything. I'd
probably just figure the hell with it. Look at the view or something.

17

Clint caught his fans and critics off guard when he directed
Breezy in 1973. The story concerns Breezy, a teenage hippy
girl (Kay Lenz) who falls in love with a middle-aged, divorced
businessman played by William Holden. Eastwood's only
appearance in the film is a cameo à la Alfred Hitchcock.

PAUL: *What drew you to make* Breezy?

CLINT: I just liked the script very much. The rejuvenation of a cynic
through this very young, naïve person who was all very open
and didn't understand the cynicism of this man. It was just that
simple. A love story between two generations. To see a man get
a second lease on life through the eyes of this teenage girl who
he shouldn't even be out with in the first place—by all social
standards, so to speak. He was successful monetarily, but not
being satisfied in any particular way with what he did. He was a
guy who'd been through the divorce thing and was down on not
only his marriage vows but his life. His relationship with women
was sort of anti-woman at that moment because of his divorce
situation. He realized that even the friends around him were
just boring compared to her. She has brought something special
to his life that this cocktail Beverly Hills social set didn't have.

---

[28] The critic Greil Marcus, an old friend of Paul's, gave him a similar assignment in
1979 when he invited him to write an essay, for his anthology *Stranded: Rock and
Roll for a Desert Island*, about what one record album he'd take with him to an
island. Paul chose Jackson Browne's *The Pretender*.

PAUL: *Did you consider playing the Holden part yourself at any one point?*

CLINT: At the time I did it, I didn't think I was old enough. I thought I wouldn't do it half as well as the guy who did it. I felt it needed a guy a couple of years older, a couple years more cynical. I like Holden and he's a good actor. He told me, "You know, I've been this guy," and I said, "I know that." I just kind of read it in his face that he'd been this guy.[29]

PAUL: *He's another universal part. Not maybe as universal as* Play Misty for Me, *but it's a part that most people can identify with.*

CLINT: I've known a lot of people who are like that. That's why it was easy to tell that story. And I've seen girls like that on their own. Whether they were as idyllic or as sharp as this girl, I don't know.

PAUL: *Did you have to work a lot with Kay Lenz? I thought she was really terrific.*

CLINT: I had to work a lot more with her than I did Holden. Holden's a terrific actor with great experience and background and a charisma that is all his own. But also Holden had *been* this character before, lived this character. This character was a snap for him to play. He knew every facet about him with the exception maybe of falling in love with a juvenile girl. And who knows [chuckles]—I mean, I didn't ask him ...

But she was a lot newer. We tested ten girls and her test was one of the worst. I tested other people who were much more proficient in the test but they just didn't fit the part right. She had a good acting facility—she was just extremely tense in a lot of mannerisms and stuff. When she got the part, she could afford to relax a little bit. I worked with her a little bit, and then she started getting really with it. She was very good.

PAUL: *She had a real quality about her. I've seen her in other things, but she seemed very iffy.*

---

[29] Eastwood was forty-three when he made the film and Holden was fifty-five.

CLINT: It was a short film, it didn't take a long time to make it. When you're doing a film with two people, you can work with the scenes a little bit. Holden was just terrific, always there, on-time, always ready to go. And very helpful to work with her. We'd do one take on him and we might do five or six or eight or whatever it took to warm up with her. He was always right there and cooking.

PAUL: *Some people apparently felt that it was a mistake to make the girl that young: sixteen, seventeen years old.*

CLINT: I didn't think so. Certainly, most girls at that age are young women physically, and it's a question of attitude. A lot of people objected when they read the script. I talked to a lot of older women who felt vulnerable about that script, but once they saw the movie they liked it. They fell in love with the girl, too. They fell in love with what she represented and her moving this man.

PAUL: *All I could think was, against all odds, just go ahead and do it.*

18

PAUL: *Have you acted onstage at all much?*

CLINT: No, I haven't.

PAUL: *Going to plays in New York, the acting just strikes me as so ludicrous, so broad, so fake that I just start laughing or I leave.*

CLINT: It doesn't have to be. There *have* been performances that aren't overacted on the stage. Good acting is good acting. There *is* a projection element that takes the conversation out of a lot of scenes sometimes, but there have been some actors who are just marvelous at it over the years. People expect broadness on the stage, so they'll accept it, where if you did that same broadness in a movie, they would say, "Oh my God." There are a lot of actors in theater who adapt to movies well and then there are a lot of them who don't. A lot of them are great vocal instruments, they have a nice voice and a presence on the stage, but when you see them in a close-up it doesn't do anything for an audience. You've got to move the people on a level where they want to look into your soul and your eyes and your movements and think very carefully along with you.

PAUL: *It seems to me movie acting, or at least a certain kind of movie acting, is very different. When you're in an action picture, you're also playing some sort of mythic charge, playing almost more than a man. McQueen plays roles like this and so have [James] Stewart and [Gary] Cooper. It's not like Fredric March playing a salesman—you're playing more like national myths.*

CLINT: That's true, sure. If you were unraveling a role like *High Noon* on a stage, Gary Cooper would seem extremely economical. But on the screen, with editing and timing and where the scene isn't very big, it's a very powerful presence there. It's two different worlds.

It's a very big paradox to be in, doing a play, because if the play's a hit you're tied up for a long period of time; a year later you're still doing the same damn thing. You think of the other things you might want to be doing. And if it's a flop you're tied up for only a few nights, but you spent all that time for nothing.

I've had discussions about theater before and during my career, but I like presenting things in film. The timing of film and everything I understand somewhat. I've done a lot in it but I think I've got a lot more to do in it, as a director or whatever. My ambition's that way.

19

PAUL: *Can we talk a little about* Magnum Force *[1973] and* The Enforcer *[1976]? Did Siegel not want to do the first* Dirty Harry *sequel, or did you not want to do it with him?*

CLINT: Don had not been interested in doing a sequel. He felt that once was enough on the thing and he was preparing another project—*Charlie Varrick,* I think. *Dirty Harry* was a far superior story than the other two. The other two were just taking the character into another situation.

Magnum Force, the premise of that interested me. It was based on a Brazilian death squad and that whole thing where an elite or an underground force is formed among the police force. Because of the slowness of the judicial system in that country, this group—they were sort of like Robin Hood/assassins or something—they'd go out and eliminate criminals who were tough on the public. I thought it would be a very important subject to analyze. It could be very entertaining, besides it could be interesting. The fact that our judicial system *is* slow, that's no big secret, and the fact that, because of that, an ultra-minuteman kind of group could form within a police force and start out doing heroic deeds. Which is exactly what happened in Brazil. They started doing deeds, and the public thought, what the hell, they assassinated a hit man or something like that—that saves the taxpayers' money. But at the same time in Brazil they got out of control. The whole principle of the thing got lost—if there *is* any principle, which there isn't. Any kind of nobility or good deed was shot down. And that's what happens with everything: everything's carried in a pendulum in life, everything goes to the right or the left.

So that's the way we approached this, about a group that starts out with certain ideals based on certain frustrations, and then all of a sudden they become the judge, the jury, and that becomes dictatorship, judging what everybody should read, listen to, et cetera, et cetera.

Though Dirty Harry would be the kind of guy whose help this minuteman or ultra-rightwing group, whatever they are, would think they could solicit—they think he would be sympathetic—the reason he wasn't sympathetic was because Dirty Harry had only one objective and that was to uphold the law. He's fighting it in *Dirty Harry,* but in *Magnum Force* he sees, in his instinctive, animalistic way, where it can all head to. And where it does eventually head to.

PAUL: *Did some of the leftover material from the various scripts of the first version of* Dirty Harry *wind up in* Magnum Force?

CLINT: No. The thing that happened with *Magnum Force* was that Milius came up with the idea of the Brazilian death squad. I was doing the *High Plains Drifter* shooting up in Mono Lake, and he called me. I said, "That *would* be an interesting thing to fool with." He was doing a ton of things and he made a draft of it, which had some good things but also missed a lot of things, so Mike Cimino helped me with a rewrite on it. I'd worked with Mike on *Thunderbolt* [*and Lightfoot*] in between all this and I liked his writing, so he as a favor helped me out with it.

PAUL: *Had you wanted to do a sequel to* Harry?

CLINT: The studio was in love with the idea. It did well, it did extremely well. *The Enforcer* the same way. *The Enforcer* came along, people liked it. It wasn't in the league with *Dirty Harry*, but it was another element of the character. The studio would like to have made three more of them, but there comes a time when you have to call it a day.

PAUL: *You'd have to find something pretty fantastic for you to do another one, I would suspect.*

CLINT: It would have to be the absolute ultimate story. It would have to be the greatest detective story ever written. Otherwise, you move on. It's the same thing with anything that's successful.

I suppose they'd love to do a sequel to *Every Which Way but Loose* because it was a giant box-office thing, but I don't know if I want to do one. It's too soon almost. I suppose if somebody came up with a really interesting script and I thought I could make a nice, entertaining Christmas kind of film that kids and a well-rounded audience could see—a PG—I might do it as an entertainment idea rather than trying to do a real stretching thing acting-wise or career-wise or for whatever other motivations.

PAUL: *That's what* Magnum Force *and* The Enforcer *seemed to me: they're not stretching films. The fact that you didn't direct either of them, they seemed to be, oh, not frivolous, but they got wilder and wilder as they went, it seemed like. I liked them both, but it seemed to me that there were a lot of set pieces with almost no* *real reason for some of them. A lot of the charges made against* Dirty Harry *would almost hold against the other two.*

CLINT: Sure.

PAUL: *Where he does go in with his gun and just blazes through the airplane full of passengers—that would never have happened in* Dirty Harry, *it would never have been set up that way. The picture didn't seem to be thought out on the level of* Dirty Harry.

CLINT: No, *Dirty Harry* was extremely well thought out. You can bet if it was the greatest detective story ever written and it was a sequel, if I wasn't doing it in collaboration with Don, I'd be doing it myself [laughs]. It's a character that's too close to me. I feel that, though the character was written, I put my stamp on it and I want it to be good. And the others, they were all respectable films—there's no problem with that—it's just that one I thought was exceptional.

20

PAUL: *I saw* Thunderbolt and Lightfoot *[1974] on TV the other night. Did Cimino bring the script to you?*

CLINT: Yeah. Cimino was being represented by William Morris, and my agent called me up and said, "There's a client, a new writer we've got, and he wrote this script, which he wants to direct. One of the other agents had told him the script would be perfect for you." You hear that a lot from people, but you can't just be negative or you'd turn off on everything. So I said, "Sure, send it over." I really liked it. I thought it was an adventure story with an interesting feel and interesting characters and it was a lot of fun. So we made a deal to do the picture. I looked at some commercials he'd directed—though commercial directors sometimes are deadly because they're so busy trying to do the ultimate trick—but he'd written it so visually I just felt that chances were he'd probably be pretty good. So I hired him.

PAUL: *Did you do much to the script after he turned it in?*

CLINT: No. It was much like the *Bronco Billy* script in the sense that it was pretty much all there. It wasn't a massive rewrite, it just needed a little redlining here and there. Some scripts you get are terrific ideas, but only about eighty percent or seventy percent or sixty percent of it works and you've got to figure out how to fix the rest. This one was pretty much right on.

PAUL: *Did he write it, do you think, with you in mind?*

CLINT: I don't know if he wrote it with me in mind or who he had in mind, but I liked it very much. He came in and he worked very efficiently, very economically. He went off and picked the locations with an AD [assistant director]. He did a real good job preparing the film and laying it out. I was really pleased with him.

PAUL: *I liked that film a lot. I just read an interview with Cimino in some British film magazine. He didn't really put the film down, but he sort of did. He said that "Oh, that one doesn't really count. That wasn't really mine." I thought, Jesus, you bastard, this is a much better film than* The Deer Hunter.

CLINT: He probably says it wasn't really his because it was done in conjunction with us and we rode herd on him a little.

PAUL: *For all his benefit, I would say.*

CLINT: It was done in a much tighter fashion editorially, judging by *The Deer Hunter*. He did a nice job on *Thunderbolt and Lightfoot* and he should be proud of it. I personally think the other was rather indulgent. It's a far better script than the other one and it's a far better executed job. In *The Deer Hunter* he got wrapped up in the lateral slide. Remember, we talked about that before? Unmotivated camera-moving like you see in every commercial on TV.

PAUL: *Utter confusion as far as I could tell. I have no idea at the end, when everybody starts singing "God Bless America," what my reaction is supposed to be, you know?*

CLINT: Well, it's supposed to be a big symbol. If you put enough of that stuff in a film you can fool half of the people half of the time and some of the people some of the time.

PAUL: *It must have been very brilliantly marketed.*

CLINT: It was marketed real well and a lot of people read things into it. People who don't know anything about war or combat thought that that was it, that that's what all the soldiers did over there, was play Russian roulette. There's never been an incident recorded of any of that stuff.

PAUL: *It was a real cheating aspect.*

CLINT: There's some nice production in the Vietnam stuff. It had such good production you were wishing you saw it in a different story, a *Steel Helmet* or something, a film that deserved some good production and didn't get it.

PAUL: *Did Sam Fuller ever get to shoot that massive war film he was going to make with [Peter] Bogdanovich helping him?* The Big Red *something, I think it was called.*[30]

CLINT: He talked to me one time about doing something and he sent over something that he had written, but it wasn't anything I was interested in. I can't recall what it was about. He's one of those guys who was like Don was in the old days, who did a lot of B movies and they were a notch above the other B movies. Guys like that, guys who could do a lot with a little, were never given much credit in Hollywood. Once in a great while somebody'd come along and praise a sleeper, but a guy like Don, who was famous for doing a lot with a little, was always second fiddle in his career to the guys who spent a lot.

It's a funny thing, on *Paint Your Wagon*, when they were having a serious talk about replacing the director, Don came up to visit me on other business and I let him read the script one night. He liked the story. I said, "They're talking about replacing the director on this thing." He said, "You've got to be realistic. You know they're

---

[30] *The Big Red One* was released in 1980 without the assistance of Bogdanovich, who'd been occupied with a project of his own.

going to go for another guy who's directed another musical." I never even brought the subject up to Lerner, but because Siegel had never done a show with a musical number in it, he wouldn't be considered. Yet, what the hell, what's a musical number? There were six, seven songs in a show—any imbecile can do that. Providing it's all cohesive there and the story's okay, there are a lot of ways of going about doing that. He was a man who was categorized as doing a two-million picture, not a twenty-million one. Of course, if he'd done it, it wouldn't have been a twenty-million-dollar picture, it would've probably been ten.

PAUL: *Does it cost you about five million to do a picture now?*

CLINT: I did *Bronco Billy* for five something. I was talking to the head of the studio the other day and I said, "You mean to tell me that five million dollars or six million dollars is now a *low*-budget film? You've got to be kidding." He said, "Yeah, I have to tell you, the average is in the eight area."

PAUL: *McQueen now says he won't consider a script for less than five.*

CLINT: You know what that is? He's doing that as a way of turning the guy down. I know that situation because I was approached on that same story, and what has happened is it's something that doesn't sound like a heavyweight property to him. What his agent's done is say, "I'll tell you what, we'll read it, but here's the price." They figure if they can find somebody stupid enough to come up with five, they'll say, "Well, maybe we better consider this." That's just a gimmick. If somebody came along with a great script and had a good, solid director—Sidney Lumet or somebody like that—he'd probably say, "Yeah, okay, let's see what the going rate is at the moment."

PAUL: *That* is *scary, that a low-budget film is five million.*

CLINT: We're always glorifying the guys who do fairly good with so much. I guess Woody Allen with *Annie Hall* was the last moderate-budget film that any glory was heaped on. A lot of people make pictures with no soul at all. I mean, they're happenings and they may be visually interesting, but as far as that old Frank Capra heart thing or whatever you want to call it, there are not too many of them. Remember *Bullfighter and the Lady?*

PAUL: *Oh, that was great.*

CLINT: God, that was a terrific movie. Budd Boetticher evidently was really interested in bullfighting and, I guess in the late Forties or early Fifties, he moved down to Mexico and did this picture. I remember seeing that picture at a screening when I was first in the business. I was a contract player at Universal and they used to screen movies every other day in the morning. You'd look at a movie and then everybody'd sit around and talk about this and that. What a knockout movie.

PAUL: *I like the Boetticher stuff. The Westerns are good.*

CLINT: He's another guy, sort of like Don, who never gets any credit in the Hollywood movie scene or whatever you want to call it because he does so much with so little. They released some marvelous films, but these guys were working with stories that they had to scrounge up and buy for peanuts from some writer who got twenty-five cents for his story, or that they had to write themselves.

I ran *Rebel Without a Cause* the other night. Sondra and I were looking at it and we came to the conclusion this is a real B story, really B stuff, except for the way it was presented. The only thing that made it kind of an A movie in its time—it had the cast and Dean was certainly a hot individual at the time—was the way it was laid out. But it was just B material, like Siegel, like Fuller and the guys you mentioned. Budd Boetticher and guys like that.

When I grew up in films in the Fifties, the guys who got all the big stuff were the guys who would spend the most. It seemed like guys like Josh Logan, who had never directed films before, would be doing *Picnic*s and stuff like that, and the guys like Siegel, Fuller, and Nicholas Ray were all struggling to get any kind of crummy little story that they could put their hands on. So it turns out their classic, you know, has to be *Invasion of the Body Snatchers* or whatever. When we got *Dirty Harry* down and had a good, solid detective story, we showed that it could be as classy as anybody else would do it.

We're seeing that cycle repeating itself now, the cycle of big spending on movies, spending twenty, thirty million dollars for films. Those guys, they end up getting the company so deep in the film that the company has to go on a brilliant marketing job, they have to spend a fortune on advertising. Consequently, they have to spend a fortune on trying to get awards for the film and various nominations in order to keep selling that film so that it will come out and hopefully it'll break even. Where a lot of times a film will get lesser treatment because it just happened to be done economically and well. Once in a while, an *American Graffiti* will take off in spite of the company, and then they're surprised. Then they'll go after it, after they find out what they've got. We had the same thing here with *Every Which Way but Loose*.

PAUL: *Do you ever envision yourself making one like that? Where you found a property you really loved and had to go to, say, fifteen, twenty million to make it.*

CLINT: If it called for it and I thought it was justifiable, I suppose you can envision it. The only thing I would hope is that if it cost fifteen, it would look like twenty-five. So many of them I've seen that cost fifteen, twenty, look like they cost about eleven.

21

In 1975's *The Eiger Sanction*, Eastwood is an art history professor pulled back, for one more mission, into his previous life as an assassin for an international intelligence agency. His assignment: to join an expedition scaling the Eiger, a mountain range in the Swiss Alps, and kill one of the three other climbers, who's a secret agent. Complicating matters, he doesn't know which one is his target.

PAUL: *What drew you to make* The Eiger Sanction?

CLINT: Somebody asked me to read the book. It was the kind of thing a lot of people were doing, these tongue-in-cheek spy drama things, but there was an element of it that was more interesting because the mountain-climbing stuff seemed like it actually could be suspenseful. The whole thing on height. I got wrapped up with the challenge of trying to make the picture all in the mountains, which I did. There were no papier-mâché rocks. In former mountain-climbing pictures there were a million. It was a tough picture to make.

If I'd had a knockout mountaineering story, a real knockout book or script, it would've been really something special. I've felt that way about a lot of pictures; mine some, other people's as well. Sometimes you see a sequence like, oh, for instance, that helicopter sequence in *Apocalypse Now*, the bombing and all, and you think, God, I wish this was in *A Walk in the Sun* or some great war story. That's probably the way I feel about that now. *The Eiger Sanction* was a modest story with good physical productions.

PAUL: *This seems to be the only one of your films where there is a lot of exposition.*

CLINT: And that was cut down. It was one of those plots—you're fighting it from the beginning—that has tricks upon tricks upon tricks. In those plots, if you're not careful, you end up in that Sherlock Holmes-ism or the *Perry Mason* kind of thing where you start talking about a lot of things that have happened. A lot of old movies that did it—classic movies, *The Maltese Falcon* or *Psycho*—you look at the end of those movies *now* and they don't play at all because they're just vast exposition that's drivel by today's standards. In those days it was fine, but nowadays you'd revamp that ending, you'd try to shoot it visually in some sort of an interesting sequence. At least hopefully you would. Everything progresses along.

PAUL: *Instead of playing for the James Bond tongue-in-cheek quality, did you consider changing the character from the book? To do the whole job seriously?*

CLINT: Do a straight-on thing? No, it just wasn't constructed that way. It was pretty hard to do that completely. I didn't try to play it James Bond, I tried to play it more at a serious level, but it was very hard to do because the situations were guided by going to another country, you're going to pose as so-and-so, and then when you get on the side of the mountain you might find out or you might not find out who the guy is.

A lot of people enjoyed the film. It had good response. It isn't my all-time favorite.

PAUL: *No, it's not mine either, but it's quite a good film. It's probably the best mountain-climbing film, I think, that's been made.*[31]

CLINT: It's as good mountain stuff as you can find in other than just a straight documentary. What happened is Universal had bought the book and they talked to me about doing it. I made some requests. I don't know what they were—maybe it was money [laughs]—and somehow the deal fell through. Then they came back and said, "Would you take it over?"

PAUL: *The only things that bother me about it are the morals seemingly stuck in that just don't fit, like "you don't see any difference between their side and our side?" These just seem to be like Cracker Jack prizes that really stuck out as being pretty average stuff.*

CLINT: Yeah, right.

PAUL: *And some of the stuff with Jemima was sort of trite, I thought, too. The sexual repartee.*

CLINT: Yeah, it was a little cutesy.

PAUL: *It was shot so well, it looked majestic. Did you find that it was extremely hard to convey all that height on the movie screen?*

CLINT: I was hanging from a 4,000-foot vertical precipice and the camera would be straight down. It looked steep and it

---

[31] Paul was tap-dancing around the truth. He told Jay Cocks and Verna Bloom beforehand: "It's a much better book than it is a movie. The book makes some sort of sense and the book is rather suspenseful whereas the movie isn't in the least."

looked wild, but it wasn't like it was with the naked eye. It's very difficult because you're only looking in two dimensions as opposed to three with the naked eye. We'd get shots from the clouds down below us and that would help give you that feeling. The Eiger is over 6,000 feet of almost vertical mountain.

PAUL: *You were awfully limited with camera placement, I imagine, too.*

CLINT: You *are* limited, but you run very compact. We'd start out in the morning—all the actors carried things, there was not a regular crew—with sandwiches in a bag. There'd be four climbers and four actors. In everybody's pack you had extra magazines, extra lenses, camera, all broken down between these eight guys who would go out on the mountain. We had this fixed-rope area where we'd work. Mike Hoover and a guy named John Cleare [cameramen and climbing advisors], one or the other of them would be filming and they'd hang off the cliff with us. Everything was done hanging on ropes and handheld.

PAUL: *How many weeks were you on the mountain total?*

CLINT: Five weeks I was there and that included shooting in Zurich.

PAUL: *I imagine that was probably the toughest physical picture you've done.*

CLINT: Oh, definitely. You might leave at four o'clock, five o'clock in the morning and you'd be finished shooting at eleven. You'd start shooting when the sun would come up and then you'd have to get off the mountain because they'd start bombing after eleven. The Eiger is very bad—it's all limestone, it's not solid like Yosemite or granite. As soon as it warms up, these little fine-particle rocks start letting loose. They come down from two, three thousand feet above you, and they'll hit right in front of you and bounce into your chin or bounce off your helmet. I was cut up every time I went out. It felt like somebody shooting at you with a .22.

PAUL: *Did you have to go on a several-week physical building-up for this picture?*

CLINT: No, I was in pretty good shape, but I went out and crammed on mountain-climbing. I went to Yosemite and practiced. Climbed up Lost Arrow, a pinnacle up there.

PAUL: *Had you done any before that?*

CLINT: No, just a little rappelling around as a kid. Nothing fancy.

PAUL: *And you climbed that peak, it was in Arizona?*

CLINT: The Totem Pole. That was in Monument Valley.

PAUL: *There was a scene with you climbing that needle, where you got to the top and your hand slipped at one point. I didn't figure that was planned.*

CLINT: No, that wasn't intended. That needle was interesting because it's about 1,800 feet high. It goes absolutely straight, then it goes in, and it's got little fissures in it. You think, God damn, what if that's fractured? But then you figure you're not going to be on it the day it falls off—it's going to be thousands of years. But someday it will fall off.[32]

PAUL: *God, you must've been scared to death during some of that filming, hanging from those ropes.*

CLINT: Yeah, I don't know if I'd make that one today. It was a little frustrating. It was fun. There was a lot of challenge to it.

PAUL: *Was there actual physical fear during some of it?*

CLINT: Well, yeah. You're hanging off a three- or four-thousand-foot cliff.

---

[32] The Totem Pole is actually 450 feet from bottom to top—the imposing equivalent of a forty-five-story building.

PAUL: *And the shot where you cut the rope was actually shot that way?*

CLINT: Yeah. That one I just shut my mind off.

PAUL: *But it wasn't a fake shot, I mean.*

CLINT: Huh-uh. Oh boy, if it hadn't worked. What was ironic, at the time we shot that we'd just shot the two dummies going off for the actors who were supposedly killed. You throw a dummy off that weighs a hundred and fifty pounds, and you sit there and watch it just sail and sail and sail. You think, God, if a guy ever fell from this, he'd have an awful long time to think about it. Awful long time.

PAUL: *And one guy did die.*

CLINT: A guy from Leeds, David Knowles. He was a climber. He was killed the second day.

PAUL: *What happened?*

CLINT: A rock fell. We'd been shooting there all day, hanging on this little ledge, and then we all came up because we got all the stuff we needed. Mike Hoover was going to stay down and get one more point of view, which didn't include the actors, so David stayed down and helped him. He was a good climber and had climbed on the Eiger before. Rocks let loose from up above. Knowles got hit square and Mike got a glancing blow. Mike was hurt so bad that he couldn't prusik back up. He was trying to get himself organized and he had the camera and all his stuff hanging off of him.

PAUL: *He had a fractured skull.*

CLINT: Yeah. David's hanging next to him, dead already. Finally, he managed to get enough energy to get prusik handles on and start coming up while some other people came down to help him.

22

> The title character in 1976's *The Outlaw Josey Wales* is a peaceful farmer in Missouri until Union renegades kill his wife and son and burn his farm to the ground. The film follows his journey of revenge as he tracks down the men who took away everything he had to live for.
>
> Philip Kaufman, who rewrote Sonia Chernus's adaptation of the book, was the film's original director until, early in the project, he and Eastwood clashed. Clint fired him and took over as director, and was hit with a $60,000 fine when he refused the Directors Guild of America's order to reinstate Kaufman. The incident resulted in what is now referred to as the "Eastwood rule," prohibiting a guild member from being fired and replaced by anyone else working in any capacity on the same picture.

PAUL: The Beguiled *and* Dirty Harry, *those two films along with* The Outlaw Josey Wales *and* Thunderbolt and Lightfoot, *are certainly among your best performances. Would you agree with that?*

CLINT: I think *Dirty Harry* and *Josey Wales* would be my two best performances. *Josey Wales* maybe is as good as I can do it. For that kind of character, I told a lot about a guy without telling a lot about a guy. Using a minimal amount of exposition, the picture of a man and the changing of a man as he went along, through the experiences with meeting other people, were shown without having to stop and do explanatory scenes. *Harry* the same way, though there were a few scenes—like the scene with the wife of the partner who quits—that sort of explain. But at the same time they don't explain. They touch on his life and then they don't. The most important thing in a visual art or a communication like a movie, whatever you want to call it, is telling without insulting the audience by saying, "Now, I'm going to read you a night-night story" or "I'll read you the funny papers over the radio." You tell it visually. They've come there for a visual thing and that's what they should get.

PAUL: *Can you give me some specific cases in* Josey Wales *where you did what you just said—you told a lot without telling a lot?*

CLINT: When Sam Bottoms's character dies. And the transition of Wales's attitudes after he meets the Indian. All these little events in life. He was feeling he'd become a cursed person. He didn't want to touch people because he knew that anybody he touched turned to crap. Even at the end, it's become an idyllic situation now with the little group settling down. All the stray dogs have settled down and found themselves a decent life, and Wales knows that he's going to just bring tragedy to it eventually, like he has everything else. Without explaining it—trouble seems to follow him wherever he goes—maybe just a line like "Sometimes trouble just follows a man" tells it without going into a big deal.

A lot of stories would be insulting and say, "You remember what happened here?" "And how I lost my family here?" "And how I did this here?" "And my kid and pal died?" You can be really insulting and look down on the audience by figuring they haven't absorbed it, but I've tried never to do that. I've always tried to play straight across to the audience. I feel the audience is a lot brighter than people, who set themselves above audiences in judgment, think they are. You watch previews of films, and how many times they'll catch on to things you'd never think that they would have caught on to. You realize that people out there as a *body*, sitting in a theater, have a vast amount of knowledge and a vast amount of animal vibration, absorbing your entertainment. If you're not entertaining them, they're the first ones to kick you out. And if you are, then they're the first ones to embrace you.

PAUL: *I would imagine it's hard to fake it when your face is fifty feet up high.*

CLINT: Yeah, you can fake it. A lot of actors just give the minimum shot, a lot of them read teleprompters, but it's a minimum shot and the audience knows it's not good.

PAUL: *Both Dirty Harry and Josey Wales are rather similar characters, although Wales was a more extreme situation than Dirty Harry. A lot more happens to him, both bad and good through the film. The range is much greater.*

CLINT: They both have had things that have changed their lives in certain ways. Harry's been changed already when we picked him up. We pick him up as a certain kind of guy who now is that guy. *Josey Wales* takes place over a period of time, and the various tragedies of his life unfold as we travel with him and he finds new leases on life. He goes the full circle, from wanting an idyllic family situation, losing it, then not wanting any connections and people. The more he resists connections, the more they come upon him.

PAUL: *There's dialogue in there that could almost be from* Dirty Harry: *Sam Bottoms says, "You can't get 'em all, Josey," and Josey says, "That's a fact." "How come you're doing this, then?" "I got nothin' better to do."*[33]

CLINT: It's almost like his life means so little to him at this point of the war—and this last final deceit on the war—he's just suicidal. He just figures this is the final straw. He sees his troops being deceived by this Northern group and he figures, Ah, screw it. I might as well go to the end, putting as many of them away as I can.

PAUL: *It's done so well. He's burying the dead the first half and then he's picking up these riders through the second half. You do it almost with a comic sense, but it's very moving to see four more people riding along in that shot than there were in the last shot.*

CLINT: The humor was in there, it was in the book. I fell in love with the book when it was sent to me. Phil Kaufman came up with the idea, which wasn't in the original book, of having a group of Redlegs continue after him. In the book it was just various people who continue after him. He had the thing with the Comanches and then that kind of ended it. There were other antagonists who came up along the way, but that was a regular one that related back to his early days in the Missouri Calvary.

---

[33] In *Dirty Harry*, Callahan's partner, recovering from a gunshot wound, quits the force. Harry tells his partner's wife, "I think he's right. This is no life for you two." "Why do you stay in it, then?" she wants to know. "I don't know," he replies. "I really don't."

And so you had a running antagonist—Bill McKinney and group—and that was a great asset to me as far as a screenplay because that keeps it constant.

PAUL: *As a director, what are the hardest scenes for you to pull off? Or the hardest kind of movie? Or, to take it down smaller, just particular things that you have trouble with sometimes.*

CLINT: Westerns sometimes are the hardest things to stage because a lot of times you're dealing with animals.

PAUL: *There's a legend that you once hit a horse [laughs].*[34]

CLINT: Sometimes you'll pick up a script and you'll love every part of it, but there might be some scene you'll have apprehension about. But I find that usually that scene goes better than you expect it to go and some other scene that you think is going to be a real snap will be the thing that'll hang you up—*if* there's any hang-up at all.

PAUL: *There seems to be a real nice little homage to Leone when Wales gives the speech and Sam Bottoms is dying—the rain is dropping off his hat. Was that a deliberate Leone shot?*

CLINT: No.

PAUL: *I remember one Leone film where this guy gives a twenty-five-minute speech with the water dripping on top of his head and you hear this* splat *every time.*[35]

CLINT: We have one in *Bronco Billy*, too, where the rain is hitting the hat, and the hat has a little curl on it so it just buckets the water up there. The moments you tip your head it *whoosh* goes off all over. But it wasn't purposely any homage to Leone.

---

[34] When asked by other journalists in the past, Eastwood had denied that he once became so angry at a horse on a set that he punched it in the mouth. With Paul, he simply ignored the question.

[35] Paul was most likely thinking of the water dripping onto Woody Strode's hat during the opening credits of *Once Upon a Time in the West*, though he misremembered the context and magnified its length.

PAUL: *Your films seem to have simplicity and directness, but they also have different styles.*

CLINT: Well, I hope so.

PAUL: Josey Wales *is certainly more ornate and more visual and has scenes that are quite complex.*

CLINT: To me, I don't have a style of my own, a particular style. I just think every picture draws on its own look. *Play Misty for Me* or *High Plains Drifter* or *Breezy* or whatever other films I've done look different. You might not be able to say, if you didn't know, that the same guy was involved with all of them directorially. But *Josey Wales* had a look. I wanted a saga feeling yet I wanted you to feel for the people, I wanted you to remember the vignettes as they came up and the people he met along the way.

PAUL: *It seems to be conceived so visually. The images when he sees the troops coming—when you see the flag over the hill first, the marauders through the trees—you conceived all of this before you started to shoot?*

CLINT: I pretty much had it in my mind. When I get to the sets and start lining it up, things will appear all the time that keep changing. I'm never locked in when I go in. I'm locked in to what I want to accomplish, but not necessarily shut out as to how I want to accomplish it. If I see a new idea on a scene, I'll embellish on it right there and then. Westerns are nice because you're out in the middle of nowhere shooting, especially in that picture. Most of the locations you could shoot 360 and point in the direction you want. It was a question of just lining up the whole thing.

PAUL: *Some of the visual look at the beginning seems to be like* The Beguiled, *with the misty forest and the Civil War troops.*

CLINT: I shot it in Oroville. I was hoping for fog and we got rain. I wasn't trying to pattern it after *The Beguiled*, but it's got that same feeling. I was trying to get the feeling of a gloomy period in a man's life and I didn't want the war to be high contrast, I wanted it to be a very sour time in life. As the story progressed in the movie, as life became better and you get out in the open spaces away from civilization, it became a higher contrast look.

PAUL: *Were you lucky with the weather on those shots or did you have to wait for rain and the certain kind of mood you wanted?*

CLINT: No, I knew ahead of time that in the Sacramento Valley, and the San Joaquin for that matter, there were great tendencies toward late November to get tule fog. It'll stay all day. Over on the coast, San Francisco will be beautifully clear, but in the valley it hangs in there at that time. I didn't get that, but I did get a lot of rain areas, a lot of gloomy, misty days, and that worked for me just as well. On the montage of the war at the beginning, what high contrast shots I did have I stripped down in the lab. But by and large I was lucky with the weather, yeah, to answer that. The weather down in Arizona, Lake Powell, and up in Utah was beautiful most of the time.

I shot it in the fall of the year, I started in October. The thing that is good about the fall of the year is the trees have great colors, the sun is low, and you get a lot of great cross light. You don't get a lot of overhead light, which you get in summer. And if you've got a good cameraman—a bold cameraman like [Bruce] Surtees is—then you can do a lot of interesting shots. I don't like to light faces a lot, and Bruce will go along with you on that. A lot of cameramen will like to light every face so you see everything, but I like to light the faces only for particular moments. In *High Plains Drifter* I kept my figure in complete backlight all the time—an unlit face—so as the audience you have to stare through just to find out, What is he thinking? Is he going to really go that way? Because audiences, they're always thinking ahead—not purposely—they're always trying to anticipate a little bit. Which is fine.

23

Appearing on *The Merv Griffin Show* in 1980, Orson Welles had this to say about *The Outlaw Josey Wales*: "When I saw

> that picture for the fourth time, I realized that it belongs with the great Westerns. You know, the great Westerns of Ford and Hawks and people like that."

PAUL: *That Welles quote would be like, oh, Ernest Hemingway reading something of mine and saying, "I really like that story." It would really be that equivalent for me, and I was wondering if it was anything like that to you?*

CLINT: It was very nice coming from somebody whom you respect and has done some marvelous films in his day. Both as an actor and as a director he's done a lot—has a big portfolio as they like to say—including one that is considered an absolute giant, and that's *Kane*. You often wonder what a person who does the type of films he has done, how they feel about other directors' work.

PAUL: *It's so unequivocal. He just says, "This Western should be right up there with Ford and Hawks," and "I've seen it four times," and "Clint Eastwood is the most underrated director."*

CLINT: Well, I saved it, so obviously I was influenced to some degree to save it. I don't save a lot of things.

PAUL: *I gathered that this guy probably knows your work. If he's watched* Wales *four times, I doubt that he hasn't seen your other stuff. That would be unusual, I would think.*

CLINT: That would be unusual. If I see a director's work, I usually look at his other stuff.

PAUL: *Were you an Orson Welles fan?*

CLINT: I liked *Citizen Kane* very much. *Ambersons* I liked to some degree. *The Stranger* is an interesting film, a back-lot kind of film. But he did a *lot* with a back lot. I don't know where it was filmed, but it looked like it was filmed out at MGM or somewhere on the back lot.

PAUL: *That was the film where he was trying to prove he could make a film under budget and on time.*

CLINT: It was kind of interesting, it had a lot of imagination to it.

PAUL: *Do you know who the original choice for the Edward G. Robinson role was?*

CLINT: Who?

PAUL: *Agnes Moorehead.*

CLINT: Oh, really? You mean, have a lady detective?

PAUL: *And the producer said no. Welles I guess pretty well gave in all the way then because he wanted to keep making films.*

CLINT: One thing about him, even when he failed, he failed big. He would always strike out to do something kind of wild. I thought Robinson was good in it. I liked him. Agnes Moorehead would have been interesting in it. That would have been interesting, a lady detective.

PAUL: *He couldn't stand the editing process, I guess. He loved the shooting—and apparently he shot a lot—but sitting down and putting it all together would drive him crazy. He would just take off and leave it to other people. He just couldn't face making sense of some of it.*

CLINT: The only time I ever met him, he told me that he didn't even shoot the ending of *The Magnificent Ambersons*. He said he went off to do a picture for the war or something in South America [the unfinished *It's All True*]. It had something to do with a government deal. He went off to do that and left the picture unfinished, and they got Bob Wise, who was an editor at that time and had been an editor on *Citizen Kane*, to go ahead and finish it.

PAUL: *Wise and Mark Robson and some other people. They cut it in half, I guess, basically.*

CLINT: I didn't get into that too much. I don't know if that's the case, but I know that to me, the editing process, I enjoy it.

PAUL: *I fooled around with it a little in college and I always loved editing because you could really make your own world when you were editing that film.*

CLINT: Exactly. You're in complete control of what you're doing with it, for better or for worse. That's when you breathe life into the film as it comes alive before you. All those little pieces here and there fall into place. It's the punctuation, you know?

PAUL: *Instead of making these decisions, I guess he preferred, more or less, to go off and then say the studio edited it and they didn't do it right.*

CLINT: That happens a lot of times, too. It gives you an out. I don't know if that was his case, but I've seen people do that where it gives them an out. If something goes wrong or is wrong, they can say, "They didn't know what they were doing putting it together. Didn't they know what I had in mind?"

PAUL: *It's just hard to imagine a man, who had made* Kane, *which is a great film, and* Ambersons, *which [might have been] equally good or better in its total version, walking out in the middle of it and saying, "You guys finish it." It's fairly inconceivable.*

CLINT: It's hard to know without knowing what was going on in the man's life at the time.

PAUL: *Have you talked to Leone since he's gotten into American films?*

CLINT: I had a glass of wine with him a year or so ago, before he started this other film [*Once Upon a Time in America*].

PAUL: *I guess it's going to be two films now.*

CLINT: The only trouble with two films is, what happens if the first film is not a hit? Then how do you attract people to the second half? It's one thing to do *Such-and-Such 2* after *Such-and-Such 1* has been proven to have a certain amount of interest. It's a very dangerous thing to do, two films.

PAUL: *On the other hand, he's got, what, four and a half, five hours or something in the hopper?*

CLINT: People can cut things down. What I like to do is I make a cut for myself—it may be a little long or something—and then what I'll do is I'll go in and make what I call a cruel cut.

PAUL: Cruel *like in vicious?*

CLINT: A *cruel* cut. It's not a cut you show to anybody, it's just a cut you make for yourself. Just tear out things. Tear out this, tear out that, try it with this. I remember talking about that with Steven Spielberg, and he likes to do that, too. It's where you just rip away at everything you can and then you say, "Wait a second, this takes away from the story." After a cruel cut you can go back to putting in elements you left out. You step away from it a few days, come back to it. Maybe sometimes you split the difference on something and you come out at a reasonable length.

I make crueler cuts now than I did in the old days. In the old days, you figured, "It took me a day to do this scene and I really like the scene, it's well done, the actors are good in it." It's a day out of your life, so you go, "Gee, I don't want to take that out of the picture. I worked hard that day." But sometimes you have to do that. You have to take a day, a week, out of your life and just say, "Okay, that doesn't work in the film now the way it is. Some other sequence took away from it and ran with the deal." That's just the way you have to be.

It's very hard to do that. It takes a lot of pictures to get to that point because a lot of you will fall in love with every shot and say, "God, isn't that beautiful, the way that the camera pans across there and the sun is setting and the birds are flying and the people are walking toward you?" But that shot you can see in commercials all day long because that's the *only* shot they have to make before they put the deodorant product's name up there. People are sitting there saying, "Okay, I'm sitting here. Entertain the hell out of me."

PAUL: *You don't usually over-shoot. I'm always amazed when I read that the director's original cut for a two-hour movie was five hours and thirty-five minutes long or something. Doesn't he have any idea how long the movie's going to be?*

CLINT: Either that or they just tack on everything and have pauses that last fifteen minutes. I try to make it come in to where it plays. If it's two hours and ten minutes and it plays, if it's an hour and forty minutes and it plays—it just depends.

PAUL: *You had extra stuff for* Josey Wales, *I remember you said.*

CLINT: Sure. I had several sequences I had to rip out of that.

PAUL: *I thought the Chinese girl's part could've gone from* Magnum Force.

CLINT: It could've. But there are a lot of ways you can go. Any film you look at—ninety percent of them anyway—you can *almost* say, "Hey, this film would've worked just as good without that sequence or this." A lot of films that are long, you can take and just halve every sequence. You could just cut away at a certain time and stylize it a little differently, and chances are it will work just as well and progress the story just as fast.

24

Eastwood found himself once again bearing a badge in 1976's *The Gauntlet*. His character, the dimwitted and drunken Ben Shockley, is ordered to escort a prostitute (Sondra Locke) from Las Vegas to Phoenix so that she can testify at a mob trial. He discovers too late that it's all a setup, orchestrated by a corrupt police commissioner. The film is probably best remembered for its over-the-top shootouts, wherein a house and a bus are literally shot to smithereens.

The film's finale finds Eastwood and Locke's characters, with several hundred spent rounds in their wake, driving an armored bus through a gauntlet of armed police officers (seemingly the entire force) in downtown Phoenix. Paul Nelson wasn't the only viewer left to wonder why one of the cops simply didn't shoot out the bus's tires.

PAUL: *What drew you to* The Gauntlet?

CLINT: I just thought it was a good script. I liked the character and the relationship it turned into. It was kind of outrageous—the overkill aspect I played up a little more than it was in the script—but it was a nice two-people story and had that old-fashioned adventure, of two people of opposite philosophies and styles forced to travel together, that they used to make in the old days. *The African Queen* and that kind of thing.

PAUL: *That seems to be a quality that you're drawn towards. It's also in* Bronco Billy.[36]

CLINT: Yeah, it is a little bit in that, though in a totally different way. What draws me to them, I don't know. Maybe I like old movies or something [chuckles]. The basis of drama being conflict, it gives you so much more to work with rather than just being a tour guide of some area.

PAUL: *Did you see* 48 Hours?

CLINT: I liked some of it. That was offered to me at one time. It was a time when I just wasn't in the mood to do a detective thing. It was too close to—it was like a spinoff of—*Dirty Harry*. But it was okay.

PAUL: *I thought* 48 Hours *might've been a viable* Dirty Harry 4. *I thought* The Gauntlet *even might've if they had changed it drastically, where Harry hits the bottle and all that.*

CLINT: You'd have to change it quite a bit. *The Gauntlet* cop is, of course, much less secure with himself, never been in the big bust. Dirty Harry's been in on all the big busts.

PAUL: *Did you intensify that aspect of the part or was that always there?*

CLINT: It was there. There were suggestions here at the studio that we could make it a Dirty Harry character, and I just felt that

---

[36] In the 1980 film, Bronco Billy McCoy, a one-time New Jersey shoe salesman who has reinvented himself as a modern-day cowboy, travels around the country with his Wild West show.

it would never work with Dirty Harry. I felt that Dirty Harry would never have allowed himself to do the things that the guy in *The Gauntlet* allowed himself to do. He would've headed off the situation and come to a much better conclusion earlier.

PAUL: *You've looked for that a fair amount in later scripts, to play vulnerable guys and guys with flaws.*

CLINT: You have to play it a little flawed. Even Dirty Harry has certain personality flaws; that's why he's the kind of guy he is. But *The Gauntlet* was a pretty good script the way it was, and I wasn't looking to play Dirty Harrys then. The idea of changing it turned me off. In the first place, I'd done as much as I could with the Dirty Harry character at that time—and probably at the present time. I just felt this was a whole new cop.

PAUL: *Oh, they're very different.*

CLINT: Just as day and night. People either liked it or didn't. Some people thought it was too outrageous, the shooting at the end, but there's a certain kind of an overkill philosophy that exists in the land. It's like if you train fifteen rounds every day to box and you never box. There would be a tremendous frustration if you trained all the time and never went in the ring. When you did get in the ring, it would be like, "*Wow!*" The adrenalin would be so *high* and you'd think, Well, here's now my chance. It's like being a fireman and you never put out a fire. Imagine what it's like for a cop to be out there training all the time. The big *if*: what's going to happen if I have to pull the gun? You may go twenty years and never shoot anybody, but yet you're packing a gun all the time, you're always training. It's always in your mind. The mayor of Los Angeles brags that he never had to pull his gun in thirty-five of service, and that's probably true.[37] But a lot of cops *do* have to, and when they do, what happens?

All of a sudden it comes over the radio that there's a house with, say, some known criminal, armed and dangerous, shooting. Something wild's going to come down. Every cop in

---

[37] Tom Bradley, who served five terms as mayor of Los Angeles, had been a police officer for twenty-one, not thirty-five, years.

town is going to descend on it because they all want to be in on the act. If they show up with shotguns and automatic weapons and somebody says, "Open fire!" you know they're going to turn that place into Swiss cheese, you know that there's not going to be one round of ammunition not expended. It's happened too many times. Sure, it was fantasy when the whole roof just goes right down, and that adds a comedic element to it, but there *is* a little statement on overkill there.

PAUL: *It was exaggerated so much, I took it that there was supposed to be an element of comedy at the end.*

CLINT: Sure. It was like, what more could they possibly go through?

PAUL: *The picture had an unbelievable quality at other points, too. A lot of people—not a lot—but I heard the comment that it was just too unbelievable at the end.*[38]

CLINT: Don Siegel made the comment when he saw it: "If I was making it, I would've made it more believable, but I don't think it would've been half as exciting." I said, "My feeling about it, Don, is that I wanted a certain believability about the story, but at the same time there had to be an entertainment quality about the story. If you're just going to tell a documentary about a hooker and a cop drifting across a few little minor incidents, it could be a pretty flat show."

PAUL: *One person made the point that in* no *town in the United States would that situation* ever *have happened—that* many *police shooting on a public street.*[39]

---

[38] The comment had actually originated with Paul, in private conversation with Jay Cocks and Verna Bloom: "It's a terrible scene at the ending. I had read somewhere that he really considered that a really, terrific, perfect screenplay that he didn't have to do anything with, and I thought it was a terrible screenplay. There were portions of *The Gauntlet* that were just so fantastically unbelievable and un-suspenseful. That whole helicopter scene where they're shooting at the motorcycle for ten minutes—and they couldn't possibly miss it."

[39] That "one person" was Paul himself, again in conversation with Cocks and Bloom. "No city in America is going to do that," he said. "In *no* city—even the worst police-state type of city—would that be plausible."

CLINT: They should look at the television coverage of the SLA [Symbionese Liberation Army] shooting in Los Angeles, in which they not only shot the house to pieces, they burned the house down and damaged about six other houses in the neighboring area. The situation of just unloading on somebody they think is armed and dangerous, it happens occasionally. We just theatricalized it and had some fun with it.

PAUL: The Gauntlet *had a very striking poster. It draws you right in.*

CLINT: I called Frank Frazetta and asked him if he'd do a poster for it. It took me twenty minutes to convince his wife that it was me because a lot of friends used to kid him, they thought he looked like me or something. I didn't realize there was an inside joke, but I finally talked to him. He asked me what I wanted and I said, "Read the script and then try and sketch just whatever comes to your mind." I sent him the script and he read it, and then he started working on it. He drew up a bunch of watercolors and stuff and sent them to me. I liked a combination of several.

I was back East, and he was only partway done but the likenesses were all done from photographs and everything, so I said, "Well, I'll just come up and I'll sit for you and you can finish it." So I went up there and he finished it. I sat and drank beer in his backyard.

PAUL: *My favorite scene in the movie is that wonderfully moving one between you and Sondra in the motel where all of a sudden you make future plans and she calls her mother.*

CLINT: That was a fun scene. It's like they're both dreaming about something that's never going to happen.

PAUL: *You get the idea that it might. The dreams are so whole-hog and instant, they're not tiny ones. One minute they're like "We're not anywhere" and the next minute "We're going to shoot for the moon." It was a really nicely played scene.*

CLINT: It's always that hope for things to work out. The audience holds out that hope.

25

Every Which Way but Loose (1978), a comedy, provided another departure for Eastwood. The movie follows the adventures of Philo Beddoe (Clint), an easygoing truck driver and bare-fisted fighter whose best friend is Clyde, an orangutan, and whose love interest is a country-and-western singer played by Sondra Locke.

PAUL: Every Which Way but Loose *seemed to me to have some Hawksian elements to it. All the reversals seem to be like Hawks.*

CLINT: *Loose* was a strange project. Fritz, who works for me, he liked it and thought we ought to do it. I liked it. My agent and my lawyer said, "Don't do that. That isn't the kind of thing you want." I said, "It's the kind of show that could have a slightly hip twist to it, but at the same time it's something my kids can go to. Don't bend the brain too much, just have a good time with it." "Yeah, but you're not the winner. Maybe we should rewrite it and have you get the girl." "No, just leave it like it is. The writer wrote it that way. It's a bizarre twist that he's an open, naïve guy and she's a gal in kind of a kinky world. It's a world he doesn't understand. Let it unravel."

PAUL: *It had a* Bringing Up Baby/*screwball comedy feel. Your image, you put a real spin on that. You turn around and lose the girl, lose the fight. The motorcycle gang, instead of being tough, never wins a single fight. The mother isn't sweet.*

CLINT: Everything is just totally twisted from the Walt Disney idyllic fashion. A lot of reviewers didn't particularly like it, but maybe that's because I have a primate in there. Maybe they couldn't associate. There was no way they could say that "that was a symbol," that "this was the Darwin creature before and here is the present, and together they're roaming the land," or some theory like that.

PAUL: *The long monologue about going after the girl, which is one of your longest speeches in any movie, it's sort of made to the orangutan. Some resonance is set off. I don't know what, but something like Ionesco. It had mythological resonance. To me, it*

*was sort of a statement, like, "I can do this stuff. I can do it so
well I can do these scenes with an orangutan." A real chip-on-your-
shoulder type of statement. I don't know if you meant it as that.*

CLINT: [bursts out laughing] Maybe I did. I don't know, maybe it
was my cockiness coming out or something.

PAUL: Dirty Harry*'s not your all-time money-grosser; it's* Loose, *right?*

CLINT: Oh yeah, *Loose* is. *Dirty Harry* did really well, but *Loose* got
a wide range of audience. People go back three and four or five
times just to have the laughs and pick up the laugh they missed
here and there. Though *Loose* had a lot of critics. The critics
either liked it and took it in the spirit it was intended, or else
they hated it and they got very uptight about it. Rona Barrett
came on her program—I didn't see it, but I heard of it—saying I
owed my audience an apology, it was a terrible film and all this
stuff. The audience didn't feel that way at all obviously, because
they went to it in droves. And it wasn't just in this country, they
were going to it all around the world.

PAUL: *[laughs] Rona Barrett makes this statement?*

CLINT: Though on the other hand she turned around and thought
Alcatraz was the greatest. In the old days people used to make
films like *Loose* all the time and nobody thought anything about
it. It's an ironic thing that all the people who criticized me early in
the Seventies when I was doing the so-called tough-guy roles are
the first ones who get mad at me if I do something a little on the
sensitive side. Not that *Loose* is the example of that, but they all
start saying, "But that isn't like you were in *Dirty Harry*." "Yeah,
but you didn't like *Dirty Harry*." They start waffling around. "It's
not that I didn't like the film. That was for political reasons" or
for some other reasons. Who knows where it all unravels.

PAUL: *Fritz told me about your first meeting with the orangutans
and their trainer in Las Vegas.*

CLINT: We went out to see Bob Berosini and his wife Joan. They had a
place outside of Vegas because they were performing at the MGM

Grand there. They brought three of the orangs in to meet us, and they all came bopping in. Pretty soon they were all flocking around. The one male that really liked me, Manis, the one that played most of the lead, he just walked right over to me, took my hand. So I just talked with him, sat with him a bit. He got so he could travel along with me fine. Orangutans are like human beings in that they have dislikes and likes. Berosini said they're much like kids: you don't want to over-push yourself on them. Some people they don't like. It would be a sad thing to do a picture with one that didn't like you, because it *is* a wild animal and you'd always be wondering when it's going to tear your head off.

PAUL: Loose *seemed to have sort of a* Hard Times *feel to it, the* Charles Bronson *film by Walter Hill.*

CLINT: I thought *Hard Times* was pretty good. That was a much more serious thing, of course, but Hill's quite clever. He's not a bad writer. He writes extremely lean and right-to-the-point kind of stuff. Some of his films maybe haven't worked quite as well because of various elements, but there are so many elements that can go wrong in a picture. Once you have a story—presuming a story is good, you go to cast it right—presumably you cast it right, then presumably you get the right crew. So you work under the best atmosphere possible and the film unravels with the most excitement up to its potential. Hopefully, it'll exceed the potential.

PAUL: *Your last three films, they have been moving towards comedy and moving towards almost what movies were like when they had a national character, when everyone was going to them. Like in Capra's time, before television. Has this been conscious on your part and reflective of what's happening in your life, or just the way the scripts have been falling?*

CLINT: It might be a little of both. I'd like to say that it's been some conscious thing—that might sound like I was heading in some great direction—but that probably isn't the case. It's probably just the way they've fallen.

It's so hard to find good material, material that stimulates your imagination, that sometimes you read scripts that are fair and you almost get tempted to try do something with them.

Then you start going, Wait a minute, if it ain't on the page, you might be able to embellish it, but it's going to turn out to be just fair. Writing is the creative art, directing and acting are the interpretive arts. The writing is the nucleus, the center, and the core. *Loose*, I read it and I laughed at it and I enjoyed it. It's got charm. You see a lot of people *working* at charm, or stories that are charmed, but they're not really charming like Capra's were or some of the early films that you were mentioning.

PAUL: *That whole consciousness back then was so different. I went to the Radio City in New York—I don't even remember the film, but it was a film you could take your kids to—and you felt what it must've been like in 1930 or 1940 when the movies were* the national art. *It was almost like in the Sixties when the Beatles would come out with a record: you knew what twenty-five million kids would be doing that Saturday night. A lot of your recent films have got this feeling.* Bronco Billy *certainly does and* Loose *has that feel to it, too.*

CLINT: *Loose* had that and it showed that people were ready to go for it. There's room for all kinds of films. I've made the hard-action Rs and I've made the little war movies and I've made the cowboy things, and there's nothing wrong with them.[40] I still like them. If someone shows me a good script with one now, I'll be the first guy to say, "Okay, let's roll." It just seems that, from unknown writers in recent years, I've come up with a couple things that were provocative. They gave me a chance to do something a little different without having the audiences say, "The hell with this guy. He's getting boring."

PAUL: *As a director, you've been as imaginative and as different as any American director I can name. You haven't followed any pattern at all as a director.*

CLINT: There's no pattern. And because there's no trend, it makes it all the more noble to do it. To do it on its own value and not to be influenced by what the so-called experts say is the movie of the moment. Because there are no experts. Every movie that's a

---

[40] "Hard-action Rs" refers to R-rated films as designated by the Motion Picture Association of America.

hit, there have been fifty people who've said, "Don't make this film." And for every movie's that's flopped there have probably been fifty people who said, "God, you've got to make this. It's going to be the greatest thing since *Gone with the Wind*."

26

PAUL: *When you started out, did you have somebody who was guiding your career?*

CLINT: I had a business manager—I'm still with the group, though he's passed away—a guy named Irving Leonard. He advised me even when I didn't have any money to pay him. A terrific man. He was like my LA father, so to speak. He gave me a lot of advice and he handled business and tax things for me. I had no dough. But he lived to see me make it. In fact, I think his name's on *Hang 'Em High* or one of those as associate producer or something, which is kind of fun.[41] He was a wonderful guy and he always instilled a lot of modern concepts of business on me. But the basic thing probably came from my father, just the general upbringing.

PAUL: *Your father became quite successful.*

CLINT: Yeah, he did. All those years of work that he had during the Thirties and the Forties—career-wise nothing was happening for him—he finally managed to make it pay off. He had to live through some rough times, times we don't know of today.

PAUL: *I suspect we may find out, though. Boy, living in New York now is real hard.*

CLINT: In those days it was depression, but now it's inflation. One of these days we're going to have to, as a people, face up to the fact that this country has to be run like a business. Most businesses would go under if they were run like this country. We

---

[41] Irving L. Leonard received associate producer credit on *Hang 'Em High*, *Coogan's Bluff*, and *Kelly's Heroes*. Until his death in 1969, he served as Malpaso's original president.

see Chrysler in trouble, we see various people in trouble, and you cannot just print up money every time we run low or every time it's tough. To make the dollar value maintain, we're going to have to step on inflation. The interest rates go up to fifteen and three-quarters on the prime rate, and then we sit around and say, "It'll go down." Everything slows down and then, boom, we drop it down again and then everything pops up. So inflation just see-saws along.

Because of our political system, every president, as soon as he gets in, he has to start running for the next four years. One of these days we're going to have to get somebody who's tough, who doesn't want to be popular, who's going to have to get in and stop this inflation.

We've become a country that is so interested with what the union can get us as far as benefits and pension plans. What difference does it make if the dollar's not worth anything? What difference does it make if you can retire on fifteen, twenty thousand dollars a year—if you can retire on that—if the dollar's only worth a tenth of what it was ten years ago? It's not going to make any difference at all. We've got to get back to values, where people start taking care of themselves and managing themselves, and we have a country that manages itself.

One of these days the bottom's going to be tough. Rather than face that, I'd rather see some management along the way. Maybe face reality. But we live in *Alice in Wonderland*. The United States is the biggest business in the world, and we should run it like a business. I've always thought that maybe, if they had the election a six-year thing with no possibility of reelection— and everybody who was elected would have to get in and do the job and do that job only and never run for another office again, or at least never run for that same office—we'd have a different deal. Or even the congressmen: maybe a one-shot deal. Get in, do the job, and not sit there and massage the constituents. And they should do what the constituents *want* them to do, live up to the platforms they're on.

Maybe we could impose upon the greatest businessmen in the country to take the job for a period. The way it is now, the greatest businessmen in the country don't want the job. Only people who are power-hungry want the job. Because the greatest businessmen can make a lot more dough doing something else, they can have a lot more satisfaction doing something else than fight the frustration that the kind of office the presidency is in this country. We live in a very cynical age for that one reason.

PAUL: *We're not that different in age. I remember when I was working through college I was making fifty bucks a week. I had more than enough money for rent, food, going to the movies, buying a new record or a book. God, now I'm making $25,000, which is not great but it's not bad either. In this city you have to almost make that to be one level above poor.*

CLINT: Fifteen years ago you probably would've said, "God, $25,000! Man, I could have the best car, I could have a penthouse overlooking everything, I could do everything I wanted, go anywhere I want." That's what happens to America. And this is not just you, these are the people who support this country, who are Mr. and Mrs. Middle America, middle-income bracket people who maybe some years ago made ten grand and then they made fifteen and now they maybe make eighteen or whatever it is. They've been saying that thing all along: "Gee, if we ever got to eighteen, wouldn't that be something? Man, we could put some money in the bank and send the kids through college. There'd be no more problems." They're seeing all the dough just going on all these frivolous programs we've got. The Social Security program is going broke, and here we've been promising all these senior citizen groups that this is the way it is and this is what you'll have after you reach a certain age.

The system is going broke and the dollar is devaluating. We're going to have to take some knocks to beat this inflation back. [President Herbert] Hoover took the knock on the Depression, but it wasn't his fault, it was many, many years of workings. It doesn't come up over four years, it comes up over twenty years.

What we've got to do is instill in everybody in this country that government ain't gonna be able to do it for you. The government isn't that strong. You're going to have to do it for yourself and manage for yourself. Like I said, the guy and the girl, or the family, they're really panicking because when it all comes down they're the ones who are stuck with all the faces to feed. When you've only got yourself, you can always figure you can handle it.

PAUL: *Yeah, you're not going to starve. You know if you're a writer you can always stay alive. You're not necessarily going to do well, but can always earn a meal.*

27

PAUL: *What does it mean when people call you a* reactor *rather than an actor? They always called Gary Cooper a* reactor. *Is this a meaningful term at all?*

CLINT: I don't know what that means. I never have. I think where that comes from is John Wayne used to make statements like that. He said, "I'm not an actor, I'm a *re*actor." You don't just sit and react, though. You have motivating forces that drive you on as an actor, as a performer performing that character. There's no such thing as a reactor. It's not a very concise statement on what acting's all about—*if* there is a concise statement on what acting's all about.

There's no way to teach people to act. There are ways to teach *you* to teach yourself to act, but there's no way that somebody can say, "Okay, now you've finished your apprenticeship. You lay these bricks perfectly now, so you're now no longer an apprentice, you're a full-fledged bricklayer." There's no way to do that with an actor. All of a sudden, when people start believing him in the parts, then they start accepting him in the parts. He's an actor.

PAUL: *There's no way to do it with a writer either.*

CLINT: You're right. You can teach yourself the certain pitfalls, certain techniques. Whether it's a profession or a hobby or art or whatever, it's one of the most unusual things a person can do, and some people enjoy it immensely and other people find it very frustrating. Some people get very disturbed by playing the roles that they play and they can't get out of it, or they get wrapped up in egos of the business and they get wrapped up with their importance. If they reach a certain stature, the importance kills them—and this is not only actors, it's directors, producers, whatever.

PAUL: *You seem not tempted by this. It seems alien to your character completely.*

CLINT: It's just we're all human beings and we're no more than that. You fly over the country and you look down at the little ants there—they're not even visible—you might see some homes or something. What happens if you weren't there and what difference would it make to the planet? You have to look at yourself on a level that is reality, the level that we're an animal species that is lucky enough to be existing in this time. Enjoy it, do the best you can by it, and then you move on and make room for other animal species to inhabit the planet. Hopefully, mankind, having the ability to create so many things, doesn't create the ultimate wipeout. But actually the threat of that is probably what keeps us *from* wiping ourselves out.

PAUL: *I was talking to Ross Macdonald last year, and he said in an odd way he considered it an advantage that he wasn't an overnight success, that his apprenticeship, say, lasted ten years. He was allowed to experiment and grow as an artist out of the public eye for the first ten years. Though monetarily that wasn't good at all, he said in the long run he was really glad that it had happened. Do you feel any similar feelings? You were twenty-eight years old before you got on* Rawhide.

CLINT: I was lucky to have a series on television that could give me a paycheck so I could afford to study. When I was doing *Rawhide* I would go to classes in the evening. I'd keep studying. I'd study the directors who came in and I'd study the screenwriting and whatever. Not as consciously as a student going to a class, but just *absorbing*. I was lucky for that reason. I got many, many years of where I could work at the profession and be considered a professional actor and be paid for doing a job—and learn an awful lot. I think a lot of people feel, "I'm a big deal on TV. Everybody runs up to me and says, 'Hey, you're the guy who plays so-and-so,' and 'Aren't you great,' and pretty soon you say, 'Yeah, I'm great, I don't have to do anything anymore. I just sit back and be great and collect the dough.'" Well, it isn't that way. You read about it all the time, these people wanting out of series. "So-and-so wants out of this series." I think you should ride them and enjoy them and learn from them. Then when you go out and do something else, you're better. One year on *Charlie's Angels* ain't going to make you the greatest actress in the world, but ride the whole thing down, absorb it, work with guest actors who are great and bit players who come in and are great, and find out what the business is all about. The business isn't looking in the mirror.

Acting is something that takes a while to do. Some people are fortunate and I guess naturally have it at a young age. Kids *have* it at a young age. Some people are fortunate to get it back at a young age. It's taken me a while to create the characters I've created. I'm not the most expressive guy in the world, but if a person really analyzes them, they're different.

PAUL: *Neither are you at all the "granite face" that you're always claimed to be.*

CLINT: [chuckles] The "granite face." I've played some roles that are, through dense expression, very held-back roles and therefore they present a mythic or a mystical image or an image where people can't quite find out on the surface exactly what a guy's thinking every second. For that reason some people haven't enjoyed me as much as they would Fredric March or [Jason] Robards or any of these people who are much more openly expressive, you-get-it-all-right-in-front type of actors, who are terrific. I admire them. I've loved March's performances over the years. I remember seeing him on Broadway and enjoying him—in fact, enjoying both those actors I mentioned—in *Long Day's Journey [Into Night]*.

Being subtle is the toughest thing in the world to do, and the great performers over the years—people who could do subtlety well like Cary Grant, for instance—never really received the critical recognition that they did with audiences. And he was brilliant. He was never winning the New York Critics Circle award or the Academy Award or whatever. He was too good.

At the same time, you do what you do best. I was never an extrovertish character as a kid. I held back my emotions a lot, covered my emotions a lot, so it becomes easy for me to play that kind of a character because I have a tendency, unless I know a person, to be a little on the shy side, I suppose.

PAUL: *Do you still get nervous before you start films?*

CLINT: I don't get nervous because I'm in my element, I know what

I'm doing. My palms don't sweat. It's like a musician. That's what G [Benny Goodman] used to do: forget how to work the valves and, once you're out there [snaps his fingers] and they say, "Go! One, two, three!" and *boom!* You're sitting there and you're playing and all of a sudden you're doing what you do. And this is what I do—at least what I've done for the last twenty-seven years or whatever. When the flag goes up, that switch goes off in your brain and you wail.

PAUL: *In what movie did you kick Sondra in the leg to get her to cry?*

CLINT: *Bronco Billy*. It was a scene where she was having trouble concentrating. There were tons of people on the set because it was a whole barroom scene, and she was complaining that this was distracting her. I just kept saying, "Come on! Come on! Concentrate now! Think!" [laughs uncontrollably] I'd been coaxing and coaxing and coaxing and it wasn't coming out quite the way I wanted it, so I kicked her—I had rubber shoes like yours—underneath the table, and I pounded my fist on the table and I said [growling], "C'mon now, God damn it!" My veins were all popping out and she was going [mimics her reaction] "Wa-wa-wa-wa." Finally, she came through terrific. But in every picture there's always some scene that somebody has a problem with.

PAUL: *As an actor, what's the hardest thing for you to do? And what's the easiest thing for you to do?*

CLINT: Boy, that's a hard one. I remember when I used to go to acting classes and bounce my head on the floor and scream and yell, I always figured that that was the easiest thing in the world to do. It still is. Most anybody with good concentration can muster up a furor. You can break down and bawl. It's glossy and showy, but it's not hard to do. I was always very good at it, but I don't have that many occasions for it, at least in a lot of the roles. It's always small things that are the hardest to do. Subtle things.

PAUL: *Jay said you were really a Cagney fan, that Cagney was your favorite for a long time.*

CLINT: I grew up on all the Cagney movies. I enjoyed those. I guess I liked those guys because they weren't afraid to do wild things. They weren't running around worrying about their image for selling toy dolls in stores or something like that. Bogart would shave the back of his head up into a stupid looking haircut for *The Treasure of the Sierra Madre*. They were very bold kind of performers, they were not just different kinds of roles.

PAUL: *Cagney climbed into his mother's lap in* White Heat.

CLINT: You have to be that bold to pull those kind of things off. He wanted to be a heavy, too. He'd shoot holes in the trunk of the car with a body in there. Stick a grapefruit in some gal's face.

PAUL: *He made a Western even with Bogart. I can't remember the name of it, but he looked totally ludicrous in a Western outfit. It's an odd movie, but it has its moments.*

CLINT: No, it wasn't a very good movie. For some reason—their background, their kind of attitude, their kind of staccato movements—his especially and not necessarily Bogart's—they just didn't seem to lend themselves to it. They could've done it with Cooper and Wayne maybe, but not Cagney and Bogart.

PAUL: The Oklahoma Kid, *I think that's the name of it. Most of it is just a mediocre, real conventional Western except it's almost like Cagney and Bogart were derricked in from a different period to jazz it up or something. They play around with it and almost turn it into something else. It doesn't work as a whole, but it certainly is interesting.*

CLINT: I love offbeat casting, but that did not work out. It backfired on them.

PAUL: *Cagney looked really like a stocky little barrel in that cowboy outfit.*

CLINT: I'm sure there were a lot of short cowboys, but for some reason that tall-in-the-saddle image was created by movies and seems to have stayed for some years.

PAUL: *I guess Wayne and Cooper and all those guys were all six-three, six-four, six-five probably. Although the screen does funny things, too. Sondra looks so fragile and tiny in person, and onscreen you get the feeling that she's much larger than she is.*

CLINT: That's the same way if you see Bette Davis or somebody like that. She's a little tiny lady. She's small-featured and small-boned, but she has that kind of presence. There are a lot of them like that. I saw Claudette Colbert the other night, and she's a moderate-sized little lady.

PAUL: *Sondra's really attractive.*

CLINT: I think she is, too. She's got a nice, earthy attractiveness, it's a *real* attractiveness. It isn't a made-up kind of thing. Sondra has a good presence, a good voice, a lot of the stuff that the old-time actresses used to have but in a lot of the new ones you don't see so much. Everybody was very different then, it seemed like. Extremely different.

PAUL: *You used to use a video truck for your performances, right? But you gave that up after* Misty.

CLINT: I used it again on *Drifter*, but I found that I had to lose it on films like *The Eiger Sanction*, where you're hanging off the side of mountains. *Breezy*, I didn't need it because I wasn't in it; I could always be a third eye myself. But I found that you can get *locked in* with a thing like that, you can get locked in to looking at every shot and analyzing it. I've also seen it bog everything down. The other actors all want to come in and see themselves in close-ups, and say, "Oh my God, my hair wasn't this," and "Can I do one more?"

High Plains Drifter was the last picture I used one on, using it on dolly shots and movement shots and masters, not looking at it on close-ups. I'd just say, "Print" and that was the end of it. They'd rewind the tape and I'd never show it to the other actors. I might look at it on my own, a close-up on myself, if I had doubts. Either I've gotten unwarranted confidence as I've gotten older or else I understand a little more about myself and the characters I'm playing.

28

In 1979's *Escape from Alcatraz*, Eastwood portrayed the real-life character of Frank Morris who, along with two other prisoners, may or may not have escaped from the Rock in 1962.

PAUL: *One of the main lures of* Escape from Alcatraz, *I imagine, was doing another film with Siegel.*

CLINT: Don and I had been talking about doing a film for years—we hadn't done one since '71—and most of the projects he had I didn't care for, and most the projects I had he didn't care for. But he read this thing and he said he thought it had good potential. He asked me what my opinion was, and I said I liked it very much.

PAUL: *Do you think he could have gotten that film financed had you not been in it?*

CLINT: Oh, I think so eventually. I know that Paramount, who had backed him and had bailed him out of his option money, wanted me in it very badly and felt it was the logical picture for us to be doing.

PAUL: *In a role like* Alcatraz, *which is a more realistic, flatter, quieter role, and a role like* Bronco Billy, *where you're playing more of a national mythic figure, what do you do different?*

CLINT: I adjust to the thought pattern of one or the other, and I take on the character. Bronco Billy is very open, absorbing, believes in sunny days over the next valley, believes that his group is great, is terribly loyal to friends, and has a morality that you don't see much anymore. The character in *Alcatraz*—the futility of his life. The intelligent man who's gone and become a loser, a guy who has been involved with crime and is sent to an ultimate institution where there's no way of ever being in society—at least until he finishes twenty years or whatever he's supposed to do. You take on a certain being and just embellish it. Like I said before, it's not an intellectual art, so I can't intellectually, analytically tell you *how* it is done. It's just that you just start doing it. It takes on a different life.

PAUL: *So the physical stuff in* Alcatraz, *was that all instinct or what was that? Your physical appearance seemed hunched and sort of Elisha Cook Jr.'d up almost. You looked smaller, you looked beaten down, and you were a lot less sure of your movements.*

CLINT: In *Alcatraz* you just take on the attitude. You go out there to the prison and you look at it and you imagine what it's like to be there. You look into the life of the character. From the only information that we could get out of the FBI files, Frank Morris was very much like that character: alone and very introspective, he teamed up with people occasionally but had been convicted of a lot of his crimes by himself. I sat down with the agent who was in charge of the case, which is still open. He told me as much as he could about Morris. I read everything he had on it. I didn't need to go back and talk to his mother—if there is a mother—or a parent or a grandparent or a great uncle. That was all I needed just to get in the feeling of the crimes he'd committed to the type of life he was leading. You just start *feeling* it. You think about it enough, it starts getting into you. Your actor's technique, whatever.

Going out to the prison, which has a special atmosphere of its own, then touring around the island, you take him on. I became him. We had the run of the place in the evening. There were no tourists, there was not another soul. Not a human being on Broadway, which is the main cellblock. You'd sit there and you'd just *feel* it and think, My God, what it must have been like to spend night after night—what must've been twenty-two out of every twenty-four hours—in this little crummy cell.

PAUL: *I would imagine that got you in the mood real fast.*

CLINT: Yeah. That was the basic research, and then I read a book on various escapes called *Escape from Alcatraz*, which had the Morris story and several others. I talked to an inmate who was there. He came on the set, a guy who was there from 1932 to 1941. He was sent there when he was twenty-one. He told me a lot things about the attitudes of the people there. That had an interesting effect on me.

But that was it. As far as telling you Step A, Step B, Step C, and then all the sub-steps, one, two, and three, there were none.

When you're in an acting class as a student actor—and let's face it, you're *always* a student actor, you're always learning and absorbing things in life that will be used down the line in performances you do, hopefully, if you have the opportunity to use them—you're analytically trying to think out, Now, how does this guy feel because he's a prisoner now? How do I think? And where has he been? You're making up a background for him. Where you do that kind of on a very analytical level, after you've been doing it for years you just instinctively do it. You go to the place and it takes you over.

PAUL: *Did you look like him at all?*

CLINT: None of us looked anything like any of our counterparts. He was a smaller man than I am and during the escape was maybe a few years younger than I was. He had sharp features and was rather tough-looking but bright-looking. All his mug shots had a screw-you kind of attitude.

PAUL: *You called Jack LaLanne to check about the escape.*

CLINT: I called him to check about the water and the currents and the tides, and how he felt they would have fared, because he's done it.[42]

PAUL: *Your conclusion was that they probably didn't make it.*

CLINT: Well, that was his conclusion. My hopes are that they would have made it—not that I root for every prisoner to get out of prison—but just because I was involved with that character and the scheme was so unique that you think, Wouldn't it have been nice if they'd gotten away and just gone straight somewhere?

---

[42] Fitness guru LaLanne actually swam handcuffed from Alcatraz to Fisherman's Wharf in 1955 when he was forty-one, then again in 1974 when he was sixty. Once again handcuffed, this time he also towed a thousand-pound boat.

You never know, maybe someday he'll drop me a letter from Uruguay.

PAUL: *I would think you took a chance on doing* Alcatraz, *which in a way is a* Beguiled *type of picture in that it doesn't have action, doesn't have sex.*

CLINT: I thought it was a chance. I felt it wasn't as commercial a film certainly as *Every Which Way but Loose,* but I felt that if it was executed well it could be provocative to the imagination and people might enjoy it. There's a certain amount of humor in the script in among the tension of the escape. I just don't feel that you have to be wielding a .44 Magnum every second to be commercial. It's fun to do that if the story's right.

PAUL: *It's very bleak and thoughtful, sort of Robert Bresson up close as an action director.*

CLINT: It's more a thoughtful thing. There are very few action sequences in it, but even in an action film you've got to like the people. There's got to be a soul to a movie, whether it's a Frank Capra type of film that has people caught up in a certain kind of thing or whether it's an action film. If there is no soul to it, it becomes an exercise in technique. A lot of the biggest, most thought about pictures in years gone by are just exercises in technique and not necessarily soul movies. People get faked out by fads of the moment and shooting styles.

PAUL: *Did you do most of the editing on* Alcatraz?

CLINT: I did some of it. Don had some ear-infection problem, was getting ready to do another film and had that hovering over him, so I worked on postproduction a little. He did a lot of it really. But we were in sync in concept to the film anyway, so there really wasn't anything for anybody to worry about. He and I were pretty much in agreement—in fact, we were in exact agreement—on the final screenplay before we started shooting.

    The only thing that we ever differed with in the early production was the amount of artificial sets to use as opposed to practical sets. In the early days of the picture, I was for shooting all of it on the island and building, if we needed, a set for a jail cell; building a small one and having it right there as a cover set. He was for building more sets than I was, in Los Angeles.

The interior corridor, which the guys climbed up in reality and the one that we actually used, is only about a yard wide and it goes down the full length of the cellblock. I thought it would be prohibitive expense-wise to build that and I thought it was so beautiful the way it was. He thought it would be impossible to shoot in it. So one day I just walked through it with him, and I said, "Don, let me just show you a few of the possibilities here. I think they're enormous, especially when you get up on top. You've got the real top, you're not going to have to cut scenes—people leaving a shot here, then cut to the real top up above, and then coming in and doing a lot of splicing together. We can be on top of the cellblock and see guards down in the cell yard below, which you couldn't do with a set because to build that set would be millions of dollars." We got in there and we paced it off and talked about the potentials and the camera, and then all of a sudden he loved it. He said, "Great. Let's do it." It was just a case where it worked well, of the two of us not butting heads but just talking out situations.

On the other hand, on the other side of the fence, using the real cell at all times like I had suggested doing, using diopters and stuff to move the camera in there, was really confining, and his idea of building some smaller set cells that could be taken apart, from a practical standpoint, was right also. If we had done it my way, we'd have been in there with much more limited angles probably, because the cells are only six feet wide and eight or ten feet long or whatever. It would have been much less practical to do that element my way. It was just a blend, the way the picture came out.

PAUL: *I would imagine that's a supreme compliment, that a director would let someone else cut his film.*

CLINT: Oh yeah, he thinks I'm good. I do the same thing with him: I solicit his comments on films. I've run him rough cuts of films I've done and said, "How do you feel about the pacing here?" and so forth. And he does the same with me. In fact, one time he even suggested, "Why don't someday we direct a film together? We could find the type of picture where you weren't in all the sequences. You could do a certain part of it and I'll do part of it and we'll do it all in sync. It would be just a slam-bang kind of thing." Of course, we never did this, but we've worked in a collaborative way for a lot of years. He's done some of his better films with me and I have done some of my better films with him. It's been very productive. I'm sure that we both have as much ego as anybody else, but we seem to be able to shed it when it comes to each other's participation. He likes me as a director and I like him as a director.

I like him as an actor. I used him as an actor in *Play Misty*. I thought he did a good job. He was an actor in *Alcatraz*, he played a part and I cut him out [laughs]. I not only cut him out but I cut myself out of it. It's just that, in the interest of the overall picture, in the pacing and the drama, it didn't in my estimation work. So I cut two [scenes] of my own out and one of his, and we joke about it a lot to this day.

PAUL: *The* Times *ran the dumbest review I've ever seen of that film. I mean, it was favorable, but it was like "This film isn't very good, but they'll be studying it in film class for twenty years."*[43]

CLINT: Yeah, I couldn't understand that really. You read the first sentence and you thought the guy doesn't like it, and then in the next sentence he thinks it's the greatest thing ever made. I don't know what he had in mind there.

PAUL: *It was just a* New York Times *big cultural attitude, that they shouldn't be praising prison movies or something.*

---

[43] Vincent Canby's review began: "Don Siegel's *Escape From Alcatraz* is not a great film or an especially memorable one, but there is more evident skill and knowledge of movie making in any one frame of it than there are in most other American films around at the moment. It's the kind of movie that could be more profitably studied in film courses than all of the works of Bergman and Fellini combined." About the star's performance, he wrote: "Mr. Eastwood fulfills the demands of the role and of the film as probably no other actor could. Is it acting? I don't know, but he's the towering figure in its landscape."

CLINT: I guess so. I was reading an article by Burt Reynolds—he's a nice guy, I like him, he's a friend of mine—but he seemed to be obsessed with reviewers and what they think of things. Some of them are really good writers who don't get a fix on the film, some of them get a good fix on the film but aren't very good writers and can't put down their feelings on it, and then there are others who are neither. So it's really a flip of the coin. I think what bothers him is that, because there are some guys who reside there and come from there [New York], they get a better shake; and because he's been commercial, he feels he hasn't gotten a shake from them. I guess I *could* feel that way if I let myself—in the early days anyway—but I never harbored any ill feelings.

PAUL: *The comment the* Times *made on your performance was very similar: "Nobody could have played this better, but is it acting?" Why isn't it acting? You're not a prisoner on Alcatraz.*

CLINT: After *Dirty Harry* especially and even during the Western period, the Leone films, I would meet people—not only reviewers but general public—and they would say, "God, I expected you to be so different." I said, "You mean you expected me to have the .44?" "Yeah." Even intelligent journalists, well-educated people in their field, would say it, and I'd say, "It was just a part. I was acting." It was the highest form of left-handed flattery, because they expect you to come charging in with the exact same attitudes that you played in the part.

PAUL: *Saying, "Asshole! Asshole!"*

CLINT: Yeah, putting the gun in the guy's face and saying, "What do you think about that, asshole?" It's a funny thing because I'll get college kids coming up to me and saying, "Do me a favor. Just tell me I'm an asshole." I'll go, "What for?" and they say, "Because I like the way you say it." One time Muhammad Ali came up to me and said, "Tell me I've got ten minutes to get out of town." [laughs] I said, "I haven't got a gun."

But it's a high form of flattery, though they might not be meaning it that way. You affect them with the role you're playing to the point where they think you *are* that person, and that to me is what acting's all about. That's what [Constantin] Stanislavski, [Michael] Chekhov, and whatever other so-called classic acting teachers would dream for. What they tried to inspire their students to achieve is that kind of believability.

PAUL: *A lot of it is, too, an actor like, say, Fredric March, again, wouldn't achieve that intensity because he doesn't play the national myth parts.*

CLINT: Yeah, right. If you don't play the national myth parts—like Jason Robards or somebody, to take a contemporary actor—you're not as subject to being ridiculed on that level because he plays character roles, comes in and hits them hard. He does a nice job with them and moves on. Somebody who plays a national myth type thing—Steve McQueen or whoever, just to drop a name out of the woodwork—could do just as good a job on their particular end of the thing and wouldn't receive the credit for it because they do have the ability to play this other aspect that you're talking about.

PAUL: *This larger-than-life business.*

CLINT: They have that ability, but a lot of times it isn't accepted. It's much easier to accept Woody Allen, who plays a guy who's having problems dealing with life, in the type of roles he plays. He does them well and I happen to be an admirer of his, but he doesn't play by the nature of his physiognomy or whatever you want to call it. He plays what he knows best—growing up under adverse circumstances—and he doesn't play those larger-than-life deals, so it's much easier for people who consider themselves intellectual to side along with that and say, "That's more reality." Maybe it *is* more reality, I don't know.

PAUL: *I doubt it.*

CLINT: But it's easy to praise that.

29

Whether out of deference to Clint or because perhaps he'd been told up front that the subjects were off limits, on tape Paul never asked about Eastwood's relationship with Sondra Locke, and his failing marriage only came up, briefly, twice.

Eastwood had been married to Maggie Johnson since 1953, and they had a son and a daughter together: Kyle in 1968 and Alison in 1972. Though Maggie filed for divorce in 1978, the year before these conversations commenced, the divorce didn't become final until 1984.

PAUL: *So I just wanted to ask you, you know, what the facts were about the divorce, the separation or whatever, and whatever you wanted to say about it.*

CLINT: Oh, well, I'm just legally separated. Not divorced, but the same thing. Practically the same thing, depending on how you want to interpret it with contracts or what have you. But, uh, my wife and I get along fine. We've got a very good agreement on a lot of policies as far as the kids are concerned. And we're getting along. But it's fine.

PAUL: *Do you think it will eventually lead to divorce or do you have no idea?*

CLINT: I don't know. I suppose if one or the other of us ever wanted to sign up with somebody [nervous laugh] or something like that, it might lead to it, but at the present everybody seems satisfied with the situation.

PAUL: *I really felt for you around Christmastime. I know I got separated and divorced, and it's particularly rough with the kids. I had a son about three at the time and, God, it was tough.*

CLINT: Well, I had a very good Christmas last year. I took the kids skiing the week before Christmas. They were home the week after Christmas, and I was on a road trip. We had a good time. We had it worked out rather well, and they're enjoying themselves. They're not watching two people argue particularly in front of each other, and it's probably a healthier relationship in the long run.

30

The night before this conversation, Muhammad Ali, defeated by Larry Holmes, had failed in his 1980 attempt to win a fourth world heavyweight boxing championship.

Almost ten years earlier, at 5:30 one morning in 1971, Paul happened to be in front of his hotel in Chicago when Ali suddenly came down the street on his morning run. The boxer approached him and they talked for a while. Paul later described the meeting as "just two guys sitting on some steps at dawn."

PAUL: *I was talking to Fritz, and he said you guys watched the fight last night. I was trying to find somebody with Select TV, but it didn't turn out.*

CLINT: We watched it. It wasn't too much.

PAUL: *That's what I hear. I've been really emotionally wrapped up in Ali for years and I've seen all those fights. I was really hoping he could pull it off.*

CLINT: Everybody's making such a big deal of the fact he's thirty-eight. I don't think that's the deal. You just cannot lay off for two years and then come back and train for three months and say, "That's it." If anything, at thirty-eight, you would have to train a longer and much more extensive period of time. He was going to have to depend on stamina and a lot of things that he didn't have to depend on at twenty-five years of age. As a young man it came very easy for him because nobody was even in the same class with him. A guy who's had such a fabulous career as he has, he probably didn't *have* to train as hard as a lot of guys because he had such great natural talent. I would've rather seen him take a year or so off. He'd be better off coming back and fighting the fight at forty and doing it really right—if he really had that burning ambition to fight again—rather than just do a crash course and come back.

PAUL: *Three months ago he looked grotesque. He practically looked like Orson Welles three months ago. Losing the weight—the photos were stunning, he really did look like he did ten years ago—that's possible, but that doesn't mean that you're in shape.*

CLINT: You can lose weight without even working out. The two don't necessarily go together. Everybody got fooled this time because, what, he dropped down to two-twenty, two-nineteen or something like that?

PAUL: *Two-seventeen.*

CLINT: But that isn't the point. People don't realize that when he first fought, back when he was in his early twenties and he was really so smooth as a fighter, he used to only weigh about two-six, two-seven, two-eight. That was his fighting weight, and then in later years he started fighting at a heavier weight because he didn't want to turn down challengers. But you've got to be trimmed down to your ultimate if you're going to fight at thirty-eight as opposed to twenty-eight. That just seems like basic physical math.

PAUL: *Fritz was saying that it sounded like Ali was going to try to fight Mike Weaver now.*

CLINT: I thought that he would've fought Weaver first and then had this fight. You know, it was a great payday and everything.

PAUL: *I don't think he did it just for that, though. I'm sure he may somewhat need the money—I mean, with all that entourage— but I really do think some of it was him thinking, My God, no one's ever done this. He's the kind of guy who loves to risk it all on something to see if he can pull it off.*

CLINT: I think he would like to have it back. I know how he could feel. I know him slightly. He's lived a good life up till now, he's used to going places and meeting heads of state and things. What he's done now is probably the wisest thing. If he could train up now, really seriously train up, then fight Weaver, he'd own the other half of the championship. Then there'd be a tremendous gate, combining the two championships and the rematch.

PAUL: *I doubt that he wants to go out a loser. I'm pretty sure that he'll try to figure out something.*

CLINT: I know he stated that he wanted to be the first black man to retire undefeated. So he did. But he's back out now, so this will give him an incentive to do some kind of deal. He'll have to fight.[44]

PAUL: *It was a sad paper this morning, with Ali and Steve McQueen on the front page.*

CLINT: I didn't see the paper, but I heard about it secondhand from the news.

PAUL: *Apparently McQueen does have this asbestos cancer or whatever it's called. He's taking treatment from somebody who's had pretty good success using Empirin or something. But he's not a trained doctor, so all the doctors are coming down on him. It apparently stopped the disease for now. He's getting better. Apparently when he checked in, some doctor said he had two weeks to live. That was ten weeks ago. There was this sidebar from the medical people, saying that the mortality rate is a hundred percent.*

CLINT: So he's hanging in there, huh? Where is he?

PAUL: *He's in Mexico. It actually sounds like he was getting better.*

CLINT: At least he's probably getting fresh air. If he was here this week, it would probably finish him off.[45]

---

[44] Ali never did fight Weaver. His next fight—and his last—resulted in his loss to up-and-comer Trevor Berbick in 1981.

[45] McQueen, diagnosed with mesothelioma, had flown to Mexico to receive untraditional treatments for the cancer that had metastasized throughout his body. He died a little over a month later.

31

CLINT: How's Warren doing?

PAUL: *He's fine. He just came back from Hawaii on vacation. He's got a live album due in November. He's much healthier now than he was. He's stopped drinking, probably for good this time. He was an alcoholic. I don't know if you knew that.*

CLINT: Oh yeah. I remember he came over here one time and he had a flask, the old time flask, and he was doing everything but drinking out of the heel of his boot. He came in and we talked about some music ideas and then he left. Then he called back. I wasn't here, and he started telling about the same ideas all over again, to Bob [Daley], like he hadn't even been here. He halfway blacked out what we talked about.[46]

PAUL: *He tended to play at the Scott Fitzgerald/flaming youth thing and it caught up with him. He went to Pinecrest, which is a drug rehabilitation center in Santa Barbara. He would lose practically whole days toward the end there, but he seems settled in now. He's doing weights again. He's lost thirty, forty pounds probably.*

CLINT: Oh, fantastic. Good for him.

PAUL: *He realized that he was playing a role that he couldn't afford to play because the logical ending to that role was death, the way he was going at it.*

CLINT: Just the way it happened with Scott Fitzgerald. I tell you, for a young guy in this town hanging around the music business, Jesus, it's tough. Music people and rock stars seem to be a lot like movie stars were back in the Twenties. In the old days, movie actors were all out partying all the time, they were driving around in Rolls-Royces or Packard Phaetons or whatever the cars were at the time. Now you see people driving around in

---

[46] According to Zevon's ex-wife, Crystal Zevon, he and Eastwood met together in 1977. "I know they were talking about writing a song together and Warren was, of course, very excited about it."

Rollses in Hollywood and they're all music people. Actors you see driving around in pickup trucks or modest cars of sorts. It's reversed itself. Even the most well-known movie actors will be driving something fairly logical looking.

PAUL: *What I would like to do, if it's all right with you, is I'd love to have Warren come over for the last forty-five minutes today and just sit and talk with us. I've done this in the past and found out it's useful because he's liable to ask a question that I'd never dream of asking. He's got his own point of view about your movies and he's liable to really come up with a surprise or two. And I think he's a little embarrassed. The time you met him, he was a mess.*

CLINT: Oh well, he was all right. He was having some problems there, but I liked him. Sure, have him come over.

Later, after Zevon arrives, the three men dine on cheeseburgers that Eastwood has ordered in to his office.

CLINT: Not bad. Big sumbitches.

PAUL: *Is it true that when David Geffen was involved in films that you showed him* Josey Wales *and he said, "I think it's too long"?*

CLINT: No, I don't think I've ever showed it to David Geffen. In fact, I don't think I've ever met David Geffen. The only person I ever showed the rough cut to was Jerry Fielding, who did the score, and he fell in love with it right away. He was just ecstatic about it, so I said, "Everything you've ever wanted to do but nobody else would let you do, try tinkering with that now."

WARREN ZEVON: *That would be quite a thing to be handed those instructions.*

PAUL: The Outlaw Josey Wales *was the first movie that Warren taped on his VCR, I remember. We both went video happy at the same time.*

CLINT: Off the TV?

PAUL: *Network, yeah.*

CLINT: At first they [NBC] wanted us to add twenty minutes to the movie and run it as a three-hour movie. We could've done that because I had a very good sequence that I had to take out just because of length, and had two, three other things I could embellish on. Then they came back and said, "No, now we only want two hours," so then we cut back the other way. They come down with a whole list of everything they want removed. The big question is how do you satisfy them and at the same time not just wreck the movie?

PAUL: *I wish they'd done that with* Wales. *I'd like to see the extra stuff.*

CLINT: There were some good sequences I had to take out. I'm just glad that I'm the one doing the cutting because some of the earlier films that I had cut for television were just butchered. *High Plains Drifter* was cut for TV and the network sent it over for me to look at. I called the network and I said, "I think you ought to get your money back. I feel bad getting all this money." The gal went, "Oh?" I said, "The movie isn't there, the story isn't there, it doesn't make sense. It's going to come off like crap. It looks like a crappy movie." She said, "What can we do?" I said, "Let's readjust the timing," and came up with some compromises. There are a lot of things I would've redone differently, but at that time we weren't editing for airing on TV.

> The conversation about editing continues, with Zevon swapping a story about having to deal with his record company while producing his latest record, *Stand in the Fire*, a live album.

WARREN: *We took about three weeks mixing it down and just fixing little things. When the gal came, she said, "Wait a minute. What are you going in the studio for?" I said, "We're just going to fix a few things." She said, "Fix?! This is a live album! You can't fix anything!" I said, "Well, dear, you see, we're making a piece of entertainment here and we measure it by how entertaining it is*

when we get done. You know, it's not a documentary exactly."
That upset her. It's true to the performance, but there won't be
a huge clam that doesn't seem to need to go down in history.

CLINT: I'm a lot rougher with my films than I used to be. I used to
fall in love with shots. I imagine it's the same way with you and
records. You spend a lot of time on a certain thing, it's really
painful to get, and you finally get it the way you want it; then
all of a sudden, in the overall spectrum, it doesn't quite work.
In *The Eiger Sanction* I had about five hours of the greatest
mountain footage you could imagine—fabulous shots—but they
didn't mean a thing to the story.

WARREN: *That's some shot on the needle [the Totem Pole]. You*
must've enjoyed the book.

CLINT: I tried to stay as close to the book within reason.

WARREN: *I told Paul my sweeping theory is that you should've done*
Heart of Darkness—*which I guess, when they made* Apocalypse
Now, *they didn't think was a sufficiently interesting book to*
bother staying to.

CLINT: They would've been better off if they'd stayed true to it. I
remember when they first started with it, they didn't have the
ending. I read the script, and they didn't have quite the *Heart of*
Darkness in it. I guess they started out with that and then they
kind of talked their way out of it. They talked their way into a
non-ending to it.

PAUL: *You were offered the [Martin] Sheen part?*

CLINT: I was. I guess two or three guys were offered the part.

WARREN: *It would've been great if you had the Kurtz part.*[47]

---

[47] Shortly after the release of *Apocalypse Now* in 1979, Zevon summed up his
dissatisfaction with shaven-headed Marlon Brando's portrayal of Colonel Kurtz—
supposed Evil incarnate—by saying the movie was like spending three hours going
upriver to discover that the devil is Mr. Clean.

CLINT: The Kurtz part would've been fun. In fact, McQueen called me. They'd talked to him about doing the Willard part. He was saying, "You're perfect for Willard and I'd like to play Kurtz," because he was trying to work a deal where he worked for two weeks. He would've had a deal much like Brando had, only I think it was a richer deal, an enormous amount of dough for two weeks' work. He said, "Why don't we do it together?" I said, "One problem is that the Willard part doesn't work two weeks—it goes on forever—and it looks like this is going to be quite a long movie." And then I talked to Francis [Ford Coppola]. I'd just moved into a new house and I had some personal reasons for not wanting to leave the country for what turned out to be two years, but at that time was a prediction of sixteen or eighteen months.

PAUL: *Coppola's production company is doing* Hammett *now with Wim Wenders. It's in its fifth year—not shooting, but altogether.*

CLINT: *Hamlet?*

PAUL: Hammett.

CLINT: Oh, *Hammett*! Dashiell Hammett, yeah.

PAUL: *They have ninety percent of it. They don't have an ending and they don't have a beginning.*

CLINT: That's nuts.

PAUL: *Wenders has been on the film for two years. They've gone through seventeen writers or something like that and now they've hired another guy. Coppola told them, "Take the ninety percent and really fine edit it, and then we'll figure out how to start it and how to end it."*

CLINT: I guess maybe you could do that. It's kind of a crapshoot. It would seem to me, though, that if you're going to tell a joke that you should know the end of the joke yourself before you present it to the audience. I would never do a picture without a conclusion—though I did do one *almost* that way at one time, this thing called *Joe Kidd*.

PAUL: New West *did this piece a couple weeks ago on* Hammett, *and it sounds like that's where they are now: the more they talk, the more confused it gets, and it just goes on and on.*

CLINT: Then all you can do is just bring in somebody you respect from the outside and say, "Give me a new opinion from scratch." If you start talking it too long, you're intellectualizing at it. The audience isn't going to be intellectualizing at it, they're going to want to be entertained by it.

PAUL: *That's how Coppola must work, though, because he had a similar problem with* Godfather II. *He didn't know how he was going to end that. So if you get involved with a project with him, I imagine you're probably signing over about three or four years of your life right now.*

CLINT: Sam Bottoms was in it [*Apocalypse Now*, as well as *Bronco Billy*]. He said that he got sick and he lost about thirty pounds, and all this happened during the picture. So he said now the scenes don't match up.

PAUL: *He told me a great story about Brando. They had two cameras turning simultaneously and Brando gave a ninety-minute monologue, of which they kept four words, "The horror! The horror!" which is right from Conrad anyway.*

CLINT: He didn't ask for a cube of butter and another roll, did he? Ask the girl to run three fingers up his ass [laughs]?[48]

WARREN: *He might've had a separate picture there, right?* Last Tango in Cambodia.

CLINT: [still laughing] Might've come up with the right ending.

---

[48] Eastwood is referencing the infamous scene in Bernardo Bertolucci's *Last Tango in Paris* wherein Marlon Brando uses butter as a lubricant. Pauline Kael's rave review in *The New Yorker* praised the film for "alter[ing] the face of an art form."

WARREN: *That's a good analogy, I like that: about telling a joke without knowing the punch line.*

CLINT: Have you ever had somebody do that? Start a joke and they get halfway through it and they realize they've forgotten what the joke was? And everybody's sitting there just slack-jawed.

WARREN: *Anything that passes as art/entertainment should stand up to the analogy of being a joke. That's all I can tell people when they want to know how I write. They say, "Why did you write that?" Well, it's like making up a joke. I can't explain why something struck me as funny.*

CLINT: It struck you at the moment, sure. Whether it's funny, pathos, or whatever.

WARREN: *Stretching the language of the entertainment value of a joke.*

CLINT: Hell, a lot of people forget about the entertainment value. If somebody calls somebody an *artist*, the word sometimes goes to the wrong part of the brain on certain people and they start thinking that they're out on a desert island with their canvas and brush, and they just go free flow with it all. You *can* be artistic, but it's still entertainment.

PAUL: *I know what I was going to tell you about* Josey Wales. *At the end of the year they asked a number of people what were the best films of the Seventies in their opinion. One person named* Josey Wales, *and it was Abbie Hoffman.*[49]

---

[49] In a 1980 article for *High Times*, Hoffman was interviewed by his former Chicago Seven coconspirator Jerry Rubin. Rubin told Hoffman, who was still hiding from the law, "I find it impossible you're not discovered." "Maybe I have been," Hoffman replied. "My neighbors are very shrewd people. My model is the Clint Eastwood movie, *The Outlaw Josey Wales*. He's a fugitive renegade from the Civil War who's chased by a posse but eventually arrives and settles in a valley. His neighbors protect him when the posse shows up. There's no gun battle. They just point a different way: 'He went thataway.'"

CLINT: Well, it has comments about government and wars and the futility of it all.

PAUL: *His list didn't seem to be at all political. It is one of the best films of the Seventies and it should've been on more lists. But the fact that he would be the one to name it I thought was just wonderful.*

CLINT: He's very much an individualist, so he would have the nerve to name it. A lot of people wouldn't have the nerve to pick that one because they'd probably want to check somebody else's list first. It's like a school kid looking at the other guy's test before he marks down the answer. That's the way a lot of people operate when it comes to that sort of thing.

WARREN: *It's funny, I started out—Paul knows this, of course—in classical modern music, which if anything gets the capital A, that's it. I observed right away as a kid that there was no amateur audience for this kind of music. There wasn't any audience but the people who were involved in it. So I've felt, since I was a child, that if there's one thing that doesn't intimidate me it's the idea of Art. Because if anything's pure art—that's really almost completely pure bullshit—that's it. So I got hold of the idea that entertainment people must know something to do with setting out to be an artist.*

CLINT: It would be something to sit down and always be playing for a set of fears and constantly be scrutinized on that level rather than just on the emotional level of the audience you're trying to reach. It *would* put a different stigma on it, you're right.

PAUL: *I got a great quote from you being interviewed by David Sheehan on HBO: "If a guy goes to a movie with his girl, I should take him on a trip somewhere."*

CLINT: That's right, I think. You look at a newspaper today, or *any* day, and it's "inflation this" and "the economy this" and "this is awful" and "the war" and "the Iraqis, Iranians, and Afghans and the Russians," and you think, Holy shit, isn't there anything to really give me a lift? If you go to a film, you don't only want to watch the Iraqis and the Russians fight it out.

You take the guy and his girl on a trip. Make total use of it, so they both can go out after work sometime and have a few laughs, have a beer, talk about the film, talk about something. The trick to do it is to make people feel they're going along on a journey but they're not conscious of the technique of it. As soon as they're conscious of the technique of the shot, then they're out of it.

It's the same way in music. You associate records and things with moments you've had in your life. Every record, whether it was Nat King Cole or whether it's Warren Zevon or whoever, it's always associated with some moments you had, whether it was in a gym or a concert or whatever. That song.

I saw Mel Torme last night and he said, "Hi, how do you do?" and that was the end of the conversation. Right away it was "Blue Moon" and right away it was Seattle, Washington, and it was a certain year and the chick and everything. It all went right by in front of my face—the gal I was with, the gal I was nuts about at the time—everything just flashed right there like a whole little twenty-minute vignette in about a third of a second. [to Zevon] And I'll be doing it with yours.

WARREN: *I never thought of that. I mean, I think of it with every-thing else.*

PAUL: *[to Eastwood] You said John Wayne approached you to do a movie once. Was that later in his career?*

CLINT: The first time I ever met him, he said, "We ought to do a movie, kid." I said, "Yeah, it would be great." We never did come up with one. Originally, the producer at Universal who did *True Grit*, he had the idea of me playing the part that Glen Campbell did, but it wasn't much of a role, and I was occupied.

PAUL: *I didn't much like the movie, to tell you the truth.*

CLINT: Then I gave Wayne a story I'd read once, which wasn't complete. It was a far-out Western idea. I sent that to him, and he didn't like it. He went on and on about how it didn't represent the men and women who settled the West. He got into some area where I didn't understand what he was talking about. I didn't say to him that it intentionally represented the men and women who settled the West. I was looking at it as something as a *potential* vehicle if developed, and somehow I wasn't very good at explaining myself when I sent him the covering notes. We never went anywhere with that. After that he became ill.

PAUL: *He might've been difficult anyway. I think he weakened* The Shootist *by toning it down and insisting that his moral values wouldn't permit him to do certain things.*[50]

CLINT: Don told me one time he wanted him to shoot this guy in the back. Wayne said, "I don't shoot guys in the back." He said, "But the guy just tried to kill you. Why wouldn't you?" Wayne had different ideas about the image and the look he wanted. The cameraman, Bruce Surtees, uses a lot of darks and he was trying to set a mood, but Wayne had worked with a lot of other guys over his many, many years in the business who would go for a much brighter and straighter kind of lighting. Eyeballs always lit to the hilt. Bruce has worked with me a lot. He's just the opposite. It was just a different way of working. He couldn't explain it to Wayne.

PAUL: *You got the feeling watching it, though, that Siegel had his hands tied behind his back during that film, that there were certain things he couldn't do that he probably would've done.*

CLINT: I don't think I'm talking out of school, I think he'd agree with that.

PAUL: *It would have been interesting if you had made one ten years ago when Wayne was still interested in films. He seemed to be walking through a lot of them towards the end. He made an imitation* Dirty Harry *that was just embarrassing.*

CLINT: I know. In fact, one of them was originally written for me: *McQ.* I passed on it.

---

[50] Directed by Don Siegel, 1976's *The Shootist* was John Wayne's final film.

WARREN: The Shootist *bothered me. It's a cruel picture.*

CLINT: I didn't read the book, so I don't know whether it's in there anyway, but I didn't understand why they invented a scene about these villains who are never set up to have really done anything wrong, and he kills them.

PAUL: *He sets those guys up to be his executioners so he can die with a gun in his hand, I guess.*[51]

CLINT: That is kind of cruel. I mean, what happens if everybody who is sick just went out and killed somebody else on the freeway?

WARREN: *The villain in the picture is cancer. To me, the idea of using an illness as violence is pornographic.* Marcus Welby's *pornographic to me now. Just that whole thing is what bothered me.*

32

PAUL: *God, I've been reading all sorts of things in the* New York Post *about "Eastwood mad as hell about* Bronco Billy. *He swears to do nothing but bloodbath pictures from now on" and all sorts of stuff like that.*

CLINT: Those guys. I don't know why these magazines insist on lying like that.

PAUL: *I think they just make it up and print it.*

CLINT: They make it up, yeah. In the first place, I've never made a statement like that. I loved doing the film, like the film, and I have no regrets at all about doing the film. When I started the film, I didn't intend it to be a film to out-gross *Every Which Way*

---

[51] A similar plot device provided the ending to Eastwood's *Gran Torino* in 2008, only its protagonist, Walt Kowalski, sets up some gang members so that he can die *without* a gun in his hand.

but Loose or *Dirty Harry* or what have you. It was intended to just broaden the field or to appeal to maybe another audience that might not like the other things. I do a few films now and then that my kids could like or have other values to them. You have to do that or otherwise your sanity goes. What's the use of me being successful in the motion picture business if I just sit there and do the same old thing? The *Post* has gotten as bad as the sheets that are sold in the supermarkets. They've printed a lot of lies about me in recent years.[52]

PAUL: *They claimed that* Dirty Harry 4 *was coming up.*

CLINT: There's no such plan at all. It's a funny thing about those newspapers: every time anybody ever attacks freedom of the press, paranoids start going, "Oh my God, the First Amendment! The public's right to know!" Well, this is the public's right to know these are just out-and-out lies made up by journalists. It brings down the legitimate press, who are trying to do responsible stories and informative stories. The public's beginning to learn that it's all lies. I've talked to a lot of people and they'll say, talking about supermarket rack-type papers, "I know it's lies, but what the hell. It's fun to read anyway." That's fine. If you approach it that way, that's great. But they still go under the guise that they're legitimate.

PAUL: *A. J. Liebling said, "Freedom of the press is guaranteed only to those who own one." Which is true, I guess.*

CLINT: I don't think anybody disagrees it's a very important facet of democracy, but the press, the legitimate press, is going to have to come down on the illegitimate because it's making them look bad. People lump supermarket papers in with the *Times*. The magic of seeing it in print. It's in print, so it's the truth.

And I'm not mad as hell. In fact, I loved doing *Bronco Billy*. I have absolutely no regrets in the world. It's going to be a profit-making film. I don't think I have to prove to anybody that I can

---

[52] Eastwood won a lawsuit against the *National Enquirer* and in 1996 was awarded over $800,000 in damages, attorneys' fees, and expenses. A previous lawsuit with the tabloid was settled out of court for an undisclosed amount.

make a commercial film. It was just made for certain reasons of my own.

PAUL: *I played back some of the tapes we had done, and you'd said that maybe it's a film that is ahead of its time or behind its time or maybe won't have any time at all. "I don't know," you said.*

CLINT: Who knows, yeah. But I felt that way about any of them. When I made *Dirty Harry* back in the Seventies, I didn't know. When I went to Italy to do the *Dollar* films, I didn't know. I just did them because I wanted to do them at the time, and they worked out. When I did *Loose*, I felt it could be a commercial film. I didn't realize it would do as well as it did. It exceeded my expectations, let's put it that way.

People get on kicks writing-wise and they don't understand why you do things. Then, when they do understand, you get the other side: you get reviewers who will say, "I wish you'd do something new." Then when you branch out, they'll say, "What the hell?" When I did *The Beguiled*, I had a critic once ask me, "Because *Beguiled* wasn't successful, is that what drove you on to do *Dirty Harry* and all these others?" I said, "Hell, no. I did those because I wanted to do them." I had no regrets about *Beguiled* just because it wasn't a commercial success. The thing is, with *Bronco Billy*, it *will* be a commercial success.

PAUL: *I don't know how it was out here, but in New York there was such viciousness involved in all these roundups about summer flops. Exactly one week after* Bronco Billy *had opened, this moron named Harry Haun in the Sunday* Daily News *said, "The picture's dead in the water completely. Eastwood's all over. Forget about him." And I thought, Jesus Christ, he's just come off his biggest grossing picture of all time,* Every Which Way but Loose, *and now his career is over?*

CLINT: My career will be around a lot longer than Haun's, I guarantee that.[53]

---

[53] New York journalist Harry Haun is currently a staff writer for *Playbill*, a theater magazine.

PAUL: *Are we so jaded that something is dead in the water after a week?*

CLINT: We had great notices. The American reviews were very good and the picture's doing nicely around the world. We had really great notices in London and great business, and the French notices were marvelous. There's nothing wrong with the film at all.

The thing is, the type of people who would go to *Bronco Billy* are not the type of audience that would necessarily queue up on the first day for a more blatantly commercial-type film. But there are a lot of films that everybody queues up for the first day and they don't two days later. Some films people don't line up for. You look at an ad in the paper and say, "Hey, I'd like to see that movie," but that doesn't mean you go out *that* night and go see it. You say, "Well, maybe next Wednesday." A more sophisticated audience, for instance, may be doing five or six things that week and maybe going to a movie is just one of those that's going to be postponed till the next week. Maybe they're people who take in two or three things and they've got sort of a program set up for themselves. Because I've done that.

PAUL: *Word of mouth has something to do with it.*

CLINT: Yeah. Your neighbor comes back and says, "Hey, I saw this movie last night. It's really good."

PAUL: *The American reviews were among the best you've ever had. The film, from what I understand, is a modest hit and it's done fourteen, fifteen million or something like that.*

CLINT: Everything is related to what a film costs. If I had spent thirty million dollars like a lot of these people, well, then I would say the film was a flop. But if you make a film for five million dollars and it grosses fifteen domestic and—I'm just picking a figure because I don't know—suppose it goes to ten foreign. So you do twenty-five million dollars. I mean, where is that so bad?

Every Which Way but Loose did over fifty domestic. That's the company's third largest grosser of all time, but those don't come around often for anybody. If you go back in history and look at Clark Gable and Gary Cooper and Humphrey Bogart and you name it, every picture didn't do the exact same amount of business. Every film has its audience, its height and where it's going to go, and once in a while you do one that doesn't go anywhere. But I've had more in-the-black films than anybody in the last decade or two.

PAUL: *And this will be one of them certainly.*

CLINT: This'll be in the black, too, because there's nothing really wrong with it. Now, some of the other films that they've lumped us in with cost fourteen or fifteen, sixteen million dollars a shot, and truly, when you consider the interest on fourteen or fifteen million dollars—or over twenty million dollars, in the case of *The Shining*—then you start thinking, well, that plus interest, now there *is* a question of when it's going to make it in the black.

PAUL: *Also, it has a negative effect. Instead of letting the film build naturally through word of mouth, which was very good on this film, people read that, wow, this one's all gone. It had barely opened, so some people didn't go see it.*

CLINT: True that people line up for *Empire Strikes Back*, but it's the sequel to *Star Wars*. It's got great anticipation to it. Of course, compared to *The Empire Strikes Back*, nothing was a hit because that probably was a hundred-million-dollar film or whatever it's going to eventually do. That was *the* summer movie. That's fine and there were a lot of other movies in there that did well, too. I mean, there are a lot of pictures that people think are hits that aren't really hits because the trades will forget to say that it cost thirty-five million to make.

You take a film, for instance, like *Apocalypse Now*—it's had a pretty good run in New York and a pretty good run in San Francisco and some areas—a film that will probably do twenty-six, twenty-seven million dollars domestic, which is very, very respectable. In fact, it's a hit gross depending on the cost of the film. But if you're talking about the cost of the film at thirty million, it's *not* necessarily a hit gross. It would be a hit gross if you'd made the film for five or six, seven million dollars and did twenty-six domestic.

PAUL: *It just seemed like, God, the absolute height of ridiculousness to write a movie off one week after its opening.*

CLINT: Have you ever met Tom Allen?

PAUL: *No, I haven't. But he wrote an excellent piece on* Bronco Billy.

CLINT: Jesus, he wrote two pieces on it. They were just marvelous. I just was wondering about him. I wonder what kind of a guy he is.

PAUL: *The one I saw was in the* Voice, *where he said, "It's really time to take Clint Eastwood seriously. He's one of the best directors in the world."* [54]

CLINT: The other one was recapping several films, including *Billy,* saying it was one of the better films from the season.

PAUL: *I didn't see the other one.*

CLINT: Somebody asked me the other day, she said, "What happened? You used to get all those bum reviews and now you get a couple good ones." I think what's happened is, a lot of it, there's a whole new generation of reviewers now and a lot of those people have grown up on my films. They were in high school when the *Dollar* films came out, and so I'm not so much an oddity. But when I came in out of left field—European films and everything—to the old generation of critics, Kael and those people, I was a real oddity because my performances were stylized in a way they didn't understand. But to the newer generation I'm more of a familiar thing.

Nowadays there are so many cinema groups and cinema schools that a lot of reviewers are really becoming reoriented on films and making a study of them, where in past generations I think that people became reviewers because they had

---

[54] Allen wrote that "now it's time to take [Eastwood] seriously, not just as a populist phenomenon, but as one of the most honest, influential, personal filmmakers in the world today."

nothing else to do. Either they couldn't write feature stories or they couldn't do other columns in papers. A friend of mine in Oakland was the son of a publisher. When he was working his way up, to learn the journalist's business, that was the job they gave him to start out. They said, "Here, you're going to be the film reviewer."

PAUL: *Either that or the big honchos were the guys who also reviewed books and plays, and they looked at movies from a purely literary value, not a visual medium. So they just completely dismissed any action films. They were guys like Dwight Macdonald and Stanley Kauffmann and John Simon who were, you know, so rarified.*

CLINT: Right. They looked down on it as a sub-art to literature and to the other things that they were reviewing.

PAUL: *That's why Siegel and Sam Fuller and all those guys went totally undetected for years, because guys like Macdonald and Kauffmann never even bothered to go see the films.*

CLINT: Nowadays it's a much more serious thing. I think they've become a little more appreciative of what it takes to put one together.

PAUL: *I also read in the* Post, *which may or may not be true again, that Warner Bros. bought a novel that isn't out yet about a guy who's dying of cancer and wants to become a country-western singer, and that that's going to be your next movie.*

CLINT: No, that isn't true. It's true that they did buy a book that isn't out yet called *Honkytonk Man*. It's something that we've been looking at, but whether it's the next picture or not, I don't know. I don't think it will be.

PAUL: *You think you might do it, though?*

CLINT: I like it. I'd love to have you read it sometime and see what you think.

PAUL: *Is that the plot of it, then: the guy finds out he's dying and his dream is to become a singer? Or is that scrambled totally?*

CLINT: No, that isn't it. He *is* a country-western singer, but he's never made it big because he's just kind of crazy. He's kind of a wild guy—he doesn't really have any driving ambition. He's seen through the eyes of a nephew, the effect he has on everybody's life. Rather than ruin it for you, I'll just send you a copy of the galleys.

PAUL: *Have you got a next picture planned?*

CLINT: Not set. We're exploring three possibilities. After Christmas I'll make a decision. Something that won't interfere with the ski season.

PAUL: *Did you find a new thriller? I know you were looking for one.*

CLINT: Nothing yet. I read the one you gave me. I enjoyed that very much. I didn't quite know how to do it, though.

PAUL: *I don't know if it's filmable. I just liked the concept of it: the one white guy down South in a black city. It was kind of nice. It has its corny aspects.*

CLINT: Yeah, but it was nice. An enjoyable read. Have you ever read the book *Firefox*?

PAUL: *No, but I know the title. Is it a detective novel?*

CLINT: No. I would like to not talk about it.

PAUL: *You don't have to.*

CLINT: I meant I'd like not to do anything in the press about it at the moment because I'm laying low so I just don't get a lot of calls and solicitations on it. But I'd love to have your opinion on it because it's an exciting book. It's like a Hitchcock thing, but it's not confined like that. It's hypothetical. The Russians have come up with a plane that's twenty years ahead of anything we've come up with. It's a fighter plane that flies at Mach five or six or something, flying 6,000 miles an hour. It is invisible to radar and it also has a weapons system that is run by thought control. We're so far behind and sort of in a quandary what to do, American and British groups come up with this plan to find a pilot to go steal it. He has some sort of personality problem, which gives an element of unreliability to him. And so they send this guy in.

It's very hard to put down once you get into it and it's got several real good suspense moments. One is the whole intrigue: how they smuggle him in and all the problems that happen to him there. I think it will be a really great suspense movie with all the *ifs* put into place: execution, casting, et cetera, et cetera, et cetera.

33

PAUL: *You said you didn't really plan to do* Any Which Way You Can *[1980], but then the script was so good that you did do it.*

CLINT: It has a lot of the fun stuff that the first one had, but it's all laid out a little differently, which is nice.

PAUL: *Did Warners come up with a script and submit a script to you and you liked it?*

CLINT: No, Lenny Hirshan, who is my agent—he's with William Morris Agency—called me and said that they had a writer [Stanford Sherman] whom he wanted me to meet. So I met this guy, I liked him very much, and he had this idea. I liked it right away, I liked his whole approach. He seemed to understand what made the first one work and the whole humor of it. He said here's what he wanted to do with the second one—he laid it out [taps on the table] all in a row. When he was done, I said, "Let's go." We made a deal, and he went and wrote it. The cat's the most amazing writer. He had about eighty pages in the first week of the thing and at the end of the second week he had the whole script.

PAUL: *Your kind of writer.*

CLINT: I just tapped the script and, before I even read it, I said, "Boy, this has got to be great."

PAUL: *I chisel them in stone.*

CLINT: When I read it, I liked it. What he did was he brought a lot of stuff, and you'd slice away at the stuff you want. We changed certain things as we went.

PAUL: *What was the new slant that he had that you wanted?*

CLINT: Just keeping the same thing that the guy does, but he gets roped into one last bare-knuckle fight deal. It's kind of a biggie, in the tradition of *The Spoilers* and *The Quiet Man*, using that principle of having the fight cut away to other sequences that are playing simultaneously. So he wrote it in that vein, where all these little vignettes were going on at the same time the fight's going on.

Of course, when I told Warner Bros. they were ecstatic, because they didn't know. All of a sudden, I had it and they said okay.

PAUL: *Who directed this one?*

CLINT: Buddy Van Horn. He's worked for me before. You didn't meet him because he wasn't on *Billy*, but he did second unit for us on several occasions and he's been the stunt gaffer on most of the films.

PAUL: *This is his first directing job?*

CLINT: Yeah. He's a really nice guy and he was well organized. I was really proud of the way he handled himself on it. I felt I could go away from the set and not worry about the way things were going to get done. I think it's pretty good. I'm not objective. After being in it and hanging around it and looking at it, and I helped Buddy edit it, I don't know, I think it will be a very commercial film.

PAUL: *I know there's only one orangutan in the film, but did you use more than one when you shot it?*

CLINT: No, I only used one.

PAUL: *Is this Manis again or a different one?*

CLINT: Huh-uh. Manis has gotten much, much bigger and is about twice his size. This is one that is the exact same size as Manis was.

PAUL: *I didn't realize they got that big. They must be monsters who can hold their own.*

CLINT: They can get up to 350 pounds. Really big mamous.

PAUL: *Have you seen Manis since those movies?*

CLINT: No, we went up one time, but they took him out of the show and use him for breeding. Poor old Manis is just sort of retired there. They use him for a sire and he'll hopefully breed some.

PAUL: *Did you have to wait around an awful lot to get the animal to do whatever it was supposed to?*

CLINT: No, it was easy. That trainer just took the animal and taught him all the things that he thought he needed to know in the script. The one thing you can't do is sit and intellectualize with the animal. The animal is like a child. What you have to do is you set a light little mood and just start shooting. Shoot the slates at the end, and allow them the freedom of that spontaneity the first time.

34

CLINT: Have you seen anything new at all?

PAUL: *Not much, no. I watched a lot on TV.*

CLINT: I ran into Chuck Champlin [arts editor at the *Los Angeles Times*] yesterday for a second. We started talking about new films, and I was so embarrassed because I haven't seen anything. It's mostly because I was just away working all summer and I haven't gotten a chance to. I'd love to go see *The Stunt Man* and a few things. I'd like to see *Willie & Phil*. I like Paul Mazursky because he doesn't blow a lot of dough on films, he tries to tell the story with a certain economy of style and movement, and, I guess because he's an ex-actor, he doesn't try to intrude the directing technique in on top of his stories.

PAUL: *I keep going back to* Apocalypse Now. *I've seen it about six times.*

CLINT: That's a happening-type movie.

PAUL: *I like that movie a lot. I haven't seen much either.* Close Encounters of the Third Kind, *the new version, and* Airplane! *are all I've seen.*

CLINT: I haven't seen anything. God, I'm so far behind.

PAUL: *Do you like Spielberg's stuff?*

CLINT: I thought he did a terrific job in *Jaws*. I know he had a lot of problems on that picture with the weather and all the elements working against him.

PAUL: *And the mechanical shark, I guess.*

CLINT: My favorite picture he's done is *Duel*. I saw it in a screening room run as a movie without any commercials in it. That's another case of a guy who did a lot under circumstances where he didn't have a lot to spend. He did a nice job with it. It had a nice movement to it. It was a provocative idea. I like crazy ideas like that, I guess that's why it appealed to me. The idea of a truck as an antagonist. I haven't seen any footage on this new one that he's got out [*1941*].

PAUL: *I hear not too good things about it. I hear it's like sort of* Animal House, Part II. *Another forty-million-dollar job, I heard.*

CLINT: It cost thirty-five or somewhere in there. That would be a lot of money for an *Animal House*. When you figure that if a film grosses thirty million bucks—that's a damn good grossing film— you're banking on eighty or ninety million dollars to break even.

PAUL: *Which would put you, what, in the top ten or twenty of all time?*

CLINT: That's a long crapshoot, to say, "Look, this is going to be one of the top ten movies of all time." Let's face it, if you do a film for forty million dollars and it isn't the greatest movie of all time, then you've failed because that is an awful lot of money to spend on a movie.

It's what the picture calls for. A lot of times you can call on too much for a film. You can call on too much dough, too much indulgence for a film, then you start laying back and directing from the easy chair over there rather than standing on your feet and slugging it out. It changes your attitude. You're seeing it now all the time. A lot of people who have done really good small films are just doing big ones. Stanley Kubrick's probably the greatest example of it. Started out with a great little film, *The Killing*, and then even up through *A Clockwork Orange* he was doing films that had a reasonable limit and expenditure.

Maybe the security goes. You don't have to have any security to direct a low-budget film when you don't have the power to direct anything else. But once you get to a certain status, maybe you start thinking, Well, what the hell.

PAUL: *Kubrick seems to have lost his ear completely for American speech.* The Shining *is so stilted. I don't see why he would want it that way.*

CLINT: I never saw so many good actors, really good performers you've seen in many, many films—all these people who are old pros—come off so stiff. I have to assume that they were just beaten down by the whole overall thing.

PAUL: *Apparently everything was like eighty takes. It appears like, out of the eighty, he took the worst.*

CLINT: I think he was on overage there, on salary, and he was probably figuring, Well, what the hell, I'm making a fortune on this one. Probably, if you went back and assembled the film with all the first and second takes, the actors would be tremendous. They'd probably all have a lot more energy.

PAUL: *Why even make a film that's supposed to be a horror film that isn't the least bit scary?*

CLINT: That's the thing. I was joking the other day because Kubrick had put that byline on the movie poster: "A masterpiece of modern horror." Even some of the execs at the studio said, "Stanley, maybe you better wait and let some reviewer stick that byline on the film, because it might be considered a little forward of *you* to do it." Evidently that got overruled and he just went ahead and did it. We were talking about ads for *Any Which Way You Can.* I said, "Well, maybe we should call it 'a masterpiece in modern comedy and adventure.'"

PAUL: *I went to a screening of* The Shining *with Jay in New York. Jay knows Malcolm McDowell pretty well. Mary Steenburgen was there, too. I wondered what McDowell was going to think of this since he'd worked with Kubrick in* A Clockwork Orange. *Half an hour into it, I was praying it was going to end pretty quick. It was just deadly to sit through. Later I asked McDowell, "What did you think?" He said, "That was the biggest piece of shit I ever saw in my life." Nobody knew how to act after that. Everybody was sitting around sort of looking at their feet and wondering, Whoa, was that really that bad?*

CLINT: We had the screening here, within the company at Warner Bros. with everybody's invited guests, and it was awful. Unfortunately the scary parts were not very scary. If it had been a new director, they would've bombed it right out of the building. But the fact that the man has a certain charisma going for him, a certain background going for him, I thought the critics were really quite kind to him considering. He might not have thought so, but considering.

PAUL: *Oh, they were. A lot of them put forth the really specious argument that he's "risen above the horror genre." The fact is, he was trying to make a horror movie and failed dismally.*

CLINT: It was just a giant failure. The greatest example in the picture is that there just wasn't anything at all terrifying about it. That ax scene, coming in with the ax to hit Scat [Crothers], it's dead as a dick.

PAUL: *And to build that whole set, that hotel, was a grotesque waste of money.*

CLINT: It's ironic that it's the same man who thirty years ago would've gone up to the Timberline Lodge, which they used for the exteriors, or rented some lodge and gone in and shot the actual sets, and would've used much less pretentious photography. It probably would've been really exciting.

PAUL: *The décor and everything was so perfect, it drew so much attention to itself, that it blanked itself right out. It's a real interior decorator movie. There's no emotion left. You're just reduced to endlessly tracking up and down corridors for an hour and a half.*

CLINT: The thing is, you get a good Steadicam shot going around four corridors and you fall in love with the shot. This is something that young directors usually do. Usually as you go along more, as you get a little older, you start realizing that the audience doesn't care about that shot. They're not counting the cuts. You talk to the general public about how good it is, all they know is emotion. They're affected a certain way by the timing, the cutting, the pacing, and stuff like that. So a director *can* fall in love with his own shots. And I guess I've done it at times.

PAUL: *That's all he's involved with now. He seems not to have any rapport with his actors or any warmth left with people. There wasn't anybody likable in that film. He's more worried about "Is* *that shade of orange, one quarter inch from the top of the screen on the right, exactly the right shade of orange?"*

CLINT: The execs here at the studio were all called to England, and he kept them there for ten days, sitting in a hotel room, just standing around—you know how expensive all that is—to see the movie. The reason he wouldn't show the movie is because one or two lines had to be re-looped.

PAUL: *This man does not seem to be living in the real world anymore.*

CLINT: I guess what you're saying is absolutely true, because he's not: the guy lives in a walled-off kind of thing, never goes to town. He's afraid to fly, won't go anywhere, won't travel—expose himself to the world. The world has changed a lot now.

PAUL: *So he sits and solves these nonexistent technical problems that nobody gives a shit about. Where they got the idea that he was such a great film technician—it doesn't show up. It's not a particularly well-made film.*

CLINT: Yeah, God.

PAUL: *That scene where [Jack] Nicholson freezes to death is right out of* The Last Hunt.

CLINT: The whole picture should have been probably made in about eight weeks or less, because the setups were all relatively simple except for tracking around after the kid. I wonder if a guy like that looks back at *The Killing* and realizes what a good little film it is.

PAUL: *I'll bet not. I think he's embarrassed by it.*

CLINT: He probably thinks it's a piece of crap, that he'd do it much better now. Somebody asked me just the other day, "Would you like to go back and do *Play Misty*, your first film, again?" and I said, "If I was doing it now I'd probably do a lot of things different, but who knows if it'd be any better. It might even wreck it."

PAUL: *You can. It's pretty hard to go back and redo something. A lot of its merit was its naïveté and its youngness and its exuberance, and it's pretty hard to do that. You'd do well to leave it alone.*

CLINT: I suppose I could give it a little more pizzazz in some of the production aspects. I probably would get too slick or something, approach it with a different attitude.

PAUL: *I dug up a lot of stuff that I wrote fifteen years ago, and I'm a better writer now in a lot of different ways. But there was a real feeling in that early writing, a real naïveté and a real charm to it, that wouldn't be there now because I was younger then.*

CLINT: There was probably a certain energy.

PAUL: *I'm not that guy anymore, but I like that guy and he wrote pretty well. I couldn't rewrite that myself because I'm not that same person today.*

CLINT: You approach things differently. It's the same with a film. You'd approach it differently. Now whether you'd approach it better or not ...

PAUL: *I know we were talking about D.O.A. once, and I read someplace that somebody, I forget who, is remaking it now.*

CLINT: It's a great little idea. It could always work. I looked at it as a possible remake, but there were certain problems about it. Another thing is, to me it was kind of a classic. I loved *D.O.A.* There's something pretentious about taking a film like that and doing it again. When you do it again you can spoil it with gloss.

PAUL: *If Kubrick remade* The Killing, *I bet he'd turn it into a twenty-five-million-dollar film. I bet he would.*

CLINT: Success ruined an awful lot of people. Just because, I don't know, your feet go off the ground.

PAUL: *I would imagine it would be easier to handle later, if you've had a tougher time, like you did, for instance. Not to say that if you had been an overnight success you'd have been any different, but you might have had different temptations.*

CLINT: Probably. All the frustrations you have in life definitely go into making you up. Now, some people, it makes them more bitter and they swear to get even or whatever—an I-had-to-suffer-you-have-to-suffer kind of attitude—but some people learn by it, get character by it, hopefully.

PAUL: *Brian De Palma's* Dressed to Kill, *that was another thing I saw recently. I really thought it was bad. There's a difference between outright theft and homage, and this was just like* Psycho *tarted up and modded up.*

CLINT: If you analyze *Psycho* there are no big appliances particularly with people being cut in two. It seems like nowadays a lot of people are trying to just outdo it with all kinds of modern technique, where you get the best makeup guy for slicing legs off and all. It seems like some of the real master film guys would give you the illusion and the shock without the gore.

PAUL: *There are only really two scary moments in* Psycho: *the shower murder and when Martin Balsam goes up the stairs.*

CLINT: Really nothing much happened, but it was the presentation up to it, the way it was all edited together. I haven't seen this one that you're talking about.

PAUL: Dressed to Kill *is just all pointlessly sexed up and sensationalized up with every ten minutes, pretty mechanically, a real flash scene. It's just so mechanical—and so cold.*

CLINT: You've got to care. Too many stories don't care. That was the thing that attracted me to *Play Misty*, the fact that there was a problem that people could identify with. If you could get them to caring about the problem—the guy who's about to lose the girlfriend, and getting the two of them back together—and the insane girl being the wedge in between, then you can work it into a nice psychotic thing but still have problems that people could relate to. Even *Psycho*, as clever a film as it was in its time, if you asked someone what the story is now they'd be hard put to explain what the plot was. The plot was really incidental to those great shocking moments.

PAUL: *Actually,* Misty *has probably even less blood than* Psycho *almost.*

CLINT: [doubtfully] There was a lot of blood in there. It's not dwelled on. I didn't do any special appliances with open wounds or do anything tricky like that.

PAUL: *It's more interested in the people.*

CLINT: If you're rooting for somebody to *not* get stabbed, which is what we want, then it's the rooting for them that makes it so shocking when it does happen. If you don't care and it doesn't make any difference, you're sitting there watching a happening. There are a bunch of happening pictures.

PAUL: *De Palma gets so desperate to have these knockout scenes in* Dressed to Kill *that two of them are just dreams that the character has—that you don't realize are dreams. They're just to give him some more flash. That seems to be the cheapest possible way to get a sensational scene in: just have somebody dream one because you need one.*

CLINT: It's got to be hooked to something. Weren't cruelty against women, or crimes against women, committees all outraged about it and up in arms about it? God, I've been accused of blood, but, Jesus, those guys spill more blood than I've ever spilt in my life, and they get praised for it. I guess if you reside in the right place ...

PAUL: *Actually, Jay knows him pretty well, and I met him a couple of times.*

CLINT: I met him with Jay. I liked him, I thought he was a nice fellow.

PAUL: *I liked one of his films a lot. I liked* Obsession, *which a lot of people don't like. I thought* The Fury *was bad.*

CLINT: I didn't see *The Fury.* Is that the one with Kirk Douglas in it?

PAUL: *Yeah. It's sort of like* The Eyes of Laura Mars.

CLINT: I was offered that picture to direct and act in. This was back when [Barbra] Streisand was talking about doing the film and playing the part. It was a model then who saw all these things and it was a great excuse to wear a lot of clothing and stuff. But it seemed very much like a gimmicky kind of idea.

PAUL: *It's tricked up in the latest chicness so that you can pass it off as avant-garde and intellectual flash—therefore it* is *better than Hitchcock.*

CLINT: Did you see *Ordinary People*?

PAUL: *Not yet. In New York at least, they're lining up around the block for it. It seems to be this year's* Kramer vs. Kramer. *That and the new Woody Allen [*Stardust Memories*], which in New York everybody always goes to. In New York it's like he's everything from Buster Keaton to Charlie Chaplin to Fellini to Ingmar Bergman. I think that's rather ludicrous myself. I don't know how he does around the country, but in New York he can do no wrong.*

CLINT: His biggest hit, which won the Academy Award, was like an eighteen-million-dollar film, which is not an unrespectable gross by any means, but when you consider that that's about the biggest and the best ...

PAUL: *That's* Annie Hall, *right? That was almost as much due to Diane Keaton's performance. I don't like Allen much as a director.*

CLINT: I enjoyed *Annie Hall* very much.

PAUL: *I did, too. It was very warm, it had a real soul to it. That was the only film of his that had any real warmth to it.* Manhattan

I really didn't care for. To me, as a director you've made seven, eight films better than Woody Allen's films.

CLINT: Who?

PAUL: *You have.*

CLINT: Oh. Yeah, but he's more in a different cult now.

PAUL: *He's Neil Simon for pseudo-intellectuals. I don't know, I just don't see it myself.*

35

PAUL: *Did* The Enforcer *lawsuit get settled?*

CLINT: I guess I was a relatively good witness because the complaint was thrown out.

PAUL: *Could you go into it from the beginning?*

CLINT: When we did *The Enforcer*, I liked the title of the movie. I'd seen the 1951 movie with Humphrey Bogart. It was produced by a guy whom I worked for at one time, on *Sister Sara*, a guy named Martin Rackin, who has since deceased. It was a Warner Bros. picture, in fact, the Bogart one. So we bought the title *The Enforcer* and we went ahead and we made the movie.

A fella named Andrew Sugar, out of New York, had written a series of paperback books called *The Enforcer*. He sued, claiming that we had stolen his title and affected his business. There was some talk of settlement from the insurance company, and I just said to them, "You absolutely *cannot* settle it. If you settle every time somebody 'nuisances' you to death, eventually they're going to eat you up alive. I *believe* that this fella is wrong and that his suit is wrong." I couldn't understand why anybody would want to settle a lawsuit for something that's bought and paid for: your own picture, your own title, your own company that released it. It just seemed amoral to me. Anytime a movie makes any dough there's always somebody who wants to hop on the bandwagon the cheap way. We had it with *Alcatraz*.

So we went back there and witnessed for them and told the jury exactly how this thing came about. When I was on the stand, the lawyer asked me an open question, which I was hoping he would do, regarding the title. I said, "I don't know, but maybe the fella you're representing was influenced subliminally by seeing the 1951 movie, which came out long before his books came out. I'm just saying that possibility exists, doesn't it?" He said, "Well, yes, but we're hypothesizing," and I said, "Yes, we are." It was just enough to get the jury sitting there going, "Yeah, that makes sense. Why are these guys having to pay for it twice?"

PAUL: *And he was* Adrian *Sugar at that time? He had, uh …*

CLINT: Well, yeah. I guess he'd gone through, he'd changed his, uh, there was a sexual change there or something. It made it a little confusing because the suit was filed as "Andrew" and later became "Adrian."

PAUL: *I would imagine the jury would've been automatically against this type of thing. Probably somewhat biased.*

CLINT: Well, yeah, but I think they were probably instructed pretty heavy by the judge—

PAUL: *To ignore it.*

CLINT: But it's very hard to ignore it.

PAUL: *You kept calling him "Andrew" rather than "Adrian"?*

CLINT: Well, I kept saying, "Mister"—

PAUL: *Mr. Sugar.*

CLINT: —but that's the way the suit was filed. I'd never met the person.

PAUL: *Was he in the court?*

CLINT: She was.

PAUL: *I worked for a record company and I remember some A&R man had promised an act that they would make them big stars. When they didn't become big stars, they took it to court.*

CLINT: Damn, I could've brought that same complaint twenty years ago.

PAUL: *It's amazing that they actually got to court with it. It got tossed out, but it cost the company several thousand dollars in attorneys' fees.*
My experiences with lawyers have been nothing but the lowest.

CLINT: It's a necessary profession, and it's necessary because one thing has pyramided: the malpractice deal, the judgments have been enormous. There are so many lawyers that are coming out of law school every day with nothing to do, they've either got to chase an ambulance or hopefully the better ones will get jobs with law firms. But there are a lot of them who are less than better who are going to have to scrounge and scramble. They figure in the next couple decades in California there's going to be one lawyer for about every hundred people. I'm not anti-lawyer—I work with lawyers all the time—but at the same time everything gets so complicated because it's to the legal profession's benefit to make it complicated. They don't have any simple solutions.

PAUL: *When my divorce came up, it was all just money, money, money. No concern for the people whatsoever.*

CLINT: Oh, sure. Maybe a majority of the couples that are getting divorced continue on through with it because it's an irreconcilable situation, but think of how many times that the legal haggling has driven the wedge even further, that there's no chance of people ever sorting things out themselves because right away the lawyer for her says, "Look, you deserve three times what the guy makes," and the lawyer for him says, "She doesn't deserve half of what you have," and it becomes just a vicious thing.

I was reading in the paper the other day that Norman Mailer said he's going to write a book called *You Never Know a Woman Till You Meet Her in Court* [laughs]. That's obviously the cynicism of a guy who's been through a lot of marriages.

PAUL: *One of the best writers in America, and he hasn't got any money apparently.*[55] *It all goes to alimony payments.*

CLINT: That's the way he carved it out. He got infatuated with signing his name on dotted lines—a marriage license is a legal document—and if you're that crazy with your signature, then you end up that way. We're all that crazy, let's face it. It's just one of those things.

PAUL: *When my father died, the whole estate pretty well went to the lawyers for doing nothing much. The people who supposedly were supposed to get the money got very little of it.*

CLINT: There's a cynicism in the country—I think because of all these things we're talking about, the whole legal aspect and Watergate and Vietnam and everything—growing through the Sixties and Seventies. I think it really reached its peak a few years back, and maybe it's waning a little bit now. We're in an era where nobody believes anything.

It's that kind of thing that attracted me to *Bronco Billy*: that there's a struggling, not-too-talented guy out there whose little band of people, all sort of half-losers trying to be winners, all have a certain morality and do believe that kids should eat their oatmeal in the morning and "do as your mom and pa tell ya, because they know best. Don't ever tell a lie, and say your prayers at night before you go to bed." It's old-fashioned, but

---

[55] Paul was still passionate about Mailer's writing when, in 1991, he discussed the writer's work with singer-songwriter Leonard Cohen: "He's not afraid to look foolish, which is a wonderful quality, I think. He really tries to hit the home run every time. You don't [hit it every time], of course, and you look foolish, I guess, but you've got to take those risks, it seems to me."

the fact that there's a guy out there who believes that when he's saying it is kind of fun.

36

PAUL: *People—not necessarily the audience but executives, sometimes critics, the media—they just tend to take the mainstream for granted. They're always looking at the artists, or the* artistes, *or whomever is being praised at the moment. Sometimes rightly, sometimes wrongly. At the other end are the guys who just crank out six horror films a month and hope that one of them hits, and they're just the panderers. Nobody really pays much attention— and it's the same in music—to the mainstream guys. Thank God the mainstream is always the one taken for granted and ignored. In their time, Ford and Hawks and Hitchcock would've been considered mainstream directors, you know what I mean? No critic ever really wrote about them seriously until the late Fifties.*

CLINT: No, mostly in hindsight.

PAUL: *They were always praising the latest avant-garde genius, who may have made a good film or who may not have. But they got the ink.*

CLINT: Oh sure.

PAUL: *And what usually happens is that the mainstream artist turns out to be the one who lasts. I think you're a mainstream artist.*

CLINT: They seem to not want to like a professional like Hitchcock or Howard Hawks or Ford or those guys, where the body of their work was what meant something. It wasn't *a* picture. Some guys have *a* picture—well, that's great. But what do the other pictures look like? Those guys were probably more interested in what the body of their work looked like—the twenty pictures that they're going to do over their career—and how they all stack up. Some of them are going to be better than others, but how they stack up is why people remember them. That's why they're so good in hindsight, those guys. You start thinking, Gee, there was a ton of really great things that went on in their life, instead of just one high moment. You look back through years of Academy Awards, back through the Thirties, back to the very first ones, a lot of times the people who were up there were never heard from again. As actors and as directors. They'd go, like you say, for the guy of the moment and they're thinking, Oh boy, this new guy's really terrific. And the new guy, all of a sudden he can't ever come back.

PAUL: *With rock & roll it's the flashiest guy or the guy that has the new look, whatever it's going to be. You just want to tell these people sometime, "Look, wouldn't it be funny if the guys who are wearing the normal clothes and are the average band were the best?" It happens that a lot of times they are.*

CLINT: A lot of times they are because the guy who's in the average band is more interested in the music, and is more interested in the performing of the music and bettering the music, than some guy who's coming in wearing an ape suit or a sequin dress or something like that. There are some people who are interested in it for the music, even in rock & roll. That's why a lot of times the person who's just the normal guy comes out and looks strange, but maybe he's just a musician who wants to do the best he can and sing the best he can. He isn't out there presenting some other razzamatazz.

PAUL: *Yet the media gravitate towards the sensational part.*

CLINT: Oh sure, they go for the sensationalism. It's the same thing in films. A lot of directors won't do certain shots because they don't want to distract the audience; and other directors, who gravitate towards the shot, they *want* to distract the audience and direct it back to them, so they say, "Hey, look at that. Boy, that guy really did an interesting thing there." Rather than the other director who says, "I want the *whole body* of the picture to jump out and say, 'That was an interesting thing,'" not *a* shot here, *a* shot there, and call it a day.

PAUL: *Most of the American movies that have really lasted weren't the ones being praised by the critics in the Forties. They were the Bogart films and the Cagney films and the entertainment films.*

CLINT: Sure. If you go back and look at the notices on some of those films—not that anybody ever saves these things—chances are a lot of the best ones weren't that well-received to begin with. They become classics because of time. I've had reviewers who reviewed *Misty* poorly write articles ten years later that were raves on it. They've just gone full circle, maybe without even knowing it. They never said, "I panned this movie, but here's what I think about it today." They just, without even realizing it, went around the circle on it.

PAUL: *James Agee in his collection wrote about a lot of stuff as being really important. He'd write off* The Big Sleep *just in one paragraph as an interesting sort of smoky cocktail and spend eighteen pages on some socially relevant film of the time that hasn't lasted at all.*

CLINT: Right. Nobody cares about it now. Even the unstructured films of those days, nobody thinks of them as classics. Remember *Beat the Devil*, that one of John Huston's where everybody got juiced up and just did their own thing? Unstructured and never-ending, it just wound up and wound down. Never did get going. Everybody thought it was unusual at the time because they all free floated in it.

PAUL: *Actually,* Casablanca, *I guess they never knew how that was going to end.*

CLINT: Yeah, that was one that they were confused with at the time. Nobody liked the script.

PAUL: *And the original casting was going to be something bizarre like Ronald Reagan and Claudette Colbert, something that just wouldn't have worked at all.*

CLINT: In every picture, even if it's a classic picture, there are always one or two key things, from casting to location or whatever, that might've just thrown it off to the point where it wouldn't work.

PAUL: *Dustin Hoffman made* Straw Dogs *with Peckinpah. That was a case where an actor just didn't make that part work at all.*

CLINT: A lot of people criticized *Apocalypse Now* for not having a bigger-than-life presence in the leading role, in the motoring role of the film. The Willard role. Which was sort of an opposite tact. Usually, instead of criticizing the mythic thing, a lot of critics whom I read felt the need *for* that kind of strength to make that thing work. But the other fellow [Martin Sheen] played it fine on another level.

PAUL: *I got suckered by Pauline Kael's review into going to see* Fingers.

CLINT: *Fingers?*

PAUL: Fingers.

CLINT: She's suckered a lot of people into getting dis-employed over the years.

PAUL: *It's directed by James Toback. Toback wrote* The Gambler, *which James Caan was in. He wrote some books. He's sort of a Norman Mailer imitator. He was apparently one of Kael's escorts pretty frequently. The first 3,000 words of her review were ecstasy incarnate and then later, among the last thirteen or fourteen thousand words, were some reservations.*

CLINT: She must have been talking about the date and not the movie [laughs].

PAUL: Incredibly *excessive. No discipline whatsoever.*

CLINT: She likes that stuff. Or else butter [chuckles].

PAUL: *Twenty minutes into it I could not believe it. God, are they showing the reels in the right order? This isn't as bad as I think it is, is it? It couldn't possibly be. After forty minutes I just couldn't sit through it. I walked out on it finally.*

CLINT: You can't call it reviewing. What's amazing is that people have stood still for it. She's suckered so many people in that area of the country [New York] and that small group of people who are aficionados of various film reviews. She's really suckered them into thinking she knows something. That's what's so funny. It becomes kind of a joke. Just making a lot of outrageous statements not having any bearing on anything, but you're doing them because you've found that that's the avenue to get attention. That's exactly what the secret to Kael is: she's found a way to get attention.[56]

37

In 1962, to capitalize on his burgeoning TV stardom, Eastwood recorded an album, *Rawhide's Clint Eastwood Sings Cowboy Favorites*. Among the songs he covered were "Don't Fence Me In," "Tumbling Tumbleweeds," and "Mexicali Rose."

CLINT: The head of Cameo-Parkway Records wanted to do an album of Western music. Not country-western music—Western music. Straight old cowboy type. I wasn't really too fond of it.

PAUL: *You mean like "Jesse James" and songs like that?*

CLINT: Yeah, like "San Antonio Rose" or any of those oldies.

PAUL: *This was during the* Rawhide *days?*

CLINT: Yeah. It was just really thrown together. They had no real composer or conductor or anything. The guy who ran the session was a former bass player with Stan Kenton. He was a

---

[56] According to Sondra Locke in *The Good, the Bad & the Very Ugly*, her book about her turbulent relationship and breakup with Eastwood, he used to obsess about Pauline Kael's negative reviews of his work: "She drove Clint crazy. After her review of *The Enforcer*, Clint asked a psychiatrist to do an analysis of her from her reviews; it concluded that Kael was actually physically attracted to Clint and because she couldn't have him she hated him. Therefore, it was some sort of vengeance according to Clint. He told others that Kael had recently phoned him to apologize, saying, 'Sorry about those reviews, Clint, but you know that's what's expected of me.' But Clint later admitted to me that she had never called him; his story was a fabrication."

good bass player and I was a big fan of Kenton's music, but every man to his specialty [laughing].

PAUL: [chuckles] *I don't think Kenton played "San Antonio Rose" very often.*

CLINT: A waste of time is what it amounted to. I don't recall whether the company stayed in business much after that was released. I've done a lot of records along the way that just never got heard because they were for companies that folded or never got off the ground. I did a few singles for an outfit in Nashville. The parent company was called Certron, a company that makes blank tape, and they somehow got talked into the record business. When I got off the plane here I learned they'd terminated the head of the company as I was flying back. As I was recording, they were closing shop and we didn't know that. So nobody ever heard the singles. They took all the material that had been recorded by four or five different recording people and just threw it in the basement somewhere.

PAUL: *I remember when I was working for Mercury in the early Seventies, somebody way higher up had asked if you could do a record for them, but you didn't do it. The answer was that you felt that you were at the top of your profession in the movies, and making a record wouldn't necessarily work unless you felt that it would.*

CLINT: A lot of times they were capitalizing on television actors. If the guys are on a series they figure, well, they can get a few airplays out of them. But what it boils down to is you don't get much airplay if the product isn't there. You might get one turn from the DJ or the program director who says, "Oh yeah, I watch that television show," but by and large if they don't like the sound of it, it doesn't make any difference if it's the president of the United States.

PAUL: *Sondra said you really perk up around musicians more than any other group of people.*

CLINT: Yeah, I like musicians.

PAUL: *You were a music major for a short time.*

CLINT: Well, not really. I just kind of got into it as a kid. Either through a lack of interest or a lack of talent, I never followed through completely. I guess I respect people who did follow through with it and did more with it.

PAUL: *Mainly piano, I guess?*

CLINT: I fiddle with it. I don't fiddle with it much anymore.[57]

PAUL: *Maybe it was the* Playboy *interview, but I thought it said that you had said somewhere that for a short time you'd majored in music.*

CLINT: I was going to go to school and major in music, then I got drafted out of it. But I played the saloons as a kid—played *a* saloon in Oakland. It was a form of making a living, and free beer.

PAUL: *Did you sing as well?*

CLINT: I just played. I was way too inhibited to sing in those days.

PAUL: *Could you play "Misty" for me [chuckles]?*

CLINT: [laughs] That wasn't written then.

PAUL: *You told me that you're not too fond of country music.*

CLINT: In the old days, I don't think I understood the older country music, the Bob Wills era, as much. Maybe it was just that I hadn't exposed myself to it. But nowadays, with Kenny Rogers and the various people who are into it, and Eddie Rabbitt, who we've used before on *Loose*, there's a wide variety of people.

---

[57] In later years, Eastwood would compose the scores for several of his own films—*Mystic River* (2003), *Million Dollar Baby* (2004, for which he was nominated for a Grammy), *Flags of Our Fathers* (2006), *Changeling* (2008), and *Hereafter* (2010)—and, in 2007, another director's movie, James C. Strouse's *Grace Is Gone*.

Country music has taken such a wide spectrum today. There are just so many different types.

PAUL: *You said you were more oriented toward black music and jazz.*

CLINT: I was raised in an area where black music was a very prominent influence. We used to listen to a lot of jazz and a lot of rhythm and blues stations. But I like country music. In those days it seemed that pop music was the balladeers—the Sinatras and Etta Jameses and then the Billy Eckstines and the Frankie Laines—and they told simple kinds of stories in a melodious way. Country singers were hard to understand, more twangy, kind of rinky-dink. Now it seems it's reversed itself. It seems like the country singers are more the balladeers and singing their stories, and pop music is more hard rock, *in the total* more concerned with the sound.

PAUL: *Some of it is.*

CLINT: As well as that, the lyrics don't mean as much as they did to the early pop music.

PAUL: *Uh, it depends. Clint, I'd like to make up a cassette for you of some of the best rock & roll, because it's not what you hear on radio necessarily.*

CLINT: I understand. I like little bits of everything, but for long periods of time rock & roll doesn't do much for me.

PAUL: *Pop music is ruled by the radio anymore. You don't necessarily hear the most interesting artists on the radio or the most challenging or the best. You hear more or less the commodities on the radio.*

CLINT: That record you gave me by Bruce [Springsteen] was terrific. There are some really good people out there. It's just that you *are* ruled by the radio. Basically, on the way to and from work is where you get your education on what's going on with popular music.

PAUL: *They're not playing the challenging stuff. Interestingly enough, where rock & roll once symbolized some sort of rebellion and personal meaning, it's become completely the opposite almost and it's become a total commodity. One guy imitates the next guy who imitates the next guy.*

CLINT: Like movies, where somebody gets a hit and everybody says, "Let's do that." A little horror movie's in? "Let's make ten more of them."

PAUL: *Have you seen rock videos?*

CLINT: Some of them are quite imaginative, the MTV things.

PAUL: *God, they just seem to me like licensed narcissism in most cases, where these groups are really preening and the director has had a lot of avant-garde film class number 1A. They're going to move everything in the world for three minutes.*

CLINT: A lot of them probably are trying to do exactly what you're saying. They're saying, "Hey, look at this stuff. Now you're going to hire me to do a main feature someday."

PAUL: *Do you know how much some of them are costing these days? Up to one million dollars for three minutes.*

CLINT: Really? God.

PAUL: *Not many, but there are several that have cost a half a million.*

CLINT: I saw that Herbie Hancock one ["Rockit"] the other day where he has robots and dummies and stuff like that. There are no humans in it. That's kind of imaginative. I like that.

PAUL: *I can't stand them myself for the most part. Most of them move so quickly, and the more elaborate they are the less you get out of the song. The best ones are the rather simple ones, where the guy is singing the song, or there isn't a cut every one-quarter second to ten more images, and you actually get the feel for the song.*

CLINT: Because they are usually synonymous with rock music, they go with that beat and try to keep that energy up. Their feelings are, I think, that they want to keep a humorous aspect.

PAUL: *[chuckles] I'm really much more negative than you are about it, I'm afraid. I just think most of them have no structure at all and they have even less so when these guys get in there. I guess watching films for all these years, I just cannot stand to watch those things.*

CLINT: You're comparing them with a movie. If you don't compare them with a movie and just put them in an element by themselves, then they're fine. I wouldn't particularly dig a whole film that way.

PAUL: *A lot of them try to be miniature films. That's the new trend now, to make an entire movie in three minutes. I've read some incredible quotes that what this is, you know, is just stripping down a two-hour movie, which is "way too long," "to the absolute essence." And it's such bullshit.*

CLINT: Well, you can find a bullshit story for everything. People can write anything into anything.

38

PAUL: *You made a couple in a row pretty quick. Firefox [1982] must've been a long film.*

CLINT: That wasn't too long, but getting those visual effects shots was like pulling teeth. Tough stuff to do. The kind of film which, if I had been an indulgent soul, would have cost fifty million dollars to make. I wasn't just dying to do a visual effects movie. That's why *Honkytonk Man* [1982] was so much fun, because I jumped right into a little movie right here on the planet. Right here in the world's small picture.

PAUL: *I really thought* Honkytonk Man *was great.*

CLINT: It was fun to do. Maybe someday thirty years from now somebody will say, "Hey, let's look at that film."

PAUL: *Oh, I think so. Did you have Kyle in mind when you first read the book?*[58]

CLINT: No, I never did because when I read the book he was only about a twelve-year-old. It was written for a fourteen-year-old kid. Then I asked Sondra one day, "Do you think he could play that part?" This was when he was fourteen, and she said, "I think so." So we gave it a shot. She worked with him a while, though.

PAUL: *It's pretty gutsy in that what would have happened if he hadn't been good?*

CLINT: Oh yeah, I'd have had to fire him and go on. It would've been terrible.

PAUL: *Has he been bitten by the bug?*

CLINT: I think he likes it. I thought he was very good in it.

PAUL: *Oh, he was! He seems to have the instincts. He doesn't overplay and he never gets cute.*

CLINT: That's the tough thing with kids. Most of them are so cutesy pie, I can't stand kid actors as a rule. You've just got to find the kid with the right kind of personality and then let him go. If they go to those acting schools, it screws them up.

PAUL: *They come out sounding like confident sixty-year-olds, little Noel Cowards or something.*

CLINT: Exactly. Kids are naturals. They naturally act and, if you get them in the right mood, they do naturally what adults try to do. Usually, if you attend acting classes, you find all the actors

---

[58] Following in his father's early footsteps, Kyle Eastwood had already appeared in uncredited roles in *The Outlaw Josey Wales* and *Bronco Billy*. His sister Alison made her uncredited debut as one of the orphans in *Bronco Billy*.

are on the floor playing some sense-memory game and stuff like that. Kids do this all the time. The other day, Alison was eating an imaginary hamburger. I was watching her out of my peripheral vision because I didn't want to let her know I was watching her, and she was just going on and on about how great this hamburger was. I can remember doing that in acting classes thirty-some years ago. Silly things like that.

God, I remember acting classes where you were playing chairs and teapots and banging your head on the floor and doing crazy improvisation. They were all fun and they taught you a release. They were ways of getting you to release yourself or focus your concentration on the ridiculous, like a child can do. A child can sit there and do that, he can be anything he wants, because children are naturally fantastic actors. The moment we start growing up and we start piling all the inhibitions and all the problems of our lives on top of it, and all the things that we think we're supposed to be and not supposed to be, then we can't act anymore. What you have to do as an adult is tear all those layers back off again and go back to having the same childlike mentality you had as a kid. You can throw the switch in your head and become whatever you want to become. Much like Bronco Billy states: you can become what you want to be. "I'm who I want to be."

That is why to me acting is not an intellectual art—although a lot of actors try to pretend it is and try to intellectualize on it—but it really is an emotional art. The best thing with kids is to talk to them like adults, get them acting, and they'll live it. Play games with them, talk with them intelligently. If you try force, they become inhibited.

PAUL: *The feel for the music was great, too. That whole sequence in the studio at the end and those two monumental close-ups were really terrific. In that end scene where they sing over your grave, I got a little worried when the black guy comes out. I thought, Oh no, he's not going to soar into a long hymn. But then it turns out he's got a lousy voice, too.*

CLINT: No, just some guy who maybe does it in church on Sunday.

PAUL: *Was* Honkytonk Man *a high-risk project going in?*

CLINT: It goes back to that old *Beguiled* problem: how do you go to your strong-suit audience that queues up for all the action films and say to them, "Look, come on and see this but don't expect it to be the same"? And how do you go to the other people who don't go to see the action things, and say, "This is something that maybe you'll like because it's not along the lines of the other things"? It's almost impossible to do. I knew going in it wasn't going to be the kind of thing that people would queue up forever on, but I was just hoping we'd get a certain country audience along the way.

PAUL: *You're definitely not playing it safe.*

CLINT: My career was born out of crazy things, starting from going to Italy or Spain to make a Western, so there's no reason why not to continue the trend. At least that way you expose yourself to new things.

It was an easy movie to make, it didn't cost a lot, and with cable television sales and all the various sales elements, it'll be fine. Sometimes you get lucky and cross over. A lot of people predicted that the one with the orangutan wouldn't go anywhere because it wasn't me with a pistol, but it broke into another area. Sometimes they do. You've just got to keep branching out in your life. I'd hate to look back and say, "Gee, I did twelve Dirty Harrys and six Westerns, and that was my career," without trying other elements. It would be a very unsatisfying career.

39

In 1982, Eastwood donated $30,000 to James G. "Bo" Gritz (rhymes with *rights*), a one-time Green Beret colonel who'd served in the Vietnam War as part of the US Army Special Forces. Gritz was planning a raid on Laos to rescue American soldiers purportedly still held in prison camps there.

PAUL: *[sighs] I suppose I have to ask you something about this Bo Gritz thing. Do you want to talk about it at all or would you rather not?*

CLINT: Well, I'll tell you, the problem with that is that there have been just too many people shooting off their mouths to the press—and it was from *his* camp, *he* and his group. I do believe that anybody who's going to go over there and try to search out possible MIAs, their heart is in the right place. They're trying to do something.

PAUL: *And certainly they're over there, too.*

CLINT: Well, some people believe that there are some there, and there seems to be some evidence of it sometimes, but what happened was there were so many warring factions within that group. I was asked to help support that and I said yes I would. I know we kept a very low profile on it. The press hounded me about it and I said I would make no comment. I still haven't made any comments on it. You're the first person I've even discussed it with in the press. I don't have a publicist and, other than a few publications a year, I try to keep a low profile. I don't want to be seen a lot. It embarrasses me a little bit to have things written about me. To have people using this thing and then going off and dealing with the press on it just didn't make sense. A lot of the press would be real responsible and probably be cooperative with these people, but there's an awful lot that wouldn't be. They've got to sell papers and that's it. There's an old World War II saying, I remember as a kid seeing it everywhere: loose lips sink ships. And the only ship that these people, this group, seemed to sink was their own.

PAUL: *The approach seemed to be very sensationalistic, like "war hawk Eastwood."*

CLINT: It wasn't intended that way.

PAUL: *Of course not! But that's the approach that they took.*

CLINT: I thought these people were on to something, and I said to them, "I wouldn't be able to sleep at night if I thought there was *one* person over there. Whether he was sent over there by his own will, or whether he was inducted by the country or activated out of the reserve or whatever, and he went over there and was still a prisoner there, it would be hard for me to sleep at night knowing that was the case." I had the entrée to a lot of things for these people, but unfortunately they seemed to be grandstanders.

PAUL: *The Gritz people.*

CLINT: They seemed to have gone public with the thing without any consultation with me or anything.

PAUL: *They went so pubic that it actually appeared in an issue of* Soldier of Fortune *before the raid. Or there was a tip, so that they were waiting for Gritz over there because they'd already seen it in* Soldier of Fortune.

CLINT: I don't know if that was the case or not. There was so much loose discussion going on in that section of the world, so much loose lips going on, that if they—the other side, the Laotian countries or Cambodia or whatever—*didn't* know, it was no fault of their own [laughs].

PAUL: *Maybe not the entire story that you're talking about appeared, but something actually appeared in print before the raid.*

CLINT: Somebody over there, I don't know who exactly it was, was reporting to a representative of the *LA Times* in Bangkok. They were keeping him abreast of everything. You know reporters, their livelihood is not keeping secrets. I'm not saying they're unpatriotic or something like that, but they're in the business to not keep secrets, they're in the business to sell publications. Once you know where a person's incentive lies, then you know how to deal with them. I just don't see any reason why anybody would ever want to go to the press with something like that. They were getting comments out of some of the other people who were involved—

PAUL: *William Shatner.*

CLINT: —but I've never made a comment on it and I'm really not commenting on it now. I'm just commenting on a *philosophy,* that I think that you're not doing any good for the cause you're talking about, and you're not doing any good for anybody, if you're just going off half-cocked and making statements. You end up counterproductive to what you might be trying to accomplish.

PAUL: *You actually felt strongly enough about the POWs to call [President Ronald] Reagan and say that the government should go search for them.*[59] *That's what I read. I don't know if it's true or not.*

CLINT: That is not the case.

PAUL: *That's not true?*

CLINT: I'm not going to say what went on, but I'll say I wouldn't be adverse to at least letting him know. If there was any validity to this story that could help, to me it would be incomprehensible that the government would ignore real hard evidence that there was something there. That is the only thing that I can say. My feelings on it now, after studying it a little bit, is that the government *would not* ignore real hard evidence that anybody was there and, contrary to what anybody tells you, I feel that they are as interested as anybody else in any possible things like that.

PAUL: *I also heard it reported that you had given them money as a screen treatment payment rather than a donation.*

CLINT: No, I didn't do any of that.

PAUL: *The implication was that you were "buying a screenplay" by doing this.*

CLINT: That was what Shatner did. Evidently he was buying some life rights or something like that.[60] I bought nothing. In fact, my

---

[59] Eastwood and Reagan were both actors who had starred in films with primates (Eastwood with *Every Which Way but Loose* and *Any Which Way You Can*, Reagan with *Bedtime for Bonzo*) before venturing into politics. Clint, who supported Reagan's successful campaigns for president in both 1980 and 1984, would run for mayor of Carmel in 1986.

[60] Shatner optioned the rights to Gritz's story for $10,000.

statement to them was, "I don't want any screen rights. I'm not interested in this as a movie." I don't know whether that disappointed them or not. Now I've maybe had second thoughts, but I said, "I know you're not interested in this as a movie—you're interested in getting to the bottom of this—so there are no attachments to this. If twenty years from now you want to talk about doing something, that's fine [laughs]. But I don't even want to discuss it."

PAUL: *I could imagine what you were going through with the reporters and the phone ringing every five minutes.*

CLINT: Ah, Jesus, you can believe it. *The Washington Post*, the *Times*, you name it, every newspaper in the world called here. We just were unavailable. You just think people are smarter than that, and you give them a lesson from years of experience. You really just have to be careful if you're going to do something as delicate as they were talking about doing, that can have a lot of implications not just as far as the country's concerned—because the country can take it—but as far as people's feelings. Feelings of families and stuff like that. They get building up false hopes for people where there's no hope really and that sort of thing, and that's where I get disenchanted. Putting up dough or taking a reconnaissance, that's okay, but to give people false hope ...

40

The evening before this conversation, Eastwood invited Don Siegel and Paul to an advance screening of *Sudden Impact*, the fourth Dirty Harry picture. This time around, Callahan encounters a rape victim (Sondra Locke) who, unbeknownst to him, is murdering, one by one, the men who several years ago brutally beat and raped her and her younger sister. Her sister has been in a catatonic state ever since.

Early in the film, Harry confronts a band of robbers in a coffee shop and informs them, "Well, we're not just going to let you walk out of here." "Who's 'we,' sucker?" one of the crooks wants to know. Harry pulls out his trademark .44 Magnum and says, "Smith and Wesson and me." (A line that, when he talked with Paul, Clint claimed responsibility for.) True to his word, none of the crooks walk out of the place—but not before Callahan speaks the movie's most famous catchphrase: "Go ahead, make my day."

PAUL: *I guess you should probably just tell me about the beginnings of* Sudden Impact *[1983]—the script and the problems you foresaw in it, how you envisioned you were going to do it, the look of it, and all of that.*

CLINT: The script just sort of popped out of nowhere. It was strictly by accident. I was going to make another type of movie out of it. This guy asked me to read the treatment. It was a small script actually, with some scenes and some explanations. It was this story of this woman and there was just a small cop part in it, nothing real big. I told Sondra that I would produce this film with her—I wouldn't be in it—because it was kind of interesting. We went to rewrites and never could get it rewritten right.

So I met this young writer [Joseph C. Stinson] through mutual friends. He was a young guy from Philadelphia, and I just got a feeling that he may be able to do something, so I said, "Would you like to try rewriting this?" I told him what I had in mind. It turned out he was a big aficionado of *Dirty Harry*, so he just took a swing at it and all of a sudden he came back and it was like sixty, seventy percent Dirty Harry in the script. "Gee, I don't know," I said, "that wasn't what I had in mind." But it was pretty good, so I finally said, "Okay, go ahead and take another swing at it, but just go all the way. Go all out as a Dirty Harry." So he did. He went all out and came back in, and Fritz and I looked at it the day he submitted it. I said, "Hell, let's go ahead with it." We got our motors up and got running. There seemed to be a great public feeling about seeing Dirty Harry again. That and Westerns.

PAUL: *I was real glad I didn't know anything about it. Mikal Gilmore asked me about it, and I said, "I'm just going to speak very generally about this because you just really ought to go and let it hit you. Because it's going to hit you. You're going to think about it for hours afterwards, and I really wouldn't be doing you* *any favors to tell you what it's about. So don't read anything about it. Go see it. You're going to really be amazed by it."*[61]

CLINT: I figured maybe it'd be better to see it and then you can refer back. You'll see what we left in and what we left out.

PAUL: *Why is Harry called Donnelly in the script?*

CLINT: When this guy was writing the script, I said to him, "Don't write it as Harry," because I didn't want him to get the studio all charged up before making a decision I wanted to do it. I decided, "We'll just leave it Donnelly, and if anybody comes across the script they'll never know the difference." When I took it up to the studio and I gave them the script, I told them, "Just read this guy Donnelly as Callahan."

PAUL: *It sort of has a* Misty *look to it.* Play Misty *and* Vertigo.

CLINT: Over the years, I'd had the idea of maybe Dirty Harry going down to Santa Cruz. I've always wanted to shoot there. It still has the San Francisco feeling, the northern California feeling, but it's not as cosmopolitan as San Francisco.

PAUL: *You said you wanted this film to have a particular look and style. How did you conceive it visually?*

CLINT: I just conceived it as moving very rapidly from sequence to sequence, very glib kind of.

PAUL: *The momentum just carries you. I thought the whole movie had that sort of* rush *to it. You almost have to keep it moving fast because you're really not sure sometimes what part of the plot you're in. It almost has enough plot for all three Dirty Harrys. It's just bing, bing, bing, bing, and they're so fast that it almost becomes a texture of life for this to happen. The minor incidents flow into the major plot and it's nonstop almost.*

---

[61] Writer Mikal Gilmore remembers: "He came out and stayed at my place once for about a week when he was working on the Clint Eastwood story. We would stay up all night watching old movies."

CLINT: The steamroller gets rolling downhill and you're off and running.

PAUL: *Because of the speed and because of all the violence and so many characters and so many subplots, I thought that it had a real nightmarish vision. I know Siegel described* Dirty Harry *as wall-to-wall violence; this seemed to have that even more so. A modern urban nightmare. You walk out the door and six guys are there trying to kill you. At the risk of sounding pretentious, it's really sort of a poem of violence.*

CLINT: I wanted to have that feeling. I didn't want to make it a new old movie: Dirty Harry's back doing the exact same scenes. To me, it had to be a whole different movie. All of the Dirty Harrys, I've always thought, should be able to stand on their own. They shouldn't have to be tied to seeing one of the other ones. That's the thing with this picture, too: you get a little bit of how his *modus operandi* is and then finally you get where her [the Sondra Locke character's] problems are coming from, and you slowly bring them together. Prior to that you think maybe she's a schizophrenic, a duel personality. One minute she's a pretty sharp-looking chick about town and another minute she's out offing guys. Her life, her motivations, are all sparked by a nightmarish thing. She's like the antagonist but yet *not* the antagonist—sort of this tormented creature. And here's this guy who seems to get into trouble everywhere he goes. Chaos follows him. And they cross paths.

PAUL: *Don found part of it a little confusing at times. There were a couple points where I was wondering what had happened, but then when I thought about them later I figured them out.*

CLINT: I don't agree with him on that. I tell you, if everybody in the audience goes and watches it completely exhausted and having as much on his mind as he's had the last week, I imagine they might find it the same way.[62] He liked the pace, though.

---

[62] Siegel was almost seventy-one and in the midst of a lengthy lawsuit at the time.

PAUL: *Oh, he loved the pace. I think the ending bothered him a little bit, that Harry lets her go.*

CLINT: Everybody's going to have some different reaction to it. You like or you don't. If you don't, then you go on to the next movie, you go across the street to the theater across the way.

PAUL: *If I can just play devil's advocate, Don would seem to be bothered by the fact that she killed four people and that she wasn't going to pay for that. Granted that most of the four were pretty scummy people.*

CLINT: I can shoot holes through that, though. In the original *Dirty Harry* we shouldn't have shot the bank robbers either, then. After all, they were just taking a little cash. You can justify anything. I can go through that script and tear the hell out of it. You can go through any script and do that.

PAUL: *I don't like it when a movie just ties it up. Sidney Lumet's movies always lay it all out for you at the end: well, this is exactly why he did it. It's tied in a moralistic package and there are no overtones left, therefore there's no real mystery.*

CLINT: There should be an afterthought. I like the fact that it stirs that feeling. If people are leaving the theater going, "Do you think he should have let her go?" or "Do you think maybe he should have sent her to jail?"—if it stirs that kind of discussion—that's great because at least it's encouraging a certain interest in what goes on. And if there are pros and cons on it, that's fine.

PAUL: *Does that justify her killing four people, though?*

CLINT: I don't know, but if anybody asks the question, it's a good question. I don't know what justifies anything, but I also don't know what justifies giving killers probation.

PAUL: *But Harry does that in a way. When he lets her go, he more or less does a Turn 'Em Loose Bruce in a way.*

CLINT: Sure he does. Except that, not living in New York, I don't know the specific cases where Bruce is turning hardened criminals back on the street repeatedly. *Sudden Impact* is a specific story with specific circumstances, where normally, I suppose, if she went to trial, she'd plead insanity and get four counts of second degree murder or something like that. Who knows how it'd come out. But the way it is, Harry knows it's all over. Everybody knows. There's no doubt.

People would come up to me after *High Plains Drifter* and say, "Don't you think you should have specified what the guy was and how he was related? Because we really don't know. I think so-and-so and my girlfriend thinks such-and-such." I'd say, "Great, you're both right. I'm glad you spent that much time thinking about it."

PAUL: *There are few things more powerful in a movie than leaving a moral question hanging. Where there are two distinct sides to it and both of them are half right or more than half right. Then you've got something there.*

CLINT: Yeah. Everybody has their point of view, and their point of view doesn't necessarily have to cross over to the next person. Even the characters. Let's face it, when a villain does something in a movie, *he* thinks he's right. Everybody who's in prison, they think they're not guilty, they think that they were justified. "What the hell, I was broke, I had to rob that store. And the guy got in my way, so I had to shoot him." You can rationalize anything in the world. Everybody who's in jail right now has got some sort of rationale as to why it wasn't his fault that he's there.

PAUL: *To me, it seemed at the end he goes for justice instead of the letter of the law. The end had a lot of moral complexity.*

CLINT: He's bent the law. She is of course relieved that he's pulled off this deal, but at the same time you get the look on his face—I *believe*, and I hope it's transmitted—that this person has suffered enough in life. *I* feel that the character looks as if he's saying, "Hmm, I don't know if this is the right thing or not, but this is the way it's going to be for the moment. I like her and I agree with her. Justice should be served—and not from just the law."

PAUL: *I thought that really made it ambiguous. Is that justice or isn't that justice?*

CLINT: There are two ways to look at it. One is that he's sympathetic to her plight. She tells him about the sister and being beaten, and was it their justice that the rapists should just walk away? And here *he* is, he's just had the crap beat out of him and his best friend's lying back there dead in the hotel room. Everybody forgets that aspect. He's got his *own* reasons for saying, "Screw it." Where she *isn't* taking any shit from anybody and she says, "You'll have to rape my dead body, you'll have to kill me," he's back and he's saying, "If you think she's pissed, wait until you see how pissed off I am!" So the methodical sleuthing of the case becomes almost moot to the point where, at the end, he's so fucking pissed that even the sounds we've got coming out of him when we cut to him are primal sounds: we used a Chinese yo-yo and all this *yah-wah-wah-wah* and *growling* trombones. I told [composer] Lalo Schifrin—and he did it very well—I wanted real animal sounds, real primal screams.

PAUL: *That was in* Harry, *too, in that Kezar Stadium scene: you got animalistic. You climbed the fence like an animal into the cage with the killer.*

CLINT: Exactly. He goes right into the cage and he gets him. He's going to find out the answer because there's a girl buried somewhere. There's no way this guy's going to leave this stadium without telling me. That's why a comment like, "Should he have let the girl go at the end?"—people are forgetting *his* indignation.

PAUL: *I like the fact that it's not a black-or-white statement at the end. It gives you the same feeling as that pullaway shot in Kezar Stadium where Harry is grinding Andy Robinson's leg. You know, they're in the fog—they're in the ambiguity. But I would assume that you're going to take a lot of flak for this ending.*

CLINT: Oh, I don't care. I'll take a lot of flak.

PAUL: *It's just they're going to once again attack you for whatever. They're going to take it all as, "This character is not a character— it's Clint Eastwood."*

CLINT: [laughs] Tell them to go ahead. I've got strong skin. Hopefully there are a few people who are more thoughtful than that.

PAUL: *Most people are more thoughtful, but some of them won't be. Kael, I'm sure, will spit fire over this one.*

CLINT: You just never know about people like that. But you're mentioning there somebody who deals on a different level with movies—not movie reviewers who are interested in, like you were saying, endings that pose certain questions and stir the imagination. In the first place, was it exciting or did it entertain, then did it pose these other questions? But if you want somebody who reviews because you're friends with them, you go and have cocktails with them, then that's a different kind of reviewer and we're not interested in that anyway. But I don't think it will cause as much controversy as you're insinuating.

PAUL: *How do you project what happens between Harry and her at the ending? Is there going to be any future for them?*

CLINT: I don't know, I never got that far. To me, I'm only as far as the ending. But the audience will *will* them whichever way they want.

PAUL: *Don thought it was a semi-happy ending.*

CLINT: Some of the audience will want him to put his arm around her and say, "Everything's going to be all right. I'm going to take you off up to my one-room apartment in San Francisco" or whatever. There are going to be other people who are just going to want him to say, "You're on your own now, kid," or "Terrific, I'd love to see you now and then, but I'm going to go out to clean out a few more coffee shops." [laughs] There are all kinds of ways of looking at it.

I remember years ago, at the end of *Josey Wales*, Ferris [Webster, editor] wanted me to put in an overlay of the girl's face just so we knew that Wales was riding back to her. I just said, "That isn't necessary." He kept saying, "That's the way we used to do that," and I said, "Hey, I don't care if you used to do it." To me, the audience is *willing* him back there. Even if you take him out of the north side of town and he came in the south side, the audience will say, "He's going to ride around the outskirts and come back and head back there." I took him back the exact same way he came in, and that was the end of it. You knew that he was going to go back and he was going to regain his health and he was going to have a great existence—or a much better existence than he'd had so far.

Just like *High Plains Drifter*: if the audience wants to think the guy's the devil, fine; if they want to think it's the brother, as it was written in the script, then that's fine, too. However they interpret it, if the audience is interpreting with you, then it's just more fun for them.

And in this thing, you know that this girl is going to go on to a better existence. But what goes on between them, it's up to the audience to draw in.

PAUL: *Don felt they were going to get together. I was less sure.*

CLINT: See, he's got a nice sentimental streak [laughs]. I'm glad to know he still has that.

PAUL: *I thought it was a good scene when she says, "You want to be alone tonight, Callahan? Neither do I." That was a scene between two lonely people that connected up very well with the first Harry, I thought. A lot of the reason he's doing what he's doing is he's got nothing else to do. He wouldn't know what else to do. His wife's dead and there's this lonesome aspect to him.*

CLINT: His work is his life, so to speak.

PAUL: *It was liable to be a very strange evening. I've had a couple friends who have been raped, and the idea of sex with a man again triggers it all back. It's very hard for them, sometimes for several years, even if they really love the guy.*

CLINT: I didn't want to make it a big romance movie—you know, all of a sudden they go off into the sunset hand in hand? There was none of that kind of feel. I didn't show them in bed together, but there were those beautiful waves and this nice setting, and maybe that's enough.

PAUL: *I thought you did that well. Maybe they just held each other, maybe they didn't have sex.*

CLINT: At the end, most people are going to assume they had a little romantic interlude and that continued on and was fine. Maybe a real rape victim viewing the film might say, "They probably just held each other." But it can be anything you want.

PAUL: *Why didn't you direct* Magnum Force *or* The Enforcer? *Any specific reasons?*

CLINT: I just felt that at that time I needed somebody else to do the work on those. I liked the scripts, but I wasn't quite as motivated. Or maybe it's maturity on my part and I just decided now is the time to do the final big chapter.[63] Having made three of them and never directing one—just scenes—and acting as a producer or second-guesser or whatever in some of them, it was fun to attack this story because I liked some of the elements of this story better than the others. And, for the same reason I directed the *High Plains Drifter*—I'd been in so many Westerns—I figured I ought to direct one.

PAUL: *I watched them all, before coming out, again. It seemed to me that one of the keys to* Magnum Force, *that the major difference between Harry and the killer cops—the Brazilian death squad element—was that speech about heroism: "Is that what you guys are all about? Being heroes?" You never get the idea that Harry's in it because he wants to be a hero. While these other guys are filled with a higher vision, Harry's going about it twenty-four hours a day doing the job.*

CLINT: Like he says in this one: "Funny, I never thought of it as a game." To him it's not. Otherwise he would've been more political and probably would've been a captain or something at this point his life, instead of still being the same rank.

---

[63] *Sudden Impact* didn't turn out to be the "final big chapter" of the saga of Dirty Harry, however. A fifth film, *The Dead Pool*, directed by Buddy Van Horn, surfaced in 1988.

PAUL: *Harry doesn't seem like a power-struck figure at all in any of the movies. He seems to be working his cases, and he gets obsessed by his cases.*

CLINT: It's the maturity of the character, hopefully. Not only have thirteen years passed since the beginning one, but the character *has* to mature a little bit. Either for the better or for the worst, he has to go somewhere. He's working his cases and solving them any way he can. If it's at a standstill, he's got to get it moving.

There's nothing wrong with ambition in the world. It's great, but you're always wondering what the motivations for ambition are. People who want to be in leadership politically or be in a position to make decisions for the rest of us—why does a person want to run for county supervisor or something? So they can tell everybody else what the hell to do? Is it really an act of goodwill, or do you feel that it is your civic duty because you feel you can help better the community? Or is it because you like the power? That goes for, I guess, anything else: the presidency or the chief of police or anything. What are the motivations for being there?[64]

PAUL: *You told Don that you'd like women to see this picture.*

CLINT: I'd like everybody to go see it if they'd like to go see it. It just seemed to me that an effective storyline could be done where this is a gal who'd been put through the ultimate humiliation. She's gone on and made a life for herself even though her sister was not able to. But nobody's ever going to crap on her again. And at the end, even though she's getting punched around and overwhelmed, she's going down swinging.

I do think that, in this age that we're living in now, with more consciousness of women's rights, women will enjoy that aspect of it. I don't know, I may be wrong.

There's been a lot of discussion in the recent years about women's rights and rape centers to comfort women who've been abused. There was a period in time when women who were the

---

[64] Eastwood would find out firsthand in 1986 when he successfully served one term as mayor. He threw his hat in the ring after Carmel's planning commission denied his application to build a two-story building because the structure didn't meet the city's design-and-construction code.

victims of rape were put totally on the defensive by the police departments for those cowardly acts that were perpetrated on them. There was never any real sympathetic caring for them.

PAUL: *It marks people, too. If they get over it at all, it takes them years.*

CLINT: That's why in this particular story, you wonder how a relationship would be. That scene, the one you brought up earlier, with the two lonely figures, I didn't want to play it as "he wakes up enchanted," like it was a great evening or something.

PAUL: *Do you see* Sudden Impact *primarily as, like* Dirty Harry, *an entertainment or is it more of a political statement?*

CLINT: I never see a movie as a political thing of any sort. I'm not in the political business. Like any story that I do, it just happens to be *a* story. It's just a movie, as Hitchcock would say. It may be a strong comment on justice—maybe my strongest to date on justice or the abuses of our judicial system—but at the same time it primarily is the story of a girl who's been tormented and then it's been covered up.

PAUL: *You just seem to relate very strongly to it, the anti-rape aspect of this particular film.*

CLINT: I do relate to it because, let's face it, it's probably one of the most cowardly acts known and also it is probably the most humiliating or degrading act. They say that one out of three women in the city of Los Angeles will have some sort of an attempt at some sort of molestation before they reach the age of sixty-five.

PAUL: *That's pretty scary.*

CLINT: That's pretty scary, when you think one out of three. You know, it's against the law in California to drive away from an accident. If somebody runs into you, you're bound by law to get out, exchange license numbers so the insurance element can be sorted out. But even the police in this town recommend that a woman hit in her car *not* stop. They recommend that she moves on to a populated area—hopefully finding a police officer—before stopping because there have been cases where these punks go around and they purposely run into women. When the person gets out to say, "Jeez, you hit my fender," then they rob them, beat them, rape them or whatever.

Maybe it's going to get better with better law enforcement, but maybe not. That's why when they try to pass a gun control law in California, it's voted down four-to-one or something.

PAUL: *Do you think a gun control law would help that much?*

CLINT: Oh, it wouldn't help at all. It might take a gun out of the hands of some woman who's got one in her purse, but it wouldn't take it out of anybody else's.

PAUL: *Exactly!*

CLINT: But all those elements come together to make this kind of a story logical. Though this kind of story isn't new. They've done other stories of vengeance. They're old as time, they're old as literature. I even had the character say, which I wrote in, that revenge is "the oldest motivation known to mankind."

PAUL: *She replies, "You don't approve," and he says, "Till it breaks the law." But then he changes his mind about the last part of it.*

CLINT: Yeah.

PAUL: *Don said to me afterwards, "I wonder if there's anyone left in San Francisco to kill." [laughs] It's probably the most violent picture I've seen, which is not a criticism. It reminded me in a slight way of the almost literal hell of* Drifter *when they paint the town red.*

CLINT: It's not violent by the standards of *Halloween* or those kind of movies where they're going around figuring a way how to stick boathooks in the guy's ears and stuff like that. But it's a tough picture.

PAUL: *It's honest, clean violence rather than exploitative, porno-graphic violence like* Friday the 13th, *where you just have seven starlets and you garrote them each in a different way. They leave you really feeling shabby, like you've been had. This one doesn't at all. I don't even object to* Friday the 13th *for its violence. I just think it's not very good and it's made strictly to make money. Not that there's anything wrong with making money.*

CLINT: No. We tried to feature the story *and* the characters, rather than just have some guy in a mask running around throwing a knife around. Those are pictures that I expect to run a week.

Out of the violence in this thing, you want it to conclude in a positive way. You want the people to win out. We did some very old-fashioned things: killing the Horace character. The guy just clicks the knife, we cut to his face, and boom—we find him dead. You don't have to see some guy stick a knife into his throat and go through all that nonsense.

PAUL: *I'm sure this is going to be a megahit, but there's no question in my mind at all that you did not make this picture as an exploitative, violent film to make money. I think there will be people who say you did, but fuck them.*

CLINT: There are going to be people who'll say a lot of things, and that's fine, let them say what they want. Naturally you hope that the widest variety of people will enjoy a film, you hope it to cross over into all different types of movie-going audiences. But there's always one person out of a hundred who's going to say, "Oh, Jesus, that was too much of this or too much of that," or "He was doing that to make dough," or whatever. I don't need to make dough. I've proved I can make money making films over the years. I never set out to make a moneymaking film—in my whole life I never set out to—I just did the film because I liked the project and I did it the best way I could. Or I was working with directors and doing the best I could, and they worked on that level. But we never said, as far as making money, "Okay, we're going to do this because in one picture some guy stabs a guy with a boathook, so we'll stab a guy three times with a boathook."

PAUL: *Hey, you've got the* Firefox *of guns in this movie. What is that gun called again?*

CLINT: It's the .44 Magnum Auto Mag.

PAUL: *Smith & Wesson?*

CLINT: Not Smith & Wesson, no. It's made by Arcadia Machine & Tool in Southern California, but they don't make them anymore. They made a run on them about ten years ago and they stopped. Then somebody bought them. They all of a sudden became very popular and they made another run on them. The head of the Arcadia Machine & Tool is Harry Sanford. He told me that it was just too expensive to make.

PAUL: *What's the advantage of them? They fire faster?*

CLINT: It's a little bit faster, it's a little bit more powerful. They fire a .44 Magnum bullet but it's a higher grain bullet than you fire in the regular Model 29. No automatic has too many advantages over a revolver. Revolvers have less moving parts and less problems.

PAUL: *They don't jam.*

CLINT: But it's probably the most beautiful handgun I've ever seen. Years ago, Mort Sahl had asked me if I knew anything about the Auto Mag, and I said, "No." He said, "I've got a present for you." He gave me an Auto Mag as a gift. He was, I suppose, the first guy who suggested that it would look interesting in a movie. We talked about doing a Dirty Harry or using it in a movie sometime but never came up with a script for it.

PAUL: *How would you rank this among your films? I would rank it right up there with* Josey Wales *myself and* Bronco Billy.

CLINT: I can't rank any of the films. I like it. I guess in a year or so I'll look back and say, "Okay, I like this" or "I don't like it." I've been just too close. I've been living with it now since finishing in the summer and then all the postproduction. I've looked at it so many times.

PAUL: *Can you look at them after five, six years, say, and sort of forget you did them and see them as you would any other movie?*

CLINT: Yeah, that's kind of fun. I look at it and I wonder why I did that.

PAUL: *You said Harry matured through the pictures. Was your approach different in playing in this one in any specific way?*

CLINT: A little bit. I've matured and I think he's matured, too. He's still fighting the Establishment a little bit, he's still fighting dipshits like Briggs [Bradford Dillman], because he always hates the political element. He hates the politicking that goes along. Otherwise, like we said, maybe he'd be a captain or at least a lieutenant or something. But he'll never be anything more than an inspector. Because that's all he is, a homicide inspector, that's all he's ever going to have a chance to be.

41

CLINT: It sounds like a country song, doesn't it? "Smith, Wesson, and Me"?

PAUL: *Sounds like a Warren Zevon song, too [laughs].*

CLINT: Oh yeah, Warren Zevon.

PAUL: *He hates me now. I don't think he's drinking, but he might be drugging.*

CLINT: Really? How's he doing? I haven't heard much from him.

PAUL: *He hates me for a totally absurd reason. I wrote a negative review of a friend of his and got everybody upset—the California music scene—except him and he understood. "It's your opinion," you know? And now suddenly, years later, he hates me for that reason, which is obviously bullshit.*

CLINT: For that review?

PAUL: *Yeah.*

CLINT: Maybe he just doesn't want to admit that he ever had any problem.

PAUL: *He refused to take my phone number even. He's pretty alone. I'm afraid he's falling apart. But he won't even talk to me, so I can't find out. I made fifteen approaches and he doesn't seem interested, so that's about all I can do. It's up to him, the next move.*

> Warren Zevon died in 2003 from mesothelioma, the same "asbestos cancer" that took Steve McQueen's life and which Paul had read about in the paper the day he and Eastwood met with Zevon in 1980. After his diagnosis, Zevon expressed a desire to reconnect with Paul, but the two men never again spoke.

42

PAUL: *There's another side of you that I find really intriguing. Everybody knows you as an actor, less people know you as a director, and probably very few know you as a businessman. Obviously, you're a very good businessman.*

CLINT: You *have* to be. I enjoy it. You're in a profession where—I see it all the time—you could be lucky and have a twenty-year or thirty-year career, or you can have a four-years-and-it's-over kind of thing. You *have* to be a businessman, you have to take care of yourself. It's much like a prizefighter. How many prizefighters have you seen making tremendous dough, and then all of a sudden one day they're not making a nickel? All my formative years as a kid, Joe Louis was always *the* champ. He was the champion for twelve years. He made terrific dough and he was a big celebrity, everything was going his way. You see Joe Louis today and he's broke. He's busted. It doesn't take a lot of imagination to learn from something like that. The same thing with actors. You go back through the Fifties and Sixties and Seventies, how many guys really came on and hit it big for two, three, four years, either in television or whatever—and all of a sudden it's all over for them?

It hasn't worked out that way for me, but it always could have. I could've done *Rawhide* and that was the end of it. That could have been the last series I'd done or maybe I could've done two or three series after that but they flopped. No matter how capable I might be as a performer, I might not have just ever clicked with the right combinations again. I might not have ever had the *Dollar* films or the Dirty Harrys or the different surges—I call them *surges*—that come along in your career, where they take you off on another character that catches the imagination of the public. So you have to be thoughtful.

You can't just go out and invest your money in flimsy things. Oh, you can take a flier on something if it's within reason. You can go to Vegas and roll whatever's within your budget— whether it's a hundred dollars, a thousand dollars, or ten thousand dollars—you can go ahead and do that as long as you take it for what it is, but don't take it for a solid investment.

You can go out and say, "I'll invest in a make-believe diamond mine in South Africa," or buy some costume jewelry or desert property that doesn't exist. Or you can go for solid things and just think it out and say, "What do real solid people invest their dough in?" You just have to think that way. The president of an automobile company might have that job for thirty years or comparable jobs along the way, and benefits, pension plans, all kinds of various stock options. An actor, you have yourself and that's it. When it's over, you might have some guild—the Directors Guild, the Actors Guild—pension plan, but I've been taught never to depend on that.

My dad was a man who worked in many jobs during the Depression and I was raised during those years. My learning days were in that period where a lot of very smart people—and I considered him a smart person—had a rough time making a living. So I figured I'd get myself into a position where I'm making a fairly decent living.

To me, the ultimate thing an actor can do is say, "When it's time to quit, it's time to quit." James Cagney felt it was time to quit. Cary Grant felt it was time to quit. He thought he was of an age where he didn't fit certain roles that they were still trying to cast him in, so he quit.

I'm interested in directing. I may want to do that for twenty years, I don't know. But I was lucky to get into that. What would've happened if I hadn't made that breakthrough? What happens if I bomb out, do a few films as a director and they don't go anywhere? And then I look at the screen and I say I don't want to act anymore? These are things that haven't happened to me, but it doesn't take much imagination for anybody to figure that it doesn't last forever.

PAUL: *You went to biz ed at Los Angeles City College.*

CLINT: LA City, yeah. I was taking that, but that's a major that everybody takes when they don't know what they want to do, when they're not sure.

PAUL: *You're self-taught to a large extent, then.*

CLINT: I think so, yeah. I was at a party once when I was a young, real naïve guy. I hadn't even—well, I really didn't know anything [chuckles]. Cornell Wilde was there, the first actor I ever met who was recognizable, of note. A movie star. He was still kind of a name, was still cooking along. I was going, "Jesus, Cornell Wilde, wow." Somebody said, "Clint wants to be an actor." He just right away volunteered: "If you want to be an actor, save your money." Why, I thought, that's kind of an incongruous statement. I said, "I don't have any money to save." [laughs] He said, "Never get in a position where you have to do roles that you don't like, because that's happened to me. You do that and right away you compromise yourself and you can wreck your whole career." I always remembered that because it was the first statement made to me by anybody whom I'd ever recognized. I'd grown up seeing him in films. I thought it was a rather wise statement. Even though I've been lucky enough to do well financially, I never take that for granted.

PAUL: *You haven't become jaded at all because of it either. You kept in contact with the people. It seems like one of the major things that causes artists to die is when they just cut themselves off from reality, surrounding themselves with an entourage. I'd imagine that affects presidents, too, probably. They have no* *connection with anybody but the yes men. They have no idea what the country's like out there.*

CLINT: Watergate was a good example. [President Richard M.] Nixon had had a respectable first term. He'd gone to China and opened up all that. Then he gets involved with criminal activities, and people start losing their trust and he becomes the villain. People almost would've respected him more if he'd just burned the goddamn tapes and said, "Okay, I made some errors, but I'm not going to make them anymore. This is the way I've done it and too bad," instead of vacillating around and, like you say, getting tied in with an entourage of people who are all vying for a position within his structure. I'm sure it's the same thing with any president along through history. They've all got their little in-groups that are vying for position with him and have their self-serving reasons for doing things. And they lose touch with the people.

You see it in Hollywood all the time with studio executives. I see them all the time. They don't know anything but New York and Los Angeles. They fly first class or private airline between here and New York, and they don't know Des Moines, Denver, Dayton, Dallas, or whatever; it's just occasionally a side trip to Chicago maybe or a glamour trip to San Francisco or New Orleans. They don't really absorb people out there and what people are thinking.

PAUL: *I heard a great Hollywood joke the other day. Susan Anspach, an actress, said that it takes two people to change a light bulb in Hollywood: one to turn the bulb and the other to share the experience.*

CLINT: [laughing] I've seen it over the years and that's one of the reasons I don't reside there, though I have nothing against it. Los Angeles is as good or as bad as any other city. I'm not one of these guys who likes to go around saying, "Oh, I don't want to be in Hollywood because I want to be out in true creation" and all this bullshit. I didn't move to Monterey [County] because of Hollywood or anything about it. I'm just away, I can think in a different vein. I see movies with the general public. I go to the movie theater and I pay for my ticket and I go in and I sit down. The audience, they pay their three or four bucks, whatever it is, and they sit there and if it ain't funny, they don't laugh; and if it's funny, they do laugh. And that's just as basic as it gets. I think I know at least as well as anybody what's good—and probably better than some film mogul who might be jockeying back and forth between here and New York, who says, "The Beekman's got this and it's a big smash and that means it's going to do something." Well, it doesn't mean dick. What's playing at the National Westwood, it's nice that it grosses there, but let's look at what are we going to do now for the whole spectrum. Are we going to make entertainment for one group?

43

PAUL: *In a lot of the books on you, Siegel has this statement that you have "an absolute fixation on the antihero." Is that still true? Was it true then?*

CLINT: I don't know if it was or not. I think back in those days everybody had a fixation on the antihero. It was kind of the word of the moment: *antihero.* I came up by playing those kind of characters.

PAUL: *A lot of it—or some of it at least—may have been caused in part by your films, don't you think?*

CLINT: I had maybe a little bit to do with it, but I just don't think that you can make heroes in movies like in the old days where the good guys were all good and the bad guys were all bad. Even John Wayne in his day, one of his better roles was *Red River,* where he played a guy who had many faults.

PAUL: *Wayne was misunderstood as an actor in the same way you are. He's a real tragic figure in* The Searchers. *It was very simple-minded to point to Wayne and say, "Ah, the big, dumb cowboy hero who always played the good guy." Wayne's character in* Red River *is a very* dark *character. He didn't play the good guy in* The Searchers, *which is again a very dark film.*

CLINT: No, he played a guy who had a lot of problems. But in a lot of the other roles that people associated him with he was more the white-hat good guy. Probably it was a key to his success that he wasn't the roguish, flawed personality.

PAUL: *It seems like with your later films that you sort of played off of your antihero persona—if not turned it around and went in completely the opposite direction, doing spinoffs of it or questioning it or making it a lot harder to get to. Like in the case of the guy striving for heroism and really struggling with it. It's not very clear-cut anymore.*

CLINT: In *The Gauntlet* he wasn't quite up to it like Dirty Harry. In *The Gauntlet* he was a guy who's picked because they figured he *could* lose, because he was a guy who wasn't going to make it. Maybe a little bit of it comes through in *Bronco Billy*, too. I'm not sure. A little bit of the guy who's been working at something for a long time and it's never quite paid out the way he imagined it would. Though Billy's quite a bit different because he's more of a moralist.

PAUL: *It's vastly oversimplifying to say that in a lot of your earlier films, and films you made for other people, you seemed to play monomaniacal characters, and in your own films you seem to have either not done that or undercut that and put a lot of trim and a lot of questions around that more. Do you think that's at all a fair statement?*

CLINT: Even the ones that I've done for other people were scripts that were chosen by me and they were done by us here. I don't know, maybe it's just the way it's come out. Maybe material is being tailored more in that way nowadays. Maybe it's more of a challenge to play a guy with more question marks about his ability. It's more of an acting challenge, that's for sure.

Dirty Harry didn't have any questions about his ability, but he had questions philosophically about life and his existence and why he was there and why he was doing what he was doing. And in some of the early Westerns I played, the Leone ones especially, the guy never had any questions about anything too much. There was a *tinge* of sadness in the character, but only from his background.

PAUL: *I guess a lot of it was the kick changing from the good-guy character in* Rawhide *to the antihero.*

CLINT: Exactly. You hit it right on the head. Television is so condescending sometimes to the public, and television writing—not necessarily the writers themselves but the producers calling for this type of material—leaves the viewer just bombarded with exposition as to why everything is happening. Why do you have to explain everything? Why can't you let the audiences figure it out for themselves? But they didn't want to do it that way, and I fought that frustration for eight years. After you've done that it's very refreshing to get into an area where you can treat the audiences as intelligent, thinking people who are going to be able to catch on just as fast as they can. And they can, they can. They rarely miss. It's amazing. Just when you think you've got them fooled, they'll fool you by jumping a step ahead of you.

I'm thankful for the series years because of that. I would've never maybe learned that—at least not as fast—if I hadn't spent all those years on a series and been able to experiment and do that week in and week out, exposing stories to the public, watching their reaction, hearing their comments over the years. You get a good feeling about what's out there.

PAUL: *One of the qualities of most of the films you've made as a director—Mazursky has this quality, too—is a real, basic humanity. Basic warmth. Your own films, including* Breezy *and* Josey Wales *and* Bronco Billy, *and* Every Which Way but Loose *to a degree, they've really gone off in a different direction than a lot of the films like* Where Eagles Dare *and those that you made for other people. That quality has been there, too, in some of the films you've made for other directors, but you're not known for it in the Leone and the Siegel films. Let me put this into a proper question: [chuckles] Under the auteur theory, what quality do you think your films do have? What are your themes?*

CLINT: I really don't know. I'm not really that objective about it. I wish I was. If I was more objective, I could be more analytical. I tend to put down the auteur theory because a lot of people embraced it as a one-man/one-concept kind of thing, and making a movie is an ensemble. Go in there on Sunday and try to make a film by yourself. I try to bring the whole ensemble, the whole crew, into my enthusiasm about the film.

PAUL: *Even that statement reflects your humanism. The fact that you think that is a* theme, *in a way.*

CLINT: Yeah, I've always put that auteur theory down. Though I've been put in the position in life where I can control my destiny, so to speak, and control at least the type of projects I've been involved in, it's being lucky enough to have the right crew, cast, everybody, right on down to the guy who sweeps the floor, who share my enthusiasm. All of their enthusiasm goes to making me do what I do and, for my vision, do what they do. That's why this picture moved along so swiftly and smoothly—is because I wanted it to move smooth and swift, they wanted it to move that way, and jointly we made this picture. The swiftness wasn't that we were trying to do a Sam Katzman-Monogram early film where you're put on a two-week budget and that's it. We had more time to make this film. But when you have a crew that's enthusiastic and willing to charge the hill with you and take the positions, you win the war. Though it's not like a war, it's very comfortable. You conquer the objective, which is the filming of the picture.

It even almost seems like the weather works for you when you think that positive. It's almost like you will things to work for you that way, rather than coming out every day and saying, "Oh my God, I know it's going to rain today and screw me up." I've worked with guys like that, who'd say, "Oh, it's going to be awful." I'd say, "No, it's not going to be awful, it's going to be *great*. Don't worry about it. It's going to be clear tomorrow and it's going to be high contrast. That's what you want for this sequence. It's going to be sensational. Think that way. If it isn't, we'll go back to the drawing board and do another sequence." You'd be surprised, they'd come up and say, "Jeez, you were right. Look what a great day it is." Just believe that things are going to work for you. Naturally, you're going to get disappointments, but you can't be afraid of the disappointments. No three weeks are going to be the same. Full moon comes out and everybody loses their coordination for a day or two, then everything goes back in high gear.

PAUL: *I'd think that would be one advantage of being on location, where you're all the way from home with this one common goal to look towards.*

CLINT: It's the reason I shoot them all on location.

PAUL: *If your career were to stop right now, what films would you be the happiest with as an actor and as a director? If you could pick one or two to be remembered by, and sort of subtract one or two.*

CLINT: As far as a completed film that's out, I suppose *Josey Wales* and *Misty* or *Drifter*.

PAUL: *As a director and as an actor both for* Josey Wales?

CLINT: I suppose so. Though I like *Breezy* a lot, just as a straight director. And I like *Misty* because it was a first film and I was under the pressure to do it extremely cheap and it wasn't expected to be anything by the studio. So it was kind of a challenge in that sense.

I suppose *Joe Kidd* I wasn't too nuts about. I was having an allergy problem and I had the flu and a lot of problems like that were going on as I was making the picture. That made it a frustrating film to do. *Kelly's Heroes* was frustrating because I thought it could have been a much better film than it was, though it had great production in it.

PAUL: *There's no way to ever put these things right now once they're out, is there? Nobody will ever go back and find those missing scenes and put them back in or anything.*

CLINT: Nah, nobody cares that much really. They just keep selling them to the tube. Who knows, they might've been right. I might've put it together my way and it might be awful.

PAUL: *If somewhere that footage exists, it wouldn't be that much trouble to stick it back in.*

CLINT: It might not exist at this point. It's a lesson you learn along the way.

PAUL: *Nobody would do this with a novel, say. With rock & roll it's almost gone the other way to a point of total ridiculousness, where the artist has so much freedom he can record almost any whim that comes along. No one can tell him when to bring it in, no one can touch it if he comes out with the world's worst cover and that's what he wants. He literally has complete freedom.*

CLINT: Well, I have that now, but I didn't have that then. I made that picture for somebody else, another studio.

PAUL: *Is there anybody on the set, or in your life, who can tell you, "You're just full of crap on this"?*

CLINT: Who *can* tell me that? Yeah, most anybody as far as if they want to.

PAUL: *I mean who you'd listen to, who could change your mind.*

CLINT: Anybody can tell me that they think I'm wrong on a certain subject and I'll respect them for saying so. There's nobody who tells anybody—in my life anyway—that I run the show and "This is it, so you guys just sit tight, will ya." There's none of that attitude. If somebody thinks I'm wrong, I want to hear about it. I don't have to listen to it, I can always say, "I don't agree with you on this particular point," and that's the end of it. I think I treat my crew that way. I allow the camera operator, the focus guy—anybody—to come up and say, "Look, I've got a thing I think will improve the shot you've got." A lot of times they do. Then you look at it and say, "Yeah, well, it *does* improve it." The guy's absolutely right. I hope I can always keep that kind of objectivity.

PAUL: *I've seen it, the camaraderie on the set and people coming up and suggesting this and that.*

CLINT: I solicit that. I mean, I could do it the other way. I could say, "You take care of the sound department, you take care of the cinematography. And, actors, you just say those two lines and do that. *I'll* take care of the directing," and that's it. But I'm cutting myself off that way, I'm narrowing down the field. I'm narrowing it all down to where it becomes my statement, but has it got all the elements of the components? Have we got all the input of thirty, forty, fifty, sixty or how many other people? Why not take all those elements?

PAUL: *You're still going to make the statement you want, but they might improve it.*

CLINT: They will, actually. Don will tell you—we used to joke about it—I'd say, "Don, I've got an idea that would improve your shot. How about we move over here and do this thing?" And he'd say, "Yeah, we'll do that, but on top of that we'll go up here and do all of this." It's like a *Can You Top This?* situation. He loved it. He's always loved it, from the very first picture, and that's why we had a lot of fun making pictures together. It's just been great fun, and I try to get my people to do the same thing to me. Just jab me, keep me jumping, don't let me sit back. That canvas chair, oh God, I haven't sat down in it three times in the whole movie. After a while the guy stops bringing it out because I'm *moving*, I'm not here to sit around and to wear leggings and spats and a beret or something.

PAUL: *Wear a monocle. And a cigarette holder.*

CLINT: DeMille. Running that kind of shop. There were guys who ran that kind of shop quite successfully, but this is the way I've got to do it and it's the only way I really enjoy it. And the pictures that have come out, they've done well because of it.

44

By the time the final round of interviews rolled around in October of 1983, Eastwood had apparently been in touch with someone at *Rolling Stone* regarding the status of Paul's cover story.

In the meantime, Paul had sent Clint, who was preparing to fly to New Orleans to make *Tightrope*, the first hundred pages of a book manuscript for a movie quiz book that he was writing with his friend William MacAdams.

CLINT: Sondra and I read it the other day and it was fun.

PAUL: *I hoped it would be. We thought it would be entertaining. I hate most of those quiz books. Most of those things are meaningless. It's going to be the movie quiz book for people who love movies, and it's written for people like us and Jay—not the guys who are totally nostalgic for nothing but Busby Berkeley musicals and all that. A real film nut's quiz book.*

CLINT: That was some nice stuff. What were you thinking of doing, publishing it?

PAUL: *Yeah, we're going to try to publish it. I was going to ask [Martin] Scorsese, if he liked it, and I was going to ask you and Sondra, if you liked it, if you'd just give me a sentence or something that I could show the publisher. But if you don't want to do that ...*

CLINT: Sure.

PAUL: *Sort of a recommendation. I'm sort of embarrassed to ask, but I think it would help sell the book.*[65]

CLINT: Is that the whole book or are you going to add to it?

PAUL: *No, that's like three percent of it.*

CLINT: When you want me to, I'll just write you a letter or something on it.

PAUL: *[pleased] Oh, anytime. We're going to basically present a hundred pages like this within the next month, and if you could write me a note or something sometime, then I'd—*

CLINT: Uh, when do you think you'll be turning this [the Eastwood piece for *Rolling Stone*] in?

---

[65] They did indeed secure a book deal, but soon after the publisher went out of business. More than ten years later, in 1995, they finally published the book as *701 Toughest Movie Trivia Questions of All Time.*

PAUL: *[quavering] Oh, by December 1st, if they want to publish it in January. I'll send it to you first.*

CLINT: What is it, a January 1st publication?

PAUL: *I don't know.*

CLINT: That was the rumor, that it was going to be in the January 1st edition.

PAUL: *I'll send you a copy of it first, because they'll undoubtedly cut it. I don't have final cut.*

CLINT: Um-hmm.

PAUL: *I can just send it here care of Judie [Hoyt, Eastwood's secretary at Malpaso] and she can mail it to you down to New Orleans, I guess.*

CLINT: Sure.

PAUL: *Because I want to make sure it's accurate and all that stuff.*

CLINT: I think we ought to cut it short today.

Paul said, "Yeah, sure," and turned off his tape recorder. He interviewed Eastwood only one more time before returning to New York. Their final conversation was a good one and bore no trace of the uneasiness that had brought the previous meeting to a close.

DISSOLVE TO:

Flashback

PAUL: *It seems like Jimmy Stewart and Henry Fonda now are having trouble getting roles. I don't know if it's the age thing or what it is, but Fonda particularly is in nothing but cameos and Stewart's in advertisements.*

CLINT: You get to a certain age where you *have* to do cameos. When a guy gets to a certain age, with audiences who are mostly young people, I don't think you can base the protagonist of a film on him because there's no identification factor there. When they were in their forties and fifties and maybe even their early sixties, audiences could still look up to a guy who is an image of leadership, a father image, or whatever kind of image.

PAUL: *Are there any directors whom you would really want to work with? What if Truffaut, say, asked you to do a film? Or Spielberg asked you to do a film?*[66]

CLINT: To me, it's the writing—if the part was there. Because every good director can go on his ass and every good director has. It's just a question of choosing the right thing. If Truffaut came along and said, "I've got this great thing," and it looked like the kind of thing that fit in, I'd say, "That would be terrific."

---

[66] Eastwood has yet to act in any of Steven Spielberg's films, but the two men have worked together several times. Spielberg produced Eastwood's *Flags of Our Fathers* and *Letters from Iwo Jima* (2006), and executive-produced *Hereafter*.

PAUL: *Which directors do you follow these days?*

CLINT: I don't have any actors or directors I wouldn't miss a film of. But if they come up with a film that's a knockout, I'll be the first one to carry the flagpole up and raise the flag on it.

PAUL: *Someone, I think Jay, told me that at one time Bob Evans [then the head of production for Paramount Pictures] was talking about* The Great Gatsby *with you as Gatsby.*

CLINT: I've had some people discuss that property with me over the years, but I was never knocked out about it. In the first place, Fitzgerald's writing is very hard to convey to the screen because they all take place over such a long period of time. Twenty, thirty, forty years. They're very difficult to put on the screen correctly. I don't think the last *Gatsby* was, and the one with Alan Ladd wasn't any more exciting either.

PAUL: *That one I never saw.*

CLINT: I saw that when I was a kid. Though I enjoy reading Fitzgerald—it's marvelous stuff—I just don't see it as a screen thing. Things that are a little more of a vignette out of life and happen in a shorter span are more appealing for the screen.

PAUL: *Boy, if it were possible to make a good* Gatsby, *you would be perfect for it. Absolutely perfect for it.*

CLINT: I just don't think I ever saw it. That's why I never got turned on to it.

PAUL: *Last night at dinner you were talking—somewhat seriously, I thought—about "hanging up the holsters." A couple, three more as an actor and seven, eight more as a director or something.*

CLINT: I don't know, you make all kinds of statements, but I thought one of these days I wouldn't mind just directing some films for a while. Sometimes I think that and sometimes I turn around and say, "Aw, that's BS," you know? "Things are going really well and you can do a few films." But other times I think ...

I don't really like the celebrity part of the thing. I don't really enjoy it like some people do. Some guys, some gals, they really enjoy the whole top-of-the-heap, fight-for-it-all-to-get-there or -to-stay-there, and I never have. I enjoy the moviemaking and that's about it. Maybe it could be a more stabilizing influence not to have that pressure brewing anyway. There's a tremendous amount of pressure as an actor—as an actor of certain success—the constant badgering a lot of times. The public can be real nice, but also sometimes, in trying to be nice, they can be ...

PAUL: *Do you think if you just directed that the pressure would start to slowly go away over the years?*

CLINT: Maybe it would subside some or something. Maybe it would take another aspect of a bit more subtle position of just a guy who's making films rather than somebody whose face is appearing larger than life on screens everywhere. I don't know, maybe not. Maybe you reach a certain deal and you have a lot of films to run on TV for the rest of your life.

PAUL: *Can you perceive the day when you wouldn't want to act anymore and just direct?*

CLINT: I've thought about it a little bit. It probably will come. There'll be a day when I'll look up there and—it's not that I'll be doing it any worse—maybe I just will feel that that's enough. I can go in and play some different type of character roles, which would be fine, if I can find challenging roles all the way and play them right up till I'm ancient. But I don't know if there *are* that many great roles after you pass a certain stage, where being a protagonist makes sense or being a young action-adventurer makes sense. And I enjoy directing so much, it's very feasible.

PAUL: *You've already moved away from the action-hero adventurer role. As much towards—not exactly—character acting, but in that direction somewhat.*

CLINT: I think so. But the most interesting leads throughout the decades have been character actors, from Bogart/*The African Queen* and Gable/*It Happened One Night* to you name it.

PAUL: *Yeah, Cooper, Stewart, Wayne, those guys were a lot more complicated than they were given credit for. They weren't playing heroes all the time.*

CLINT: Some of my favorite acting roles over the years have been things like *The Last Ten Days* and Oskar Werner playing a soldier in Nazi Germany with his doubts about the way things were going. I thought that was brilliantly conveyed by him. I remember seeing *A Place in the Sun* when I was a kid. Montgomery Clift, you felt so sorry for him. He'd committed a crime and got involved, yet it was a position you could see anybody getting in. You identified. You thought, Oh my God, what *else* would you do? Here you are, you're nothing, you've got an uncle who doesn't really think much of you but you get this chance to do a job, and just when everything's going your way you get this little gal screaming—who's brilliantly played by Shelley Winters. But it moved you, so much so that, as an audience, when he had her and she was in the water out in the lake, you'd say, "Hit her with the oar!" [laughs] It just moved you tremendously.

PAUL: *Liz Taylor was awfully good.*

CLINT: She was great. She looked like an ice cream cone.

PAUL: *Did you ever meet Clift?*

CLINT: No, I never met him.

PAUL: *Do you feel that way about any actors today or any performances in the last few years?*

CLINT: No, I haven't seen anything recently that compares to those. I'm sure there is, I just haven't seen it.

PAUL: *In Monterey you're pretty well left alone, right?*

CLINT: Yeah, but they have a big tourist season there, too, sometimes.

PAUL: *You've got this ranch now up in Redding, right? That's fairly private country up there, isn't it?*

CLINT: I don't like to talk too much about that [chuckles].

PAUL: *We don't have to put it in.*

CLINT: That's kind of just a hideaway. It's the place where I can walk in the field and be by myself. Totally. Sometimes your nerves get frayed, you're working a lot of hours and it creeps up on you, that kind of stuff. It sneaks up on you when you're least expecting it.

PAUL: *I read someplace that you once used disguises to go out in public.*

CLINT: I used to put on a moustache and wear my glasses or a hat or something like that. Different things to just try to play low key.

PAUL: *You have the aura of* total *approachability. I noticed on the set that anyone can come up and put an idea to you. I would imagine sometimes this gets annoying out in public.*

CLINT: In public I don't necessarily have that aura, but on set I do because it's with the people I'm working with. I have to admit, when I'm out in the evening by myself or with friends, I like to be just left alone. I don't make a Garbo "I want to be alone" situation out of it, but I like privacy. I like to be alone. I don't mind sitting by myself in a room or a building or a house or whatever. A car. Sometimes I'll take trips driving just for that one reason: so I don't have to answer telephones and I just think. Some of my best scenes I've ever worked on were devised when I was just off driving someplace. Sitting by myself.

PAUL: *You go in the camper a lot?*

CLINT: No, not always, but sometimes.

PAUL: *Jay says people generally tend to leave you alone because you don't put on the air of a movie star. That you fit in so well that they* don't *bother you.*

CLINT: A guy who runs around with an entourage of a couple thugs because he's got to have bodyguards, well, if you have that, right away you set up that atmosphere. People are going to be more antagonistic. I've gone into saloons by myself anyplace in the country and people say, "Hey, Jesus Christ, it's so-and-so! How about that." By the time they get a few belts and start wanting to get overly friendly, I've moved on anyway. I don't have to have ten guys hanging around, and I'm not the type everybody wants to take a swing at. I don't know whether it has anything to do with the roles or whether most of the guys who'd like to do that enjoy my stuff onscreen [laughs]. It's hard to tell. The more you start analyzing stuff like that, the more you realize how little you know.

Sometimes if I'm sitting alone in a restaurant or a saloon, it doesn't mean I'm lonely, it's because I want to sit alone. But a lot of times people will go, "He's lonely. Come over and join us." It's part of the act, I don't resent it. Also, in going after it, I knew it was the key to being able to play the things I want to play and direct the films and do the all the things that I've had a chance to do, so I have no real regrets. It's just that sometimes it beats you down a little bit. It's a thing I've never really enjoyed as much as a lot of people have maybe—maybe as much as I should've. I should've enjoyed it and taken a swing.

PAUL: *You're just born with one personality. It's not going to change.*

CLINT: I can turn the switch and be on and do some of the right things, I guess, when I'm out like that in the public. I'm basically not a person who likes to expose himself or expose his emotional feelings or thinking in front of people. I'm private, I guess, and I've found it's a great pressure to be known.

PAUL: *I'm sure there are other times when your mood is like, God, if one more guy comes up and asks for an autograph, I'm going to go out of my mind.*

CLINT: Sometimes it can be a very poor invention asking you for an autograph if the timing's wrong. It's a thing that people do as a *pack* anyway. Once in a great while somebody will come over and say, "Gee, I'd love you to sign this for my daughter" or son or something, so you do it. But a lot of times the only reason ten people are doing it is because they saw two or three other people do it and they thought that was the thing to do right now. "I can go show somebody." And they lose it, it goes to the bottom of the purse and stays there [chuckles].

PAUL: *When you take your kids to the movies, are you left alone pretty much?*

CLINT: When the kids and I go to little neighborhood theaters, we're left alone pretty good. It depends on where you are. Some places people are great about leaving you alone and other places people are more demonstrative. If you're in an area where there are a lot of tourists and people are on vacations, then they're much more outgoing because it's all part of their scene. One thing about living in a small town is you can become old hat after a while and then you can fit right into a certain groove. Sometimes you walk off into a field and you think you're all alone and it's really great, and then one person will find you and they'll run over and point, "Hey, Al, it's ..." Sometimes it's just really sapping.

I'll never forget when I was doing *The Eiger Sanction*, I had to do an added scene. The first time we tried it, it didn't work and so we had a helicopter let us off on top of this pinnacle down there in Monument Valley. A thing called the Totem Pole. It's only about twelve or fourteen feet across at the top. It's actually narrower in the center than it is at the top. Really quite an unusual thing. They pushed George Kennedy and me out there. We got out and we did the scene, then I put him back in because he was terribly nervous about being out there. He had a problem with the height. I had to do another shot there, but they needed to go back and get fuel. It was very early in the morning.

So the helicopter went way back down and way behind a bunch of mountains. It was just super quiet and not a human being for miles and miles and miles—not a person, nothing—just a few early-morning birds that reared up. Not even too much of that. And as I was sitting there, it was like one of those Ferde Grofé *Grand Canyon Suite* sunrises. It was only ten minutes. I thought, My God, these moments are really worth a lot in life, just to be in a place like this. It's worth any problems or any work on the film just to have this.

FADE OUT.

AFTERWORD

Despite several requests, Clint Eastwood declined comment for this book. The answer was always the same: he was busy editing his new film and preparing for the next one. "He does wish you the very best with your book." It would have been nice to hear, from the man himself, why he kept giving Paul the benefit of the doubt.

Eastwood still lives in Carmel—with his wife Dina, whom he married in 1996, and their daughter Morgan—where, with his eighty-first birthday approaching, he has spent the last year having a 15,000-square-foot estate built for a reported twenty million dollars. Over thirty years ago he told Paul Nelson that, at a certain age, actors "*have* to do cameos," but, proving himself wrong, he starred in films throughout his seventies. His last role to date, *Gran Torino*, was made when he was seventy-eight. All told, since these conversations he has acted in eighteen films and directed twenty-one (with another, *J. Edgar*, currently in production).

Paul Nelson died shortly before the Fourth of July in 2006. He was seventy years old. Receiving Social Security and living in an affordable (albeit illegal) sublet, a short-term memory problem plagued him the last year of his life. He regularly wrote Post-it notes to himself that he was hungry, thirsty, and needed food, all the time forgetting that, for the first time in many years, he had money in the bank. Although the cause of his death was determined to have been heart disease, he had not eaten in the last week of his life. He'd been dead for a week by the time someone discovered his body.

It's not difficult to imagine how Paul felt, returning to New York after the final interview and, a week or two later, unwrapping the Sunday *Daily News* containing Norman Mailer's cover story in *Parade*. With a one-two punch, his literary hero had proclaimed Eastwood an artist, and had done so, according to the article, after only a couple of meetings, a meal together, and a visit to the set of *Sudden Impact*.

Over a year later, in February of 1985, a woman left a message on Paul's answering machine. "Hi, Clint Eastwood calling for Paul Nelson. Clint will be here for about an hour and a half. It's three PM your time on Thursday." His old friend William MacAdams remembers a subsequent telephone call. "We had got a blurb from Eastwood for the movie quiz book. It was either Eastwood or somebody in his organization, after it was obvious Paul wasn't going to finish the *Rolling Stone* piece. They told him that he no longer had permission to use the Clint Eastwood blurb for the book."

For Paul—who had once confided in Warren Zevon, "I still can't get over that Eastwood calls me up at home in New York just to talk"—his inability to transform his conversations with Clint into something more than just a memory was no doubt crushing to the ego but even more so to the soul. He'd lost much more than a cover story.

ACKNOWLEDGMENTS

Thanks to my family and friends for all their encouragement and advice, to David Barker, Katie Gallof and John Mark Boling at Continuum Books, and, for sharing their memories of Paul Nelson, Jay Cocks, Mikal Gilmore, William MacAdams, John Morthland, Kit Rachlis, and Crystal Zevon.

Jonathan Lethem continues to amaze me.

Thank you, as always, Jeff Wong, for being so much more than an illustrator.

SOURCE MATERIALS

Apocalypse Now. 1979. Directed by Francis Ford Coppola. Screenplay by John Milius, Francis Ford Coppola (narration by Michael Herr). American Zoetrope/United Artists.

Avery, Kevin. 2011. *Everything Is an Afterthought: The Life and Writings of Paul Nelson*. Fantagraphics Books.

Bronco Billy. 1980. Directed by Clint Eastwood. Screenplay by Dennis Hackin. Warner Bros.

Canby, Vincent. 1979. "'Alcatraz' Opens: With Clint Eastwood." *The New York Times*, June 22.

Carter, E. Graydon. 1983. "People: Feb. 14, 1983." *Time*, February 14.

Denby, David. 2010. "Out of the West: Clint Eastwood's Shifting Landscape." *The New Yorker*, March 8.

Dirty Harry. 1971. Directed by Don Siegel. Screenplay by Harry Julian Fink, Rita M. Fink, Dean Reisner (based on a story by Harry Julian Fink and Rita M. Fink). Warner Bros./Seven Arts/The Malpaso Company.

The Eiger Sanction. 1975. Directed by Clint Eastwood. Screenplay by Warren B. Murphy, Hal Dresner, Rod Whitaker (based on the novel by Trevanian). Universal Pictures/The Malpaso Company.

Kael, Pauline. 1972. "Tango." *The New Yorker*, October 28.

Katz, Ephraim. 2001. *The Film Encyclopedia, Fourth Edition*. HarperCollins Publishers, Inc.

Locke, Sondra. 1997. *The Good, the Bad & the Very Ugly*. William Morrow and Company, Inc.

Magnum Force. 1973. Directed by Ted Post. Screenplay by John Milius, Michael Cimino (based on a story by John Milius and characters created by Harry Julian Fink and Rita M. Fink). Warner Bros./The Malpaso Company.

McGilligan, Patrick. 1999. *Clint: The Life and Legend*. St. Martin's Press.

The Merv Griffin Show. 1980. Merv Griffin Productions.

Nelson, Paul. 1972. "Dirty Harry." *Rolling Stone*, March 2.

Nelson, Paul. 1981. "Warren Zevon: How He Saved Himself from a Coward's Death." *Rolling Stone*, March 19.

The Outlaw Josey Wales. 1976. Directed by Clint Eastwood. Screenplay by Philip Kaufman, Sonia Chernus (based on the novel *The Rebel Outlaw: Josey Wales* by Forrest Carter). Warner Bros./The Malpaso Company.

Rubin, Jerry. 1980. "Positively the Last Underground Interview with Abbie Hoffman ... (Maybe)." *High Times*, February.

Sudden Impact. 1983. Directed by Clint Eastwood. Screenplay by Joseph C. Stinson (based on a story by Earl Smith and Charles B. Pierce and characters created by Harry Julian Fink and Rita M. Fink). Warner Bros.

ABOUT THE AUTHORS

Kevin Avery is the author of *Everything Is an Afterthought: The Life and Writings of Paul Nelson*. His writing has appeared in publications as diverse as *Mississippi Review, Penthouse, Weber Studies,* and *Salt Lake* magazine. Born and raised in Salt Lake City, Utah, he lives in Brooklyn, New York, with his wife Deborah, stepdaughter Laura, and a four-legged muse named Mysti.

Paul Nelson was, in the words of Bob Dylan, a "folk-music scholar" who in 1965 went electric and pioneered rock criticism. A legendary editor for *Rolling Stone* magazine, he also discovered the New York Dolls. Throughout it all, movies remained his first love.

Jonathan Lethem is one of the most acclaimed American novelists of his generation. His books include *Motherless Brooklyn, The Fortress of Solitude,* and *Chronic City*. His essays about James Brown and Bob Dylan have appeared in *Rolling Stone*. He lives in Claremont, California.

INDEX